Studies in Central and Eastern Europe

Edited for the International Council for Central and East European Studies by
Roger E. Kanet, University of Miami, USA

Titles include:

Graeme Gill (*editor*)
POLITICS IN THE RUSSIAN REGIONS

Roger E. Kanet (*editor*)
RUSSIA
Re-Emerging Great Power

Katlijn Malfliet, Lien Verpoest and Evgeny Vinokurov (*editors*)
THE CIS, THE EU AND RUSSIA
Challenges of Integration

Stephen Velychenko (*editor*)
UKRAINE, THE EU AND RUSSIA
History, Culture and International Relations

Forthcoming titles include:

Rebecca Kay (*editor*)
GENDER, EQUALITY AND DIFFERENCE DURING AND AFTER STATE SOCIALISM

John Pickles (*editor*)
GLOBALIZATION AND REGIONALIZATION IN POST-SOCIALIST ECONOMIES
Common Economic Spaces of Europe

John Pickles (*editor*)
STATE AND SOCIETY IN POST-SOCIALIST ECONOMIES

Stephen White (*editor*)
MEDIA, CULTURE AND SOCIETY IN PUTIN'S RUSSIA

Stephen White (*editor*)
POLITICS AND THE RULING GROUP IN PUTIN'S RUSSIA

Thomas Bremer (*editor*)
RELIGION AND THE CONCEPTUAL BOUNDARY IN CENTRAL AND EASTERN
EUROPE

Stephen Hutchings (*editor*)
RUSSIA AND ITS OTHER(S) ON FILM
Screening Intercultural Dialogue

Joan DeBardeleben (*editor*)
THE BOUNDARIES OF EU ENLARGEMENT
Finding a Place for Neighbours

Stanislav J. Kirschbaum (*editor*)
THE MEANING OF EUROPE, CENTRAL EUROPE AND THE EU

Studies in Central and Eastern Europe
Series Standing Order ISBN 0–230–51682–3 hardcover
(*outside North America only*)

You can receive future titles in this series as they are published by placing a standing
order. Please contact your bookseller or, in case of difficulty, write to us at the address
below with your name and address, the title of the series and the ISBN quoted above.

Customer Services Department, Macmillan Distribution Ltd, Houndmills,
Basingstoke, Hampshire RG21 6XS, England

Russia

Re-Emerging Great Power

Edited by

Roger E. Kanet
Department of International Studies
University of Miami, USA

First published 2007 by
PALGRAVE MACMILLAN
Houndmills, Basingstoke, Hampshire RG21 6XS and
175 Fifth Avenue, New York, N.Y. 10010
Companies and representatives throughout the world

PALGRAVE MACMILLAN is the global academic imprint of the Palgrave
Macmillan division of St. Martin's Press, LLC and of Palgrave Macmillan Ltd.
Macmillan® is a registered trademark in the United States, United Kingdom
and other countries. Palgrave is a registered trademark in the European
Union and other countries.

ISBN-13: 978-0-230-54304-1 hardback
ISBN-10: 0-230-54304-9 hardback

This book is printed on paper suitable for recycling and made from fully
managed and sustained forest sources. Logging, pulping and manufacturing
processes are expected to conform to the environmental regulations of the
country of origin.

A catalogue record for this book is available from the British Library.

A catalog record for this book is available from the Library of Congress.

10   9   8   7   6   5   4   3   2   1
16   15   14   13   12   11   10   09   08   07

Printed and bound in Great Britain by
Antony Rowe Ltd, Chippenham and Eastbourne

Contents

Preface

The editor wishes to express to the authors of the chapters that appear in this volume, first, for the quality of the chapters that they have produced; and second, for the dispatch and cooperation that they demonstrated in carrying out the several revisions of the original drafts.

The editor wishes to thank the anonymous readers of the original draft of the book, whose trenchant comments resulted in changes that have, we believe, strengthened its overall cohesion and the effectiveness of its argument.

Finally, on behalf of all the contributors, the editor wishes to thank others who contributed to the collective effort that this volume represents – especially others who commented on various versions of the individual chapters and the editorial and production staff of Palgrave Macmillan.

Roger E. Kanet
Miami, Florida

Preface by General Editor

When the International Council for Central and East European Studies (ICCEES) was founded at the first international and multidisciplinary conference of scholars working in this field, held in Banff, Alberta, Canada, on 4–7 September 1974, it was given the name International Committee for Soviet and East European Studies (ICSEES). Its major purpose was to provide for greater exchange between research centres and scholars around the world who were devoted to the study of the USSR and the communist states and societies of Eastern Europe. These developments were the main motivation for bringing together the very different national organizations in the field and for forming a permanent committee of their representatives, which would serve as an umbrella organization, as well as a promoter of closer co-operation. Four national scholarly associations launched ICSEES at the Banff conference: the American Association for the Advancement of Slavic Studies (AAASS), the National Association for Soviet and East European Studies in Great Britain (NASEES), the British Universities Association of Slavists (BUAS), and the Canadian Association of Slavists (CAS).

Over the past three decades six additional Congresses have been held: in Garmisch-Partenkirchen, Germany, 1980; Washington, USA, 1985; Harrogate, UK, 1990; Warsaw, Poland, 1995; Tampere, Finland, 2000; and Berlin, Germany, 2005. The next Congress is scheduled for 2010 in Stockholm, Sweden. The original four national associations that sponsored the first congress have been joined by an additional seventeen full and six associate member associations, with significantly more than a thousand scholars participating at each of the recent congresses.

It is now a little over three decades since scholars felt the need to coordinate the efforts in the 'free world' to describe and analyse the Communist political systems, their societies and economies, and East-West relations in particular. Halfway through this period, the Communist system collapsed, the region that was the object of study was reorganized, and many of the new states that emerged set out on a path of democratic development, economic growth, and, in many cases, inclusion in Western institutions. The process turned out to be complex, and there were setbacks. Yet, by 2004, the European Union as well as the North Atlantic Treaty Organization had welcomed those post-Communist states that had met all of the requirements for membership. Not all of the applicant states achieved this objective; but the process is ongoing. For this reason, perhaps even more than before, the region that encompassed the former Communist world demands study, explanation, and analysis, as both centripetal and centrifugal forces are at work in each state and across the region. We are most fortunate that the community of scholars addressing these issues now includes many astute analysts from the region itself.

Roger E. Kanet

Contributors

John Berryman is Lecturer in International Relations, Birkbeck, University of London. He was previously Head of the Division of European and International Studies and a member of the Russian and East European Research Centre at the University of Wolverhampton. His recent publications include 'Putin's International Security Priorities', in Roger E. Kanet (ed.), *The New Security Environment: The Impact on Russia, Central and Eastern Europe* (2005). He is a member of the International Institute for Strategic Studies and the Royal Institute of International Affairs.

Robert O. Freedman is Peggy Meyerhoff Pearlstone Professor of Political Science and President Emeritus at Baltimore Hebrew University, and Visiting Professor of Political Science at Johns Hopkins University. He is the author of four books on Soviet foreign policy, including *Soviet Policy toward the Middle East Since 1970* now in is third edition. A past president of the Association for Israel Studies, Dr Freedman is currently completing a book on Russian foreign policy toward the Middle East since the collapse of the Soviet Union.

Graeme P. Herd is a resident Faculty Member at the Geneva Centre for Security Policy (GCSP), and Associate Fellow, 'International Security Programme', Chatham House, London. During 2002–05, he was Professor of Civil-Military Relations and Faculty Director of Research at the George C. Marshall European Center for Security Studies, Garmisch-Partenkirchen, Germany. His latest books include *Soft Security Threats and European Security* (2005), co-edited with Anne Aldis and *Divided West: European Security and Transatlantic Relations* (2006), co-authored with Tuomas Forsberg.

Larisa Homarac is a graduate student in the Department of International Studies of the University of Miami. She holds a BA from the University of Missouri at Kansas City with majors in Piano Performance, Spanish and German. She worked as a Serbo-Croatian linguist for KFOR in Kosovo during 2004–05.

Roger E. Kanet is Professor in the Department of International Studies of the University of Miami, where he served as Dean of the School of International Studies 1997–2000. Prior to 1997, he taught at the University of Illinois at Urbana-Champaign, where he was a member of the

Department of Political Science and served as Head of that Department, 1984–87, and as Associate Vice Chancellor for Academic Affairs and Director of International Programs and Studies (1989–97). He has published more than two hundred scholarly articles and edited more than twenty books. Publications include the edited volumes: with Edward A. Kolodziej; *U.S. Power and Global Hegemony*, in press and *The New Security Environment: The Impact on Russia, Central and Eastern Europe* (2005). He is a member of the Council on Foreign Relations, New York.

Nikita A. Lomagin is Associate Professor in the School of Economics, St. Petersburg State University and the European University at St Petersburg. From 1994 to 1999, he served as associate dean in the School of International Realtions, and Director of the NIS Studies Center at St. Petersburg State Univeristy; since 1999 he has been Researcher in the Finnish Institute of International Affairs. His most recent publications include *Leningrad v blokade* (2005) and *Neivestnaja blokada* (2002).

Susanne Nies is Research Director at the Institute for International and Strategic Relations (IRIS) in Paris, France, and professor at the Institute for Administration and Management (IPAG), in Paris. She has held appointments at CERI, Paris (2000-2002) and the Free University, Berlin (2000–2002). Her recent publications include articles in *IRIS-Dalloz Année stratégique 2007* (2006); *Révue internationale et stratégique* (2006) and *Revue politique et parlementaire*, No. 1036 (2005).

Bertil Nygren is Associate professor of political science at the Swedish National Defence College and at the Department of Political Science, Stockholm University. He has held various administrative positions at Stockholm University, including Head of Department and Deputy Head of Department 1994–2001. He has edited anthologies and published chapters primarily on Russian politics, especially foreign policy.

Ingmar Oldberg is Associate Director of Research at the Swedish Defence Research Agency (FOI) and a member of a team writing biannual reports on Russian developments for the parliamentary Swedish Defence Commission. He has written and edited many books and reports on Russian foreign policy, specifically toward Western Europe and CIS neighbours, as well as on Russian regions, for instance Kaliningrad. His most recent publications include *Reluctant Rapprochement: Russia and the Baltic States in the Context of NATO and EU Enlargements* (2003), and *Membership and Partnership: The Relations of Russia and Its Neighbours with NATO and the EU in the Enlargement Context* (2004).

Vladimir Olegovich Rukavishnikov is Professor at the Department of Global Politics and International Relations of the State University-Higher School of Economics in Miscow, Russia since 2003. Prior to 2003, he served as Head of Department of the Institute of Socio-Political Research of the Russian Academy of Sciences. Rukavishnikov has published (in Russian and other languages) more than two hundred scholarly articles, essays and papers, authored and edited over fifteen books. His recent books include *Cholodnaya Voina, Cholodnyi Mir* (Cold War, Cold Peace, 2005).

Introduction: The Consolidation of Russia's Role in World Affairs

Roger E. Kanet

Until its implosion in late 1991, the Soviet Union was one of two global superpowers that had been engaged for most of the prior half century in a competition for power and influence that ultimately engaged virtually all the other states of the world. Initially, the Soviet Union and the United States faced one another across what Winston Churchill termed the 'iron curtain' in Central Europe. Soon, however, the realities of the danger of nuclear confrontation in the centre of Europe, as well as the emergence of a host of new political units from the collapse of Western colonial empires in Asia and Africa, led to the expansion of the super-power conflict to the 'Third World', where the Soviets and the Americans engaged in what both viewed as a 'zero sum' competition for presence and influence. Both sides built up military arsenals that could destroy the entire world multiple times. They established networks of alliances and competed for clients. By the 1970s, the Soviet leadership under Leonid Brezhnev foresaw the imminent establishment of a socialist-oriented international system, resulting from the 'changing international correlation of forces', that would compete with, and eventually overcome and replace, the capitalist-dominated system headed by the United States.[1]

In the 1980s, however, the internal weaknesses of the system on which the Soviet leadership had based its superpower status became increasingly evident, as did the overcommitment of Soviet resources to support allies and clients across the entire globe. The final years of the Soviet state system witnessed the efforts of Mikhail Gorbachev and others to reform the very structures of the Soviet state beginning with the economy, but including as well the entire political system and even the foreign and security framework of the Soviet state. As we know, these efforts at reform ultimately failed and had the unintended and unexpected result of bringing down the entire economic and political structure on which

1

the extended Soviet system was based from Central Europe to the Chinese border. Even before the dissolution of the Soviet Union in late 1991, however, the Soviet leadership had initiated fundamental changes in foreign policy that not only resulted in a dramatic scaling back from the global confrontation with the United States, but also reduced Soviet military and political involvement in regional conflicts across the globe.

The collapse of the Soviet Union in 1991 ushered in even more drastic changes. Although the Russian Federation emerged as the primary successor state of the Union of Soviet Socialist Republics (USSR) and inherited its seats in various internatonal fora, for almost a decade its very identity was not clear, and its overall status, prestige, and its role in the world was in virtual free fall. Many authors have outlined the vagaries of Russian policy during the decade of the 1990s. Among them there was general agreement that Russian policy objectives were not clearly developed, that the institutions intended to make and to carry out Russian policy were poorly managed and, most important, that the domestic political and economic chaos that characterized the Russian Federation and led to the financial meltdown of 1998 greatly weakened Russia's ability to pursue a coherent foreign policy.

Initially, during the first part of Andrei Kozyrev's tenure as foreign minister, Russia pursued a policy that in effect mimicked the policies of the United States and seems to have been based on the assumption that by following the lead of the major Western states, Russia would be admitted to what the Russian leadership referred to as the group of 'civilized nations' and would receive the massive inflow of economic resources required to stabilize and restructure the Russian economy. The widespread criticism of this policy as a form of capitulation that ensued resulted in shifts in Russian policy, even before Evgenyi Primakov replaced Kozyrev as foreign minister in 1996, and in Russian efforts to pursue what was termed a Eurasianist approach to foreign policy that included the effort to build alliances with other states that shared Russia's concerns about the dominant US position in world affairs. In the years leading up to Vladimir Putin's appointment as Yeltsin's successor and his ensuing election as president in spring 2000, Russian foreign policy continued to waffle between a commitment to joining the community of Western states, including the United States, and efforts to challenge both US global dominance and the broader Western community. Early in the administration of George W. Bush the new Russian–US confrontation peaked, when Bush expelled a large number of Russian diplomats for 'spying', and the Russians reciprocated. Thus, shortly before the terrorist attacks on New York and Washington of 11 September 2001, relations between Russia and the United States had reached their lowest point in the decade since the end of the cold war and the demise of the Soviet Union.[2] But, not only had Russian relations with the United States reached a low point, Russia's ability to accomplish its foreign policy objectives, to have an impact on events beyond its borders, had declined to the point that by the end of the 1990s it could be, and was, largely ignored by the major states of the West, as they made individual and collective foreign and security policy decisions. Russian opposition to North Atlantic Treaty Organization (NATO) expansion eastwards and to NATO bombing of Serbia during the Kosovo intervention, were simply ignored. Russia was not an important factor, therefore, in the security decisions being made in the West at the time that Vladimir Putin replaced Yeltsin as Russian president.

As all of the contributors to this volume demonstrate, the terrorist attacks on the United States provided President Putin with the opportunity to reassess Russian policy toward the United States and, in fact, to reassess Russia's views of itself, its medium- and long-term objectives, and the place that Russia would once again play in world affairs. Although Russian leaders throughout the 1990s spoke in general terms about Russia as a great power and of Russia resuming its important role in world affairs, within the context of Russia's political and economic collapse one often got the sense of mere wishful thinking and nostalgia for the past as the driving force for such statements. However, since the political rise of Vladimir Putin in 1999, with his commitment to rebuilding the political and economic foundations of the Russian state, the goal of re-establishing Russia's place as a great power has become the overarching objective of Russian foreign policy. It is this aspect of recent Russian policy that leads to the title of the present volume, *Russia: Re-Emerging Great Power*. As several of the authors, in particular Ingmar Oldberg and Vladimir Rukavishnikov, make quite clear, great power status is a central goal of current Russian policy. The question remains, however, whether Russia is, or will be in the near future, in a position to play the role of a great power. Of course, the fact that Russia retains a major nuclear arsenal provides it with a position in world affairs that its overall current economic capabilities would not support. Moreover, the meteoric rise in global petroleum and natural gas prices since the turn of the century has contributed to a revitalization of the Russian economy that in late 1998, soon after the financial collapse in Russia, would have been virtually unthinkable. This, in turn, has begun to provide President Putin with the underpinnings of the economic clout – especially in what a decade ago was termed the 'near abroad' – to assert Russian interests and reestablish

Russian policy influence, as Bertil Nygren, Graeme Herd and others demonstrate most clearly in their contributions to this volume. Moreover, Putin has gone far in rebuilding the structures of the Russian state, although the means used are essentially authoritarian in nature. This has meant that the central government now commands political clout within the Russian Federation that was simply unavailable to President Boris Yeltsin prior to his resignation in December 1999. All of these developments, plus the fourishing of a new sense of Russian nationalism and self confidence, contribute to a situation in which Russia is definitely on the verge of re-establishing its position as a great power – one might even argue, as do several of the authors of this volume, that it has already reached this goal.[3]

Even though the arguments developed in the chapters that follow are based on quite different perspectives among the authors, they overlap to a significant degree in the picture that they present of Russian policy as it has evolved under the political leadership of Vladimir Putin. They describe the policies of a pragmatic, but basically authoritarian, leader committed fully to re-establishing Russia as an important, even dominant, actor in world affairs, not just in post-Soviet space – although the initial focus has been in this region – but also further afield. To accomplish this long-term objective, however, Putin must first consolidate the power of the Russian state at home, as we have noted. Thus, the reassertion of central authority, the suppression of possible secessionist pressures, the destruction of alternative competitors for domestic influence such as the "oligarchs" (the major capitalist entrepreneurs who in the Yeltsin period had come to dominate sectors of Russian politics), and the rebuilding of the foundations of the Russian economy have all been essential elements in the consolidation of Russia's role in world affairs.

The three chapters that comprise the first section of the book examine the broad outlines of Russian policy, both the objectives of that policy and the development of policy toward the other important global actors. Ingmar Oldberg, Nikita Lomagin, and Vladimir Rukavishnikov all address issues associated with the broad sweep of Putin's foreign policy and the clarification of Russia's role and objectives in global affairs. Although the tone of their analyses and the perspectives that underlie them differ, their overall assessments have much in common. They emphasize the reassertion of central authority and the rebuilding of the economic foundations of Russian society as the essential preconditions for the consolidation of Russia's role in world affairs. They also examine the relevance of this objective to Russian relations with the United States, the European Union, and East Asia.

In presenting and developing his overall argument in Chapter 1, Oldberg provides a broad-brush overview of most major aspects of Russian policy. This includes tracking the important developments in Russian–US relations, in Russian policy toward the European Union (EU) and the major individual states of Europe, as well as policy toward China and the other major countries of Asia. Oldberg notes the important effort under Putin to balance Russia's interests and objectives in Asia with those in Europe and the overlapping aspects of policy toward Europe with that toward the United States. The end result is a *tour d'horizon* of Russian foreign policy, all of which is viewed within the context of the goal of re-establishing Russia as a great power. Oldberg concludes by noting that, although 'Russian preoccupation with great power status and influence is partly a heritage from the past, partly it reflects the current authoritarian trends in the country'. For him Russia must outgrow these views 'to become a really modern and "normal" power in the Western sense, according to which greatness is mainly based on the citizens' welfare and a civil and democratic system of government'.

In the second chapter, Lomagin, unlike the vast majority of Russian analysts, who, along with Russian leaders, view the world almost exclusively from a realist political perspective, maintains that the official Russian perception of security has broadened significantly and now includes an array of concerns that both break down the division between foreign and domestic and fall into the category of 'soft' security threats – environmental degradation, terrorism, major health concerns, etc. Although Putin has in recent years re-emphasized the importance of traditional military challenges to Russia's interests and security as a great power, he has retained this broadened interpretation of Russian security. Yet, Russia's security identity is not static and continues to evolve, according to Lomagin.

Rukavishnikov presents a picture of Russian foreign policy in Chapter 3 that is similar to that of Oldberg, although he emphasizes Russia's security goals in a post-cold war environment. The tone of his assessment of Russian relations with the West is decidedly more critical of the latter than is that of most of the other contributors to this volume, but his overall picture of Russian relations with the United States, for example, overlaps substantially with that presented by Kanet and Homarac in Chapter 8. Rukavishnikov concludes by noting that the twenty-first century has ushered in 'a new world order profoundly different from that of the 1990s and the 1980s. It is no surprise that Russia is in a quest for its role in the post-cold war world order. History is accelerating. Russia has a great past, but will she have a great future?' Although Rukavishnikov does not answer the question directly, his analysis makes clear that he views Russia as well on the way to re-establishing its role as a major world power.

An important component of Putin's foreign policy has been geared toward rebuilding Russia's dominant role within the swathe of states that emerged from the former Soviet Union. This aspect of Russian policy builds on the Eurasian thrust of Russian policy advocated in the mid- and late-1990s by Evgeny Primakov, both as foreign minister and later as prime minister during the Yeltsin presidency. The first three chapters that comprise the second part of *Russia: Re-Emerging Great Power* examine Russian policy toward the countries of what was termed the 'near abroad' in the immediate aftermath of the dissolution of the Soviet Union.

Almost immediately after the collapse of the former USSR, several of the new successor states faced secessionist movements that involved significant conflict, even civil war. In all of these cases Russia was involved – nominally as a peacekeeper, but in reality as a supporter of secessionist forces and as part of an attempt to pursue Russian state interests and maintain influence over neighbouring states.[4] Russia was directly involved in the conflicts that erupted in Moldova, in Georgia, and in Nagorno-Karabakh. Three of the chapters in Part 2 deal explicitly with Russian policy related to these conflicts. Both Graeme Herd and Bertil Nygren emphasize the degree to which Russian policy has shifted away from reliance on direct use of the military instrument, including *de facto* military intervention, to the use of economic and political capabilities to influence political developments in neighbouring states of the Commonwealth of Independent States (CIS). In his chapter on Russian policy concerning secessionist Transdniestria, Herd provides an updated assessment of Moldovan–Russian relations and of prospects for a resolution of the dispute between Moldova and its breakaway eastern province. He notes that the Russian approach to the issue has shifted over time from a focus on military relations to the use of economic and political levers. He argues that not only is Russian policy driven by views of Russia's rights as a great power in the region, but also by the fact that support for Transdniestria has become a matter of importance in Russian domestic politics.

Nygren's discussion of Russian policy toward Georgia in Chapter 5, emphasizes Russia's move away from supporting secessionist groups in the latter country and to a growing reliance on gaining control over key aspects of Georgia's economy, especially in the energy sector. Russian firms have simply bought out Georgian pipeline and electricity companies and, as occurred early in 2006 in Ukraine, have been willing to turn off the flow of energy to accomplish economic and, presumably, political objectives. Nygren concludes his examination of Russian–Georgian relations by noting that 'Russian relations with Georgia have increasingly been governed by "softer" policies guided by a "geo-economic" focus, seen as a more effective way of drawing Georgia into a firm Russian embrace than the previous conflict-laden strategies ....' The use of economic pressure in Russian dealings with Georgia became most evident in the confrontation between the two countries in early autumn 2006.

In Chapter 6, Susanne Nies provides an interesting examination of three enclaves that have survived the Soviet system and of their significance both for Russian policy and for broader security issues in the international system. As she points out, Russia views its approach to these regions as part of a larger strategy of rebuilding Russian influence or control over regions formerly an integral part of the USSR. She begins with a discussion of the idiosyncrasies of enclaves as political units that differ appreciably from other state structures. She then examines Russian policy *vis-à-vis* three enclaves – Kaliningrad, which is an integral part of the Russian Federation, and both Nagorno-Karabakh and Nakhchivan, whose destinies are tied together because of their involvement in the ongoing territorial conflict between Armenia and Azerbaijan. In an interesting parallel with the shift in Russian policy toward both Moldova/Transdniestria and Georgia, Nies notes that, although Russian policies towards Kaliningrad have been contradictory since 1991, a recent shift has decidedly opened up Kaliningrad and is supposed to create a 'Hong Kong in the Baltic'. This shift has important implications for the countries of the EU, in particular those located around the Baltic Sea.

Russian policy toward the two Transcaucasian enclaves and the countries, Armenia and Azerbaijan, to which they are tied has also undergone a parallel change in the direction of a more liberal approach in which Russia has become a reliable partner in the international process of containing the conflict between Azerbaijan and Armenia.

Herd, Nygren and Nies present overlapping arguments that Russian policy has shifted, at least in the cases that they have examined, to far less reliance on coercion and conflict to an expanded use of economic, political and diplomatic instruments in the attempt to pursue their policy objectives and to re-establish their dominant position within what was once Soviet space. No doubt this results from an awareness, based on earlier experience, of the counterproductive nature of confrontation and, as Susanne Nies puts it, on the fact that Russia is not yet a great power, if by that term we mean a state with 'soft power, the capacity to initiate diplomatic processes, to contribute with new proposals – in that sense Russia is surely not a great power'.

Chapters 7 and 8 examine Russian policy toward the countries of Central Asia within two overlapping, but quite different contexts. John Berryman focuses on the revitalization of Russian security relations with the countries of the region, in particular in relationship to the growth of Chinese economic and political involvement there, while Roger E. Kanet and Larisa Homarac examine the US challenge to Russian influence in Central Asia and the longer-term viability of current US policy. Berryman traces the revitalized Russian interest in the region that had begun by the end of the 1990s. Despite Putin's willingness, as part of his new approach to the United States, to accept the temporary presence of US forces in the area, the Russians have matched US involvement with wide-spread efforts to reestablish security ties with the governments of the region and a willingness to downplay, even ignore, the repressive nature of most of the regimes. Besides the expanding security ties between Russia and the Central Asian states and despite the concerns of these governments to free themselves from economic dependence on Russia, new linkages tying the energy industries to Russia have also been created.

In the short term, in its competition with both China and the United States for influence throughout Central Asia, Russia remains at an advantage. In the longer term, however, Berryman concludes, 'It is widely recognised that, as China's economy has doubled in size while Russia's has shrunk by almost half ... the extraordinary shift in their power relations will lead to a further reworking of their bilateral relationship which will profoundly impact on their relations in Central Asia'.

Kanet and Homarac focus on the challenge to the Russian position in Central Asia presented by the United States. They put US policy in the region within the broader context of the US war on terror, including US military operations in both Afghanistan and Iraq, but also as part of US policy aimed at maintaining global dominance, including containing Russian influence, especially over the extraction and transport of petroleum and gas. Given the inherent contradictions in US policy and the much stronger position from which the Russians operate in the region, they question the long-term viability of current US policy.

In Chapter 9, Robert O. Freedman discusses Russian relations with Iran, with special emphasis on the nuclear issue. Although the Russian leadership shares the concern of key Western governments about the probable negative implications of Iran's development of nuclear weapons, its decision to provide Iran with nuclear technology for the production of energy, as well as its decisions to sell sophisticated conventional armaments to Iran, are based on economic considerations. Moreover, Russia and Iran have cooperated in areas close to the Russian border such as Tajikistan, and Russia appreciated the low profile taken by Iran during its wars in Chechnya.

Russia has attempted to balance its relationships with the United States and with the EU states, with the development of meaningful ties with other states – in particular, with those which, as China and Iran, share the Russian concern about US dominance in world affairs. Freedman traces the intricacies of the Russian effort in recent years to juggle it relations with Iran and its desire to sell nuclear technology with its relations with Europe and, especially, the United States. He notes that, while Russia 'has sought to put that day of decision off as long as possible, the time may be coming sooner rather than later when Moscow will have to choose between Iran and the West. Whether Putin will be able to finesse such a choice is a very open question.'

The contributors to this volume do not provide a simple, clear-cut answer to the question whether Russia at this point has re-established itself as a great power. However, the authors, either explicitly or implicitly, have reached a consensus that Putin and the Russian leadership are committed to re-establishing Russia's great power role in world affairs. Most would agree, however, that, despite the dramatic improvement in Russia's economic and political foundations in recent years and the fact that Russia has returned to the ranks of major world powers, its continued membership in that club remains contingent on a variety of factors, not least important of which is the continued growth of its domestic economy.

Notes

1 This argument is developed more fully in Roger E. Kanet, 'The Superpower Quest for Empire: The Cold War and Soviet Support for "Wars of National Liberation"', *Cold War History* 6/3 (2006), pp. 331–52.
2 I have discussed these developments in Russian policy in some detail in several articles: Alexander V. Kozhemiakin and Roger E. Kanet, 'The Impact of Nationalism on Russian Foreign Policy', in William E. Ferry and Roger E. Kanet (eds), *Post-Communist States in the World Community* (London: Macmillan; New York: St Martin's Press, 1998), pp. 46–61; Roger E. Kanet and Nuray Ibryamova, 'Verpaßte Gelegenheiten? Amerikanisch-Russische Beziehungen in den 90er Jahren', *Osteuropa*, 51/8 (2001), pp. 985–1001; and Roger E. Kanet, 'Zwischen Konsens und Konfrontation: Rußland und die Vereinigten Staaten', *Osteuropa*, 51/4–5 (2001), pp. 509–21.
3 Other analysts have concluded, as do some of the authors in the present volume, that Russia has regained the status of a major actor in international affairs and can be viewed as a great power. See, e.g., the perceptive volume edited by Jakob Hedenskog, Vilhelm Konnander, Bertril Nygren, Ingmar Oldberg, and Christer Pursiainen, *Russia as a Great Power: Dimensions of Security Under Putin* (London and New York: Routledge, 2005).
4 For background, see Alexander V. Kozhemiakin and Roger E. Kanet, 'Russia as a Regional Peacekeeper', in Roger E. Kanet (ed.), *Resolving Regional Conflicts* (Champaign, IL: University of Illinois Press, 1998), pp. 225–39.

Part I
Russian Strategy Under Putin

1
Russia's Great Power Ambitions and Policy Under Putin

Ingmar Oldberg

Although Russia's superpower status faded away with the Soviet Union, there is a striking consensus in Russia today that the country has been, is and will remain a great power. This claim has become a mantra for the Russian political leadership under Vladimir Putin and a prominent feature in current Russian foreign policy, which in its implementation affects both Russians and their neighbours in other states.

This chapter first analyses how the political leadership and well-known analysts in Russia define this claim to greatness by citing a number of representative statements made in the past few years, with due regard given to the situations and audiences. Second, the chapter examines how the decision-making leadership has sought to exercise power and gain recognition for Russia as a great power in international organizations and in its relations with major countries on the world arena. It also explores which problems this policy has encountered, thus assessing the realism of the claims.[1]

Russian great power claims

The claim that the new Russia that emerged from the Soviet Union is a great power was made already under President Yeltsin in the 1990s, despite the fact that the country suffered from serious economic and political crises.[2] Under President Putin, the claim has become more strident and outspoken, especially in the domestic arena. When taking over the presidency from Yeltsin at the end of 1999, Putin in a programmatic statement expressed belief in the greatness of Russia, saying that 'Russia was and will remain a great power, preconditioned by the inseparable characteristics of its geopolitical, economic and cultural existence'. He also stressed the need for a strong state power as 'the main driving force of any change' in Russia, and the value of Russian patriotism.[3] In his Address to the Federal Assembly in 2005, Putin asserted that 'Russia has been, is and will be a major (*krupneishei*) European nation, where the ideas of freedom, human rights, justice and democracy for many centuries have been determining values', sometimes even ahead of European standards.[4] According to Putin, these values have determined the desire to see Russia's state independence grow and its sovereignty strengthened. He especially wanted to stress that Russia's place in the world would depend on how strong and successful it was.[5] The great power claims are, thus, based on both material and spiritual factors and are closely connected to the strength of the state.

Great power claims are also made to foreign audiences on various grounds. At the summit of the Group of Eight (G-8) leading industrial states in 2004 Putin boasted that 'Russia is one of the world's biggest nuclear powers', and emphasized that efforts to resolve issues like non-proliferation of nuclear weapons would not be serious without Russian participation.[6] At the 2005 G-8 summit, Putin more tactfully chose to stress that 'Russia is the world leader on the energy market' with the biggest potential in oil, gas and nuclear energy taken together.[7]

In the same vein, former Foreign Minister Igor Ivanov in 2004 told the all-Arabian television station that Russia was, is and will remain one of the leading world powers because of its size and economic and military potential. It is a permanent member of the UN Security Council and, therefore, has a special responsibility for peace and stability, according to Ivanov.[8]

Similar and even more ambitious statements are made by many other Russian officials, politicians and analysts. In a comparative analysis of great powers in history Yeltsin's former Deputy Defence Minister Andrei Kokoshin in 2002 concluded that Russia is in fact a *superpower* as a result of its nuclear weapons, vast territory and natural resources. Concerning so-called human capital development, Russia allegedly was ahead of China and India, for example. Kokoshin added another criterion of greatness, namely that also strong leadership has served to win great power status for some states, as shown by Peter the Great in imperial Russia and Charles de Gaulle in France.[9]

Not least are Russian great power claims based on history. When celebrating the incorporation of the Kazan Khanate by Muscovy in the mid-sixteenth century, Putin asserted that already this historic event allowed Russia to become 'one of the largest and most influential states in the world'.[10] At the 60th anniversary of the victory in the Second World War, when leaders from all over the world were present, Putin emphasized

Russia's decisive role, claiming that 'the Red Army by liberating Europe and in the battle over Berlin brought the war to a victorious end', although he went on to hail the Allied help.[11]

Indeed, some of these reasons seem to justify calling Russia a great power. There is no denying that Russia has the largest area of all states in the world and is second only to the United States regarding the number of nuclear weapons. It has become one of the biggest oil and gas exporters in recent years and has the largest reserves of gas. Undoubtedly, the Soviet Union played a decisive role in defeating Hitler's Germany in Europe, and Russia has inherited the Soviet Union's position as one of five permanent members of the United Nations (UN) Security Council. Present-day Russia is, thus, seen as heir to both the vast Tsarist empire and the Soviet Union, the world's second superpower.

The current strong emphasis of Putin and his administration on Russian great power status, independence and national interests is probably best explained by growing Russian economic strength after the deep crisis in the 1990s, especially regarding energy exports. The claims also reflect the promotion of Russian state patriotism, which has replaced Marxism-Leninism as a unifying ideology for the various nationalities in Russia, among which the Russians are dominant. Furthermore, the great power doctrine fits well with the concentration of power in the hands of President Putin. His power at home serves to underpin his authority in the international arena, and international recognition of Russia as a great power serves to buttress Putin's power domestically.

Notwithstanding the above claims to greatness, Russian leaders, of course, at the same time recognize that the country has many problems and weaknesses, and they understand that great power status must be fought for.[12] This was especially true during Putin's first years in power. In his 1999 programme statement, Putin realized that today a great power relies more on advanced technology and high living standards than on military power. Russia had fallen behind other major powers in the 1990s and had to work hard to catch up. To the Federal Assembly Putin in 2003 said that Russia *will* (author's emphasis) 'firmly take its place among the truly strong, economically advanced and influential states of the world', but he admitted that it was faced with serious threats.[13] On closer inspection, the earlier mentioned claims to greatness are often more based on potential strength or history than on the present situation.

In the 2004 speech, Putin declared that his aim was to raise the Russian living standard and strengthen Russia's position in the world, although he also complained that not everybody in the world wanted an independent, strong and self-confident Russia. In response to Western criticism of the lack of democracy in Russia, Putin underlined that Russia builds on its own traditions and will develop them in its own way at its own pace.[14]

Russian officials and most analysts share these views. For example, Foreign Ministry official Alexander Orlov has explained that Russia will never tire of asserting its right to play a leading role on the world stage and will not accept the role of a poor relative that the West wants to impose on it.[15] Gleb Pavlovsky, a Kremlin political consultant, has stated that the main priority under Putin is to make Russia a twenty-first century world power, while admitting that it presently is a weak regional power with a weak commodity-based economy.[16] Liberal commentators such as Vladimir Nadein have, instead, regretted that Russia remains a 'free-loading superpower', which does not want to be a normal country and wishes to be feared by the world.[17] Even if Putin and his people realize the country's remaining weaknesses, this does not prevent them from harbouring great power ambitions; rather the opposite is the case.

Thus, the claim to great power status is permanent, but the motivations and foundations for it have shifted according to audience and situation. In recent years the claims have become stronger and increasingly based on economic criteria, especially in foreign forums. As will be shown below, the status is seen as having political consequences, entailing certain rights and responsibilities.

Domestic and foreign sources of power

The Russian leadership under Putin wishes to underpin and strengthen its great power position in several ways. The main aim is to make Russia strong again through self-reliance by increasing its economic potential, raising the living standard, exporting more energy, etc. At the same time and on that basis Putin has started to restore Russia's military strength by allocating large shares of the budget to the defence sector. Putin also strives to strengthen state power and concentrate it at the top, to boost efficiency in administration and planning and to fight corruption. He wants to unite the people by building on Russian patriotism and national traditions. The imperial Tsarist heritage, as well as the Soviet Union's exploits in the Second World War, are cherished.

In the international arena, which is the focus of this chapter, the Russian ambition, as already noted, is to increase its influence and prestige abroad by all available means.[18] Russian foreign policy under Putin has become more coordinated, versatile and assertive than it was under Yeltsin. It attempts to forge ties both with the most influential powers in the world and renew ties with old friends and allies in the Third World. There is a combination of bandwagoning with the leading Western powers along with the formation of alliances in opposition to them, which can be seen as balancing acts.

Rising world prices of energy and raw materials have greatly strengthened the Russian economy and improved its bargaining position *vis-à-vis* its trading partners, as will be exemplified below. The political leadership, therefore, wants to control, promote and cooperate with Russian companies abroad.

Besides economic aims and means, Putin has made the war against terrorism a central theme in Russian foreign and domestic policy, which of course has to do with the war in Chechnya and recurrent terrorist attacks across Russia, for instance in Moscow in 1999. This was the principal reason why Putin was as elected as president in 2000, after having been appointed interim president by Yeltsin, and concentrated power into his hands. When the 11 September attacks hit the United States in 2001, Putin felt justified and supported the US-led war against international terrorism and the invasion of Afghanistan, thereby garnering political support in the United States.[19] As will be shown below, Russia has made cooperation against terrorism a central issue in its relations with practically all states and international organizations such as the UN, the Organization for Security and Cooperation in Europe (OSCE), the NATO-Russia Council and the CIS. In 2004 Russia was elected to head the Counter-Terrorism Committee of the UN Security Council, and after the terrorist attack at Beslan that council supported Russia with a sharp condemnation of the terrorists. Russia has even been claimed to be 'the key country in all anti-terrorist activities'.[20] How efficient this policy has been will be assessed below.

Russia's role in international organizations

'Multipolarity' is a key concept, often mentioned in Russia's foreign policy documents, in its attempts to secure its position as a great power on the world arena. Developed by Yeltsin's Foreign Minister Yevgeny Primakov in 1996, the concept means fighting for a world in which the United States does not dominate and where Russia is one of the poles of power or influence. In the early 2000s, the concept was criticized for setting a goal beyond Russia's powers, but it is sometimes is still used, especially at meetings with potential allies such as China and India (see below). Most often Russian foreign policy under Putin is officially called 'multivector', which means an independent policy with relations and interests in many directions. As formulated by Mikhail Margelov, Putin's trusted chairman of the Foreign Affairs Committee of the Federation Council, Russia has to play the whole field, not only some of the squares, if it wants to remain a world power.[21]

To this end, Russia strives to exercise influence in international political organizations, particularly in the most exclusive ones, where its membership can be seen as multipolarity in practice and as a recognition of Russia's great power status. As noted above, Russia appreciates the importance of the UN Security Council (SC), where it has inherited the position as one of five permanent members with a veto right. As noted, this is seen to give Russia a special responsibility for peace and stability in the world. For example, Russia has used its veto right to demand that the member states' military actions must be approved by the SC, and therefore opposed NATO's bombing of Yugoslavia and the US-led occupation of Iraq. For the same reason, Russia accepted the US intervention in Afghanistan in 2001. Russia's former Foreign Minister Primakov became one of the 'wise men' working out a proposal for reforming the United Nations. Russia accepted the expansion of the SC and supported the candidacies of Germany and India, which are seen as friends. However, Russia wanted some *quid pro quo*, and it is uncertain whether it was willing to grant them veto rights. In the end, the issue did not even appear on the UN agenda, partly because the United States linked the enlargement to the creation of a new council for human rights, which Russia and others resisted.[22]

Russia has also participated in the G-8 summits since 1997, which it highly values. At the 2004 summit, Putin praised the G-8 for being a forum for coordinating positions on the key issues in the world, although he acknowledged that no binding decisions are taken in this largely informal club. Russia was entrusted with the presidency and with arranging the next summit in 2006, it made world energy policy the key issue. Concerning the touchy issue of widening the circle, Putin in 2004 talked about admitting China and India, but at the 2005 summit he did not want to suggest membership, because Russia is a new member and it was enough to invite the states into the discussions.[23] The problem is that Russia became a formal member only in the political part of the forum mainly on US recommendations after September 2001, since Russia does not fulfil the economic criteria for membership. United States Congressmen have since suggested excluding Russia again, to which it has reacted strongly.

Furthermore, Russia is a member of the Mediation Quartet for the Israel–Palestine conflict along with the United States, the United Nations and the EU, and it has become a participant in the six-nation talks concerning

North Korea's nuclear programme with the USA, South Korea, China and Japan. This too may boost Russia's prestige and power, even though the chief rationale for including Russia may partly have been to prevent it from creating problems.[24]

Concerning broader regional organizations, Russia in the 1990s pinned high hopes on the OSCE, in which every member has a veto, suggesting that it should replace NATO as an all-European security organization. However, NATO was not abolished, but rather enlarged. Moreover, Russia has in recent years become increasingly dissatisfied with the OSCE because of its promotion of democracy in ex-Soviet states and its calls for Russian troop withdrawals (see below). In order to force the organization to concentrate on other security issues like the threat of terrorism, Russia has used its veto to block the adoption of the OSCE budget.

Russia, thus, is a member of several important international organizations and forums, which can be seen as recognition of its great power status. However, Russia's real influence in some of them is quite limited, since it participates by invitation, and no binding decisions are made. Russia also participates in several regional organizations such as the Council of Baltic Sea States, the Council of Black Sea States, the Shanghai Cooperation Organization and the Asian-Pacific Economic Cooperation, and it is an observer in the Organization of Islamic States since 2003. This both testifies to Russia's global interests and reflects its geographic extension.

As for economic organizations, it should be noted that Russia to date is not a member of the World Trade Organization (WTO) despite many years of negotiations, whereas China was accepted in 2001. Russia has repeatedly complained about excessive demands on opening its markets, whereas many members do not want to give Russia special favours.[25]

Relations with Western states and blocs

In order to exert influence and be recognized as a major power, Putin, as Yeltsin before him, relies on so-called strategic partnerships with the most important western states, especially the United States, the only indisputable superpower in the world. As mentioned, the Russian support for the American war on terrorism after September 2001 improved relations with the United States and contributed to the decision to accord Russia a seat on the G-8 and to create the NATO–Russia Council (below). Russia accepted American bases in Central Asia as a backup for the war in Afghanistan and claimed that with regard to the war on terrorism, the countries are not only partners, but allies.

The countries also had common interests in certain strategic issues. In May 2002, Russia and the United States signed a bilateral treaty on reducing offensive strategic weapons, and Russia supported the American policy of nuclear non-proliferation. Russia further promised to help satisfy the growing American need for energy imports, and US companies belonged to the main investors in the Russian energy sector. The presidents developed good personal relations including a regular exchange of visits. When President Bush visited Putin in St Petersburg right after invading Iraq in May 2003, Putin was happy to say that their unshakeable partnership 'contributed to uniting the world community against new threats'. Clearly, Russia's special relationship with the United States concerning nuclear issues and terrorism serves to elevate its status above that of the other great powers.

However, Russia's partnership with the United States has increasingly come under strain for several reasons. The Bush administration started a war against and occupied Iraq in 2003 despite opposition from Russia and other states in the UN Security Council. Furthermore, the United States was seen to interfere in Russia's zone of influence, for instance by supporting Western-inspired revolutions in Ukraine and Georgia in 2003–05. Concerning terrorism, the United States refused to extradite Chechens whom Russia accused of being terrorists, and US media levelled criticism against the Russian war in Chechnya. As for nuclear issues, the United States suspected that Russian trade with North Korea and Iran contributed to the construction of nuclear weapons, which Russia denied. In the economic sphere Russia could not satisfy American energy needs in the short term, and American investors worried about the freedom of business in Russia. The American leadership also politely questioned Putin's increasingly authoritarian measures, whereupon Russian leaders started to find faults in the American form of democracy.[26] During a visit to New Delhi in December 2004 Putin denounced 'the barracks principles of the unipolar world' and 'dictatorship' in international affairs, 'even if it is packaged in pretty, pseudo-democratic phraseology' – words that clearly referred to the United States.[27] A basic problem with the partnership with the United States is that it depends on US goodwill and that the United States in many respects has more trusted partners than Russia.

Furthermore, Russia cultivates its partnership with NATO, the strongest military organization in the world. Relations have improved greatly since September 2001, resulting in the creation of the NATO–Russia Council (NRC)[28] in 2002 for cooperation on specific issues like fighting terrorism and non-proliferation. The NRC, in which Russia has an equal status with the NATO members and a veto right, is a special arrangement that no other state has with NATO. More and more often military exercises are held with NATO units. According to Putin, the cooperation between Russia and NATO states made the victory in Afghanistan possible and has 'become a real factor ensuring international stability'.[29]

However, this partnership also has clear limits. Even if Putin once talked about joining NATO, he later rejected the idea, because it would limit Russia's sovereignty and freedom of decision-making.[30] Russian cooperation with NATO could not even stop the enlargement of NATO to include even countries that formerly belonged to the Warsaw Pact or were part of the Soviet Union, notably the three Baltic States. Nor could it stop the widening of NATO's zone of engagement to the east, the creation of its rapid reaction force, and its growing cooperation with the CIS states. Russia thus in reality sees NATO, dominated as it is by the United States and now including several Russia-critical members, as a problematic partner, if not as a threat to Russia.

In order to balance its relations with the US-dominated military organization of NATO, Russia has further developed a so-called strategic partnership with the European Union and its key members. This relationship with Europe is especially stressed when relations with the United States are tense. In 2000, for example, Foreign Minister Igor Ivanov called on Europe to be united and independent in order to contribute to a multipolar system. In his 2003 Federal Assembly speech, Putin proclaimed that broad rapprochement and real integration with Europe is Russia's historical choice, and mentioned the United States only in the context of fighting terrorism. At EU meetings Putin often stresses that Russia is part of Europe and its culture. Of course, the growing integration, the widening of objectives and the enlargement of the Union since the 1990s have also boosted Russian interest.

Russia's partnership with the EU has thus developed with several new agreements and regular meetings. The EU states have become Russia's main trading partners, and some of them are quite dependent on Russian oil and gas. This is especially true for the new East European members. At the 11th summit in 2003, Russia and the EU both talked about strategic partnership on the basis of common values. They created a Permanent Partnership Council (a counterpart to the NRC) and decided to form four common spaces of cooperation, for economy, security and justice, external security, research and education. In 2005, the parties agreed on 'road maps' in these areas in order to create a so-called Common Economic Space. Russia also accepts the EU's Common Security and Defence Policy and wants to contribute to its emergent military force.

However, there are also several problems in this relationship. As with NATO, Russia has no chance of becoming a member in the foreseeable future, nor does it aspire to membership, because that would allegedly limit its independence as a great power. A key problem is that Russia insists on equality, while in actual fact the EU economic community is stronger. The EU expects Russia to adapt its legislation to the EU's, as other neighbours do, whereas the opposite would be very complicated. Russia rejects the European Neighbourhood Policy programme, which lumps Russia together with many other neighbours. With regard to military cooperation Russia wants the use of EU forces to be sanctioned by the UN and the OSCE, which would give Russia a veto right. Another basic problem is that the EU overlaps with NATO and is closer to the United States than to Russia in most respects.

Partly as a result of the difficulties in dealing with the EU as a whole, Russia at the same time continues its traditional policy of nurturing relations with its best friends in the Union, at present Germany and France, states which also are great powers. The three acted together to oppose the US– British invasion of Iraq in 2003 and formed a 'triangle' with regular summits,[31] thereby undermining the unity of the EU (and NATO). France has an imperial part and embraces similar views as Russia on multipolarity and US hegemony. Germany is Russia's main trading partner, and Putin became very friendly with Chancellor Gerhard Schröder. In the Russian view, the special relations are profitable for Russia and serve to strengthen its sovereignty.[32] In September 2005, Putin and Schröder signed an agreement on building a gas pipeline by 2010 directly across the Baltic Sea. Gazprom will hold 51 per cent of the shares and also invest in German gas companies, while the latter will invest in Russian gas fields. The pipeline will make Russia less dependent on the pipelines through Poland and other states for its export to Europe and enable it to exercise more pressure on them. Germany, which is already more dependent on Russian oil and gas than other 'old' EU states, will be even more dependent.[33] However, even though growing, this energy import from Russia still makes up a small share of total EU imports, and Russia has so far not used energy as a political means of pressure against Western states – although Russia's cutting off gas exports to Ukraine in 2005 for economic and political reasons did result in cuts in gas reaching Western Europe.[34]

Another political problem for Russia is the fact that most EU states are very critical of its war in Chechnya and Putin's increasingly undemocratic regime, even more so than the United States. This is particularly the case with the new Central and East European members, which have experienced Russian and Soviet oppression and, therefore, try to influence the

Union accordingly. Russia has countered by accusing the new EU (and NATO) members of Russophobia. As before accession, Estonia and Latvia are claimed to discriminate against their Russian minorities. Russia refuses to sign and ratify border agreements with them and does not even maintain normal political exchange with them.

Enlargement of the EU has also created new problems, both political and economic. Russian leaders criticize the adoption of Schengen visa requirements by the new members for creating new divisions in Europe and isolating the Kaliningrad exclave from the rest of Russia. As for visas, Russia – differently from Ukraine for instance – insists on reciprocity and maintains complicated visa routines for visitors.[35]

Last, but not least, Russia is worried about the EU extending its ties to former Soviet republics, notably its new ambition to solve the so-called frozen conflicts in South Caucasus and Moldova and its support for pro-Western democratic leaders such as Viktor Yushchenko in Ukraine, in this case acting in unison with the United States. Thus, even if Russian leaders officially may regret the constitutional crisis in the EU that erupted in 2005, most commentators expect that this may delay further EU expansion and engagement in Eastern Europe.[36]

Thus, Russia is recognized as a valuable partner by the EU, and many EU members have become more dependent on Russian energy. Russia clearly sees this as a prop for its great power status. Still, Russia has become even more economically dependent on the EU as a whole, and the EU countries are clearly the stronger party. The parties have some common political interests, but Russian foreign policy ambitions and domestic political development increasingly clash with those of the EU member states.

Balancing in Asia

If the Russian partnerships with Western states and groupings can be seen as bandwagoning with and seeking recognition from the dominant powers in the world, Russia at the same time tries to balance this through 'strategic partnerships' with the rising Asian giants, China and India. In relations with these countries there is often talk of multipolarity.[37] Thus, Russia in 2001 concluded a friendship and cooperation treaty with China, and the parties agree on many foreign policy issues like promoting multipolarity, fighting separatism, terrorism, US policy in Iraq, US space warfare, etc. For many years China has been Russia's main recipient of arms exports in defiance of a Western embargo since 1989, and nuclear cooperation has been resumed. Military cooperation has developed, for example with a major common exercise in 2005. Together with China,

Russia and four Central Asian states make up the Shanghai Cooperation Organization, which is partly intended to keep the United States out of Central Asia.

However, there are great problems and mutual distrust between Russia and China after the cold war between them since the 1960s. China is the most populous country in the world and may soon become the biggest economy after the United States. Many Russians fear that China will become a military threat in the future and that increasing cross-border trade may lead to a Chinese take-over of the thinly populated Siberian and Far Eastern provinces.

Therefore Russia tries to offset China by developing relations with Japan, still the strongest economy in Asia and China's traditional enemy. A sign of this was the Russian decision in 2004 to build an oil pipeline with Japanese support all the way from Angarsk in Siberia to the Pacific coast, instead of a shorter pipeline to Daqing in Manchuria, which would make Russia dependent on China as a customer and a partner for other export markets.

However, one problem with not giving China secure deliveries of oil is that this may increase Chinese efforts to get oil from Central Asia instead. There are clear limits to Russian cooperation with Japan, as well. Japan insists on making the return of four Kurile islands a condition for a peace treaty. This is unacceptable to the Russian leadership because of nationalist opinion at home and the fear of creating a precedent for ceding territory elsewhere. Japan is also allied with the United States and economically well integrated in the Western world. As a way to press Japan into giving up its demands, Russia therefore reminds it of Russia's good border relations with China. Russia also talks about building a Chinese branch of the pipeline, which may precede or even replace the longer branch to the Pacific.[38]

In Asia Russia further relies on its proclaimed strategic partnership with India, with which it has maintained good relations since the 1950s, when India was a leading non-aligned country. India has become Russia's second biggest customer for weapons after China, again defying Western restrictions. Yet, India may also be an increasingly difficult partner for Russia because of its own power ambitions. India has a population exceeding one billion, its economy is now growing very fast, and it is increasingly oriented towards the West.

Russia has finally tried to form a strategic triangle together with both China and India. At a tripartite meeting recently in Vladivostok, Foreign Minister Lavrov noted that the parties have 'joint approaches to global issues based in international law and principles of multipolarity'. They also hold similar views concerning separatism and terrorism.[39] True, the prospects for this strategic scheme have improved since Chinese–Indian relations were recently normalized. Yet, they were long marked by hostility since the war between these states in 1962, and economic competition between them may intensify. In fact, all three parties are more oriented toward the West than toward each other, and they all stress that the grouping is not directed against any third party. It seems safe to conclude that Russia's balancing in Asia has clear limits and that it runs the risk becoming a junior partner of the strong powers there as well.

Russian great power policy in the former Soviet area

Russia's main foreign political priority is to remain a great power *vis-à-vis* the other states that formerly belonged to the Soviet Union and now are members of the Commonwealth of Independent States (CIS) (excluding the Baltic States). According to Putin's Federal Assembly speech of 2003, the CIS countries belong to Russia's strategic sphere of interest and are close neighbours, with which it has centuries-long, historic, cultural, economic ties. Terrorism, transnational crime and drugs were identified as the main common threats.[40] In the 2005 Assembly speech Putin said that 'the collapse of the Soviet Union was a major (*krupneishei*) geopolitical disaster of the century', a drama that for Russia meant that tens of millions of compatriots ended up outside the country. He also emphasized that Russia should 'continue its civilizing mission on the Eurasian continent ... ensuring that democratic values, combined with national interests, enrich and strengthen our historic community'.[41] In the Russian Security Council Putin had earlier stressed security issues, saying that Russia has a significant role in maintaining stability in the CIS region and offering solutions to problems like settling conflicts, protection against common threats, strengthening borders, etc.[42]

In accordance with these aims, Russia uses a wide array of means of power in the region. In 1991 Russia took the initiative to form the CIS as a substitute for the dissolving Soviet Union, and it still maintains the organization. Yet, in view of the difficulties of keeping the CIS together, Russia has more and more focused on gathering the willing partners in smaller organizations, where it is bound to dominate due to its comparative strength, such as the Collective Security Treaty Organization (CSTO) formed in 1992 and the Single Economic Space (SES), formed in 2003 by Russia, Ukraine, Belarus and Kazakhstan. The obvious intention is to create countervailing blocs or 'partners' under Russian control for NATO and the EU and to keep other great powers out. Thus the CSTO is said to be a complementary element of global security, which should have working relations with NATO.[43] Under CSTO auspices common military exercises are regularly held and Russia sells military hardware at preferential prices to the other members.

On the bilateral level, Russia maintains military bases in several states in support of the host governments, for example in Tajikistan. In other cases it supports separatist regions in opposition to the central governments, for example in Georgia, Moldova and to some extent Ukraine. Russia also backed Armenia against Azerbaijan, for instance when the Armenian Nagorno-Karabakh enclave in Azerbaijan was 'liberated' and became a pseudo-state in the early 1990s. Since 2004, Russia also more or less openly promotes a second CIS consisting of the separatist regions with the proclaimed aim to promote state building and democratic institutions.[44]

Contrary to its democratic pretensions, Russia has no qualms about authoritarian regimes and their suppression of human rights, if only they are anti-Western. Thus, Russia defends Alexander Lukashenka's Soviet-type regime in Belarus against Western criticism.

Concerning economic integration Russia can exploit the fact that the other countries since Soviet times are most dependent on Russia as a trading partner, especially with regard to energy, raw materials and transit to the West. The Russian economy has grown faster than those of the other states and attracted millions of 'guest workers'. Most states have become indebted to Russia, which has enabled Russian companies, especially in the energy sector, to take over key companies in these states. The SES aims to create a common market for goods, services, capital and labour and to coordinate foreign trade, taxes, currency and finances on the EU model.

Nonetheless, Russia has run into difficulties in retaining its dominant power in the CIS region and in developing common institutions. Almost all members, even the authoritarian ones, want to become more independent from Russia and often seek support from the West. Thus, Georgia, Ukraine, Uzbekistan, Azerbaijan and Moldova formed the GUUAM (after the initial letters of the countries' names) in 1997. Russian backing of corrupt regimes and separatists contributed to popular revolutions in Georgia and, most importantly, Ukraine, which brought Western-oriented leaders to power. The communist regime in Moldova turned from Russia to the West in order to win back Transdniestria.

The authoritarian Karimov regime in Uzbekistan, which aspires to a leading role in Central Asia, left the CSTO in 1999 (as did Georgia and Azerbaijan) and allowed American bases to be established in 2001 so as to back up anti-terrorist operations in Afghanistan. But when the United

States wanted an investigation of a massacre in Andijan in 2005, Karimov asked the Americans to leave and got support from Russia instead.

Belarus remains Russia's best ally against the West and the two countries have formed a union, but the authoritarian president Lukashenka prevents Russia from gaining political and economic control of his country. The dictatorial regime of Turkmenistan conducts a neutral foreign policy and hardly participates in CIS cooperation.

In the economic sphere, Ukraine is afraid that integration in the SES may prevent integration with the EU, and this is a problem for Russia, too, to the extent that it wants such integration. Indeed, almost all CIS states, including Russia, have increased trade with the West at the expense of mutual trade since the early 1990s. Azerbaijan and Georgia, for example, agreed with Western oil companies to build an oil pipeline from Baku to the Turkish south coast (opened in 2005), which made them less dependent on Russian pipelines.

Thus, even if Russia has strong means of exerting power in the CIS region, it has lost influence also in this the most preferred area. The popular revolutions in Georgia and Ukraine, which are seen as inspired and fomented by the West, scared the Russian leaders that something similar might happen in Russia, thus reinforcing their determination to restore Russia's influence in these states and to maintain it in other places.

Some conclusions

The above survey shows that Russia views itself as a great power, however the concept is defined, and that this entitles it to a say in international affairs. But Russia is not content with its present position and wants to improve it at the expense of other states and to recover lost ground. The leaders nowadays act confidently and, with respect to smaller countries, often arrogantly. At the same time they are quite sensitive to criticism, which can be perceived as actual weakness and a sense of insecurity.

Even if the Russian economy has grown lately, and internal political stability seemingly has been achieved, Russia's great power status rests on a fairly narrow basis. In the world arena Russia is confronted by several great powers, which are stronger or growing more quickly, and it is therefore consigned to play its cards carefully and use all the means at its disposal. With regard to Western countries, Russia poses as an ally or partner, but it also exploits differences among them or tries to stand as a model of its own. For its position in international institutions, Russia to some extent depends on backing from the American superpower, which is looked upon with envy and admiration.

Russia's Western partnerships are balanced by partnerships with the leading countries in Asia, but these are also divided among themselves. Russian attempts to exploit these divisions have not been very successful.[45] Even in the post-Soviet region, where Russia undoubtedly is the greatest power, it has lost positions, as the other states band together, seek and receive backing from the West, or isolate themselves.

Another conclusion is that, despite all Russian talk about cooperation, trade and democratic values, foreign policy is still to a significant degree seen as a zero-sum power game. There is an obsession with security, national interests and independence. Even if Russia increasingly uses soft power like energy exports and transport, this is generally subordinated to political ends. Russia may thus be recognized as a great power in the traditional sense, but modern great powers are nowadays more broadly based and more open to international integration.[46]

Obviously, this Russian preoccupation with great power status and influence is partly a heritage from the past, partly it reflects the current authoritarian trends in the country. Thus, it may take time for Russia to become a really modern and 'normal' power in the Western sense, according to which greatness is mainly based on the citizens' welfare and a democratic system of government.

Notes

1 The author is grateful for constructive comments on a draft of this text from Professor Roger E. Kanet and from his colleagues B.-G. Bergstrand, Kerstin Castenfors, Ingemar Dörfer, Robert L. Larsson and Carolina Vendil Pallin.
2 See citations of Foreign Minister Alexei Kozyrev in 1994 and his successor Evgenyi Primakov in 1996 in Hanna Smith, 'Det förflutnas inflytande på rysk utrikespolitik' (The influence of the past on Russian foreign policy), *Nordisk Ostforum*, 3 (2005), pp. 290 f; Ingmar Oldberg *et al.*, *At a Loss – Russian Foreign Policy in the 1990s* (Stockholm, 1999), p. 16. For similar conclusions, see Richard Sakwa, *Putin. Russia's Choice* (London: Routledge, 2004), pp. 207 ff.
3 *Nezavisimaya gazeta*, 30 Dec. 1999.
4 On the Day of Russia 12 June, Putin claimed that Russia has one of the most democratic constitutions in the world. *Eurasia Daily Monitor*, 16 June 2005.
5 President of Russia website, 'Annual Address to the Federal Assembly', 25 April 2005, at <www.president.kremlin.ru> (visited 27 June 2005).
6 President of Russia, 'Press conference following the G-8 Summit', 11 June 2004, at <www.president.kremlin.ru> (visited 9 Nov. 2004).
7 President of Russia, 'Meeting with Russian and foreign media following the G-8 Summit', 8 July 2005, at <www.president.kremlin.ru> (visited 30 Aug. 2005).
8 Ministry of Foreign Affairs website,'Stenogramma interviu Ministra inostrannykh del Rossii', 20 Feb. 2004, at <www.ln.mid.ru> (visited 29 March 2004).

9 Andrei Kokoshin, 'What is Russia: a superpower, a great power or a regional power?', *International Affairs*, 6 (2002), pp. 105–7, 121 ff.

10 President of Russia, 'Speech at the ceremonial gathering to commemorate Kazan's 1000th anniversary', 26 Aug. 2005, at <www.president.kremlin.ru> (visited 30 Aug. 2005).

11 President of Russia, 'Vystuplenie na voennom parade', 9 May 2005, at <www.president.kremlin.ru> (visited 10 May 2005).

12 Sakwa, as note 2 above, p. 209.

13 *BBC Monitoring Global Newsline*, Former Soviet Union Political File, vol. 7, 16 May 2003.

14 President of Russia, 'Poslanie Federalnomu Sobraniiu Rossiiskoi Federatsii', 26 May 2004, at <www.president.kremlin.ru> (visited 28 May 2004).

15 Alexander Orlov, 'Russia will Never Accept the Role of a Poor Relation', *International Affairs*, 50/4 (2004), p. 31.

16 RIA, 3 Feb. 2005.

17 *Moscow News*, 22–28 Dec. 2004.

18 The following sections partly build upon my chapter 'Foreign Policy Priorities under Putin', in Jacob Hedenskog, Vilhelm Konnander, Bertil Nygren, Ingmar Oldberg, and Christer Pursiainen (eds), *Russia as a Great Power. Dimensions of Security under Putin* (London: Routledge, 2005), pp. 30 ff.

19 More on this in Pavel Baev, 'Counter-Terrorism as a Building Block for Putin's Regime', in Hedenskog *et al.*, ibid.

20 Ekaterina Kuznetsova, 'NATO: New anti-terrorist organization?', *International Affairs*, 3 (2004), p. 26.

21 Mikhail Margelov, 'Victory on points: Pragmatism in foreign policy', *Russia in Global Affairs*, 1/3 (2003), p. 223.

22 *Nezavisimaya gazeta*, 31 Aug. 2005; *Dagens Nyheter*, 14 Sept. 2005.

23 President of Russia, Press conference, 11 June 2004, Meeting with Russian and foreign media, 8 July 2005.

24 *Jerusalem Post*, 29 April 2005.

25 *Moscow News*, No. 34, p. 9.

26 President of Russia, Press conference by President Putin, 23 Dec. 2004, at <www.president.kremlin.ru/eng> (visited 17 Feb. 2005).

27 *RFE/RL Newsline*, No. 227, part 1, 6 Dec. 2004.

28 In Russia it is called the Russia–NATO Council.

29 President of Russia, 'Speech at the Security Council meeting', 29 Jan. 2005, at <www.president.kremlin.ru/eng>, (visited 17 Feb. 2005).

30 President of Russia, Interview, 22 Feb. 2005, at <http://www.kremlin.ru/ eng/speeches/2005/02/22/2038_type82916_8445.shtml>.

31 See, e.g., President of Russia, Press conference, 3 July 2005.

32 *Nezavisimaya gazeta*, 31 Aug. 2005.

33 *Svenska Dagbladet*, 8 Sep. 2005; *Eurasia Daily Monitor*, issue 169, 13 Sep. 2005.

34 Jan Leijonhielm and Robert L. Larsson, *Russia's Strategic Commodities: Energy and Metals as Security Levers* (Stockholm: FOI, 2004).

35 *The Economist*, 6 Aug. 2005.

36 Torbakov, *Eurasia Daily Monitor*, 3, 24 June 2005.

37 See also Sakwa, as note 2 above, pp. 226–8.

38 *Svenska Dagbladet*, 8 Sep. 2005. Lately Russia talks more about the pipeline to China.

39 *Eurasia Daily Monitor*, No. 108, 3 June 2005.
40 BBC Monitoring, 16 May 2003.
41 President of Russia, 'Annual Address to the Federal Assembly', 25 April 2005, at <http://www.kremlin.ru/eng/speedes/2005/04/25/2031_type7002912_87086.shtml>.
42 President of Russia, 'Speech at the Security Council', 29 Jan. 2005.
43 Ibid.
44 *Eurasia Daily Monitor*, No. 173.
45 This is also the conclusion of Mark N. Katz, 'Exploiting rivalries for prestige and profit', *Problems of Post-Communism*, 52/3 (2002), pp. 25 ff. Kokoshin asserts that Russia's mediation between India and Pakistan at a conference in Almaty in 2002 showed its ability as a great power. Kokoshin, as note 9 above What is Russia p. 123.
46 See also Iver B. Neumann, 'Russia as a Great Power', in Hedenskog *et al*, as note 25 above, pp. 25 ff.

2
Forming a New Security Identity Under Vladimir Putin

Nikita A. Lomagin

Russian history in the twentieth century was full of political upheavals. During the last century Russia has been through three revolutions, two world wars, seventy years of communism, and the collapse of the Soviet empire.[1] This meant that the Russians had to reinvent themselves: their law, their personality, their sense of security were not stable. The mentality of a 'besieged country' after the October Revolution[2] changed for partial partnership with the Western democracies during the Great Patriotic War, and again came the prewar 'normality' of confrontation in relations with the West during the cold war. Finally, the collapse of communism and the break-up of the Soviet Union resulted for Russia in the search for itself in a new world order (or maybe more correctly – disorder). Russia, having undergone so many great seismic shocks, now faces the problem of identity, trying to understand her national interests, first of all in the area of security.

The ending of the cold war transformed the two security dilemmas that have confronted states historically. The first locates the security dilemma in the unhappy circumstance that 'many of the means by which a state tries to increase its security decrease the security of others'.[3] The second concerns the allocation of national resources between economic welfare and military security. The division of resources between guns and butter and the actual level of consumption of both goods are determined by two factors, the productive capacity of a society and its preferences.[4]

Fifteen years of political and economic reforms in Russia have laid the groundwork for a market economy and a change of the political regime. Steady economic growth over the past six years, mostly because of extremely high oil prices and rapprochement with the West after 11 September, have forced Russia to face a fundamental question of policy: will she continue to pursue a great power security policy and, *in fact,* ignore the demands of a changed and changing world in the field of non-traditional security, or will she construct and implement a proactive and even preventive soft security policy? In the end, the fate of Putin's regime may depend on its ability to offer the Russian people better, and safer, living standards and to reverse the shocking decline in life expectancy.

This chapter explores the current stage of security identity formation in Russia. Although a majority of experts argues that Russian security policy under President Putin falls in the category of *realpolitik*, some important moves in the security area by the Kremlin cannot be explained merely by realism or neorealism and need further analysis. Official documents and Putin's speeches reveal a peculiar combination of security threats representing two traditionally different schools of thought in Russian security thinking. The first reflects traditional (or military) security thinking and, assuming the growth of traditional threats to national security, and calls for a greater emphasis on the need for substantial increases in military capabilities in Russia. The second perspective deals with the so-called soft security issues that are almost totally new for Russian security thinking. For instance, in setting the agenda for the G-8 summit in St Petersburg, Putin, to the surprise of many observers, put forward the global struggle with infectious deceases as one of the three most important issues of the Russian presidency in the club, despite the fact that just two years ago Russia itself was criticized by the World Bank and leading experts in the field for neglect of this issue.

A number of important questions emerge and require answers. What happens to a nation's sense of identity when its enemies no longer provide of a threat to that nation's very existence?[5] Does a new Russia need a new enemy? Why and how has the widening[6] of the security agenda in Russian politics taken place? Are mass identities based on the actor identity favoured by its political elite? And finally, what is a dominant security identity at the end of Putin's tenure in the Kremlin? In answering these questions, we draw from the constructivist approach to international relations theory and analysis which emerged in the last decade of the twentieth century. It advanced a sociological perspective of world politics, emphasizing the primacy of normative over material structures, the role of identity in the constitution of interests and action. Constructivism assumes that the identity of a state is a dependent variable determined by the historical, cultural, social and political context. State action flows from a particular state actor identity, which is shared by a policy elite and an understanding of the international context, both of which are viewed as socially constructed and historically contingent. Constructivism focuses not only on the policy elites' construction of the identity of the state as an actor, but also on the construction of national identities by elites, as well as the self-construction of individual political identities.[7]

The contemporary Russian political elite may embrace and act to sustain a variety of Russian identities as an international political actor (Russia as a great power, Russia as regional hegemon, Russia as a modern, European-style democracy and so on). The question of which form of identity is the dominant one must be tested empirically. A state's behaviour is viewed as an intention to reproduce its identity as a state actor conditioned by shared norms – for example, if a state identifies itself as a great power, it will act to reproduce that identity in terms of the prevailing norms regarding great power behaviour. While realists assume that the anarchic character of the international system is an objective reality that shapes the behaviour of states, constructivists assume that anarchy is what states make of it. The constructivist approach entails investigating the Russian sense of state actor identity, as well as the Russian/Putin's understanding of the international context and the identity and security interests of other states.

The 1993 foreign policy concept and national security concept

In the early 1990s some foreign affairs experts in the United States warned that the Soviet threat would reappear in a revived nationalistic, authoritarian Russia, with the natural resources, people, and nuclear weapons again to challenge American principles and threaten American security. It seems that by 2006 this prognosis has become a reality. By the end of the twentieth century, however, Russian economic stagnation, demographic decline, conventional military weakness, pervasive corruption, and fragile political authority put a pause to images of America as Russia's possible other and/or enemy.[8]

To a great extent the construction of a new Russian security identity was anticipated by the authors of the new (1993) Russian Constitution and of the new partnership between Russia and the European Union (EU). The constitution stipulated that the key priority of Russian foreign policy must be the integration of Russia into the 'civilized world'. By this it clearly meant, first of all, support for the values of Western civilization. Historically, it was quite logical. Since the era of Peter the Great (1689–1725), Russian diplomacy has without question looked towards Europe first and foremost.[9] Indeed, geographic proximity, the long-term cultural ties between Russia and Europe, and the fact that today's Europe is the major trading partner of Russia made it a major partner of Russia in the international arena. Integration into the civilized world (first, Europe) meant, *inter alia*, sharing some basic values, including those related to security.

But this was an uneasy process. The bankruptcy of a simple communism-to-democracy conversion, as implied by the Russian Foreign Minister Andrei Kozyrev in 1992–93, was reflected in a debate over the national interests of Russia. In general, national interest is a slippery concept, used to describe as well as prescribe foreign policy. In a democracy, the national interest is simply the set of shared priorities regarding relations with the rest of the world. It is broader than strategic interests, although they are part of it. A democratic definition of the national interest does not accept the distinction between a morality-based and an interests-based foreign policy.

In Russia the consensus of 1993 resulted in the drafting of the Foreign Policy Concept that signalled the emergence of a post-perestroika Russian foreign and security policy.[10] First, the national tradition of the unchallenged domination of national security and foreign policy priorities over domestic economic, political and social development was reversed. For the Kremlin, economic progress and democratic stabilization emerged as the key objectives by which Russia's external activity was to be subordinated. Second, the Russian state, whose emergence had coincided with the era of colonial conquest, was decoupled from the Russian Empire after more than four centuries during which the two were inseparable. Third, also gone was the messianic component (the Third Rome, panslavism and world socialism) which for centuries had been a guiding principle of foreign policy making. The process of 'secularization' of Russian foreign policy, its liberation from the 'special spiritual mission' of the country, finally seemed to prevail. As Trenin and Lo stated, Yevgeny Primakov, who succeeded Kozyrev in January 1996, adapted Palmerston's dictum in claiming that Russia 'does not have permanent friends, but permanent interests'. This thesis of permanent interests can be sustained as it relates to such broad objectives as national security, territorial integrity, and economic prosperity.[11]

According to the new Foreign Policy Concept (1993), at a time of growing uncertainty and unpredictability with respect to the development of the international situation, any actions in the political sphere aimed at undermining the integrity of the Russian Federation and the integrative processes in the CIS, vilolations of human rights and freedoms and armed conflicts in adjacent states, and steps intended to weaken und undermine Russia's international prestige would be viewed as threats to the security of the country and the vital interests of its citizens. In the economic sphere the chief danger stems from the fact that the process of opening up the Russian economy could be accompanied by a weakening of Russia's economic independence, degradation of its technological and industrial potential, and its permanent specialization as a source of fuel and raw materials in the world economy. In the new concept, a completely new sphere of ecological threats inhereted by Russia from the USSR received special attention. It was noted that the 'ecological disaster in Russia' had to be dealt with, first, through deep international cooperation at all levels; the amendment of Russian environmental laws in accordance with international standards was envisaged, as well as the development of a rational ecological policy at the national level. Russia's leaders believed that international support would be provided to tackle the most pressing ecological problems, and in its turn, Russia was going to fulfil all of its international obligations in this sphere.[12]

Russia's December 1997 National Security Concept not only repeated the main provisions of the Foreign Policy Concept of 1993, but also put even more emphasis on Russia's internal conditions as a major source of threats to Russia's security. Since Russia's internal threats arise from economic decline, instability and societal problems such as poor health and unemployment, they must be addressed through economic reform.[13]

It is astonishing that the national security policy of such a large and important country considered internal threats to its security more significant than external threats. Traditional international security threats were noted, but these were secondary to the internal threats. Similarly striking, the means for achieving Russian security at the international level was 'partnership' with the West and, while Russia's defence capabilities were mentioned, it was in the context of reasonable expenditures rather than the kind of dedicated investment required for any ambitious military reform and restructuring.

Thus, almost ten years after the end of the cold war, the traditional security dilemma based on the perception of military threats between Russia and the West had largely given way to a variety of new challenges related to *non-military security*, and the so-called *soft security* threats.[14] These threats were not merely problems internal to Russia, but also constituted existing or potential problems for other countries. The Common Strategy of the EU towards Russia stipulated the crucial importance of soft security issues for relations between Russia and the EU:

> Nuclear safety is an essential issue ... the sustainable use of natural resources, management of nuclear waste and the fight against air and water pollution, particularly across frontiers, are priorities ... Russia

and the Union have a common interest in stepping up their co-operation in the fight against common scourges, such as organised crime, money-laundering, illegal trafficking in human beings and drug trafficking. The fight against illegal immigration is also major preoccupation. The Union proposes to put increased co-operation in place in these areas by creating the necessary tools and forms of co-operation between the competent bodies and by developing exchanges of experts ...[15]

In the late 1990s, Russians also were much more concerned about soft security than about traditional (or hard) security. Russians believed that drug addiction, crime, corruption and terrorism were the most dangerous problems and the main curses of their nation. Among other problems that troubled Russians, those interviewed named low living standards, unemployment and the situation in Chechnya (27 per cent each), inflation (14 per cent), uncertainty about the future (13 per cent), environmental problems and the economic crisis (10 per cent). A majority of the population assumes that the environment in Russia is a problem. Just 1.3 per cent of respondents are fully satisfied with the state of the environment and another 19.1 per cent is generally content with it. However, 75.5 per cent of the people find the state of the environment unsatisfactory. However, 39.1 per cent of respondents are in favour of economic growth above the preservation of the environment, while 32.3 per cent are of the opposite view. The remaining 28.6 per cent could not answer this question.[16]

However, much depended on the question whether the gap between declaratory and operational policy can be closed.[17] The Russian record of achievement in concrete soft security issues was not impressive. None of the problems was solved, and some even increased. In fact, the two things – hard and soft security – rarely go together, and the institutions in charge of them even compete with each other. Most Russian senior security professionals remained reluctant to accept a broader definition of national security even when the facts cried out for such a definition. Indeed, if Russia is a haven for several million illegal migrants, if one-sixth of the Russian land mass is so polluted that it is unfit even for industrial use, if Aids/HIV spreads at the same rate as it is spreading in the poorest states of Africa,[18] and if radioactive and nuclear waste poses a risk of a hundred Chernobyls, then the mere survival of the Russian people is at risk or will soon be at risk.

For instance, according to World Bank data, Russia, grappling with one of the fastest rates of HIV infection in the world, faces a huge bill that it can ill afford if hundreds of thousands of people develop full-blown Aids in the years to come. A report prepared by the chief economist of the

World Bank's Russia office, Christof Ruehl, on the likely economic consequences of Russia's looming Aids crisis, paints a bleak picture of an economy continuing to grow but straining to pay for public medical treatment as the epidemic spreads.[19] Russia's biggest challenge will be to offer expensive anti-Aids drugs free to patients in a country where most people are far too poor to pay for them out of their own pockets. The World Bank estimated that treating the HIV-infected population at a cost of $900 per person per month would soak up more than 80 per cent of Russia's current annual federal budget. However, if treatment can be provided for only US$30 per month per patient, the cost would be less than 2.72 per cent of the budget.

National security under Putin, 1999–2006

Russia's National Security Concept of 2000 and her Foreign Policy Concept of the same year are important for understanding Russian security policy, because they reflect the priorities, assessments, compromises and negotiations within the Russian political and security elite. They are evidence of the government's assessment of the international system, Russian national interests, the sources of threats to those interests, and the means by which Russia can secure its interests.[20]

As we have seen, a quite remarkable shift from traditional realist/liberal thinking to a broader understanding of security took place in Russian security thinking in the 1990s and was embodied in the first two National Security Concepts issued in 1993 and 1997. The new National Security Concept signed by President Putin on 10 January 2000, as well as the Foreign Policy Concept (28 June 2000) embodied this change, as well. Alongside statements about the need to 'fight for a multipolar world' that were redolent of the Primakov era, both documents stressed that most risks to Russia's security are of internal origin. The novelties were twofold; first, the cumulative weight of all the threats and risks to the national security reached their highest point for the whole post-Soviet period. Second, practically all spheres of life have been viewed through the lenses of security. The most important aspect of the new security concept is that it elevates the importance and expands the types of external threats to Russian security, at the same time as devoting a great deal of attention to internal threats. The new security concept no longer states that there are no external threats arising from deliberate actions or aggression, as did the first Security Concept issued in 1993 under Yeltsin and Kozyrev. It provides a substantial list of external threats. Given the greater significance that it gives to external threats, it is not surprising that it calls for a greater emphasis on traditional security instruments. The main task of Russia's security policy in the external realm, it says, is to secure the country's territorial integrity, especially in preventing terrorism and threats to Russia's international borders.

The process of developing the new security concept was influenced by events and problems such as the enlargement of the North Atlantic Treaty Organization (NATO), the 1999 military action in Kosovo, the second war in Chechnya (since 1999), and disagreements with the West on offensive and defensive nuclear weapons. However, its roots lie deep within Russia's political and security establishment. Were Russia to suffer another leadership reshuffle, the basic outlines of the policy would remain. Given the greater significance that it gives to external threats, it is not surprising that it calls for a greater emphasis on traditional security instruments.

However, the partnership with the West was resumed in September 2001 after the terrorist attacks in the United States. Russia became a full-fledged ally of the United States in the war on international terrorism. A new format of cooperation with NATO, the NATO–Russia Joint Council, was introduced in May 2002, symbolizing a new momentum for real partnership on a number of hard and soft security issues.

The Bush Administration was sure that the perspectives of cooperation in the newly created NATO Council of 20, as well as in a global energy alliance, were more important for Putin than the risk of confrontation over Iraq. However, in February 2003, Schröder and Chirac managed to win over Putin to a common anti-war stance. Moscow feared incurring greater losses for its economy as a result of the war. Oil prices would drop in the long term, Russia would lose the oil-production and industry-delivery contract that it had signed with Hussein, and, all in all, Russia's losses due to a regime change in Baghdad would amount to US$48 billion.[21] In the Iraq conflict, Putin managed with the help of Germany and France, to build foundations of a regime of soft containment of the United States,[22] although he never wanted an open conflict with the United States. Partnership in the anti-terror coalition, joint responsibility for non-proliferation and for general stability in the world remained for Putin top priorities of his security policy. It seems that Putin has also succeeded in repudiating future criticism of Russia's treatment of the Chechen problem by arranging the referendum in the Chechen Republic (March 2003), which has revealed a broad Chechen approval of remaining in the Russian Federation. The fact that both the EU and the United States acknowledged the referendum, demonstrated, at least formally, a sort of rapprochement between the West and Russia over the most crying issue of Russia's domestic politics of the 1990s.

Thus, over the first term of Putin's presidency, Russia demonstrated varying preferences in its foreign policy/security thinking, but the main trend was in favour of a reassessment of the nature of the threats to Russian security and the adoption of a concept of its security that was close to that of the EU.

The re-election of Vladimir Putin in 2004 coincided with an enormously favourable situation in the world energy sector. Alongside Russia's rotating presidency in the G-8, this factor produced some changes of understanding by the Russian leadership of Russia's place in the international arena in general, and in the field of international security in particular. Also, the situation in the Russian Caucasus became more or less stable. Over the past two years, Putin's main goal has become clearer. On the face of it, it is simple and reasonable. Putin wants Russia to be a strong country: economically powerful, politically stable and internationally respected. What is in dispute is what those goals mean to him, the methods he uses to achieve them, and if he is as powerful as he seems.

The economic independence of Russia was viewed by Putin as a major prerequisite for a new role for the country on the world stage. In Putin's 2004 'State of the Union address' to the Russian Federal Assembly, the Russian president noted proudly that 'Now, for the first time in a long time, Russia is politically and economically stable. It is also independent, both financially and in international affairs, and this is a good result in itself. We want high living standards and a safe, free and comfortable life for the country.'[23]

However, economic interests do not stand alone in defining Russian foreign and security policy: they stand alongside the strategic interests in how Russia defines its security and status, that is, Russia is an accepted great power. Putin made this clear in the same address to the Federal Assembly by pointing out that:

> We want to strengthen Russia's place in the world ... We must grow faster than the rest of the world if we want to take the lead within today's complex rules of global competition. We must be ahead of other countries in our growth rate, in the quality of our goods and services and level of our education, science and culture. This is a question of our economic survival. It is a question of ensuring that Russia takes its deserved place in these changing economic conditions.

As C. Wallander suggested, 'Russia's is not a foreign policy driven by economic growth for economic growth's sake. This is a foreign policy driven by economic growth for the sake of political autonomy, and global position.'[24]

In general, Russia ended 2005 with its seventh straight year of growth, averaging 6.5 per cent annually since the financial crisis of 1998. Russia has also improved its international financial position since the 1998 crisis, with its foreign debt declining from 90 per cent of GDP to around 20 per cent. On 29 June 2006, Russia came to an agreement with the Paris Club of creditors to pay her debt in full (including the Soviet debt) by the end of 2006. Strong oil export earnings have allowed Russia to increase its foreign reserves from only $12 billion to some $180 billion at mid-2006, not to mention a huge stabilization fund. These achievements, along with a renewed government effort to advance structural reforms, have raised business and investor confidence in Russia's economic prospects and let Putin generously pump money both into the army and navy, in order to cope with new security challenges and into civilian sectors responsible for so-called soft security.

Fighting Aids/HIV provides a good example of the new approach in dealing with soft security problems. As for today, the situ-ation in Russia has changed for the better. Although fighting Aids/HIV falls under the category of a broader federal programme dealing with the whole range of the so-called social deceases, its funding in 2002–06 exceeds $100 million, which made it possible at least to freeze the problem. The turning point in the healthcare system in general and in fighting Aids/HIV in Russia was 2005. For the first time in post-Soviet history, this issue became a central concern for Russia's Security Council debate in September that year. This debate resulted in approval of several documents related to the problem.

The Security Council has developed a plan that defines a niche not only for traditional actors such as hospitals and other medical institutions but also to all establishments of education in order to put essential information about Aids/HIV prevention into the curriculum. Another important step supported by the Security Council was a multilateral agreement between the Ministry of Social Development and Healthcare, on the one hand, and the Federation of Trade Unions and the Union of Employees, on the other hand, to cooperate in the prevention of Aids/HIV among workers. Radical improvement of the healthcare system became one of four so-called national projects offered by Putin in his annual address to the Federal Assembly on 10 May 2006. Besides the development of medical services on the spot, the project calls for making the most sophisticated medical treatment available for those in need. As for funding, for fighting Aids/HIV, and some other most dangerous diseases, the Russian budget provides more that $120 million in 2006 alone. In addition to this, another $45 million will be spent on special drugs needed for infected persons. The same amount of money is allocated for diagnostic purposes and treatment. In addition, Russia has received $87 million from the Global Fund on Fighting Aids/HIV, tuberculosis and malaria in 2002–06. In March of 2005 the Global Fund supported those who were HIV positive in Russia by another grant of $120 million. All of these measures will change the situation for the better. All citizens of Russia will get needed medical assistance regardless of their incomes and place of residence; the quality of life of those who are HIV infected will improve. Finally, all infected pregnant women will be provided with the most effective drugs that will almost totally exclude the transmission of the infection to infants.

Finally, in April 2006, the State Council of the Russian Federation endorsed the programme 'On urgent measures for fighting Aids/HIV in the Russian Federation'. Taking into account the severity of the problem, the State Council advised the president to develop a common strategy on fighting Aids/HIV and to build a special institution 'with high authority and broad interagency capacity'.[25]

Thus, it took the Russian leadership almost a decade until it adopted a new strategy to deal with soft-security problems. Initially, it was promoted by the EU, but more recently, in the favourable conditions of high oil prices, Russia not only accepted this problem as its own, but also included it in the agenda for its G-8 presidency. But this does not mean that Russia has changed its security identity. For economic reasons and because of long-term pressure from the West, it has adopted a broader approach to security, while paying even more attention to traditional threats.

Closer attention by Putin to traditional security concerns may be traced to the Beslan tragedy in September of 2004, where terrorists killed hundreds of children and adults. It was the first time after 9/11, when the Russian leader referred to forces in the West willing to catalyse further disintegration of the country. After the tragedy in Beslan, Putin issued a declaration of war, calling for his country's mobilization. Putin blamed the breakup of that 'vast great state', the Soviet Union, for Russia's sorry condition. 'Despite all the difficulties', said Putin, 'we have managed to preserve the core of the colossus that was the Soviet Union'. And that core has come under attack. 'Someone' wants to destroy what remains of the USSR. 'We showed weakness', Putin explained, 'and the weak are trampled upon. Some want to cut off a juicy morsel from us while others are helping them … because they believe that, as one of the world's major nuclear powers, Russia still posing a threat to someone, and therefore this threat must be removed.'[26]

Putin's evaluation of the situation in Iraq, and the crisis over Iran, indicate his further move into the camp of security traditionalists. Addressing the Federal Assembly in May of 2006, he presented a detailed threat assessment that Russia is facing and to which it must respond.

Some observers have pointed out that, as expected, the Russian president used the speech to respond to the strongly worded speech given by American Vice-President Dick Cheney at a conference in Vilnius, Lithuania, just a few days before. In his speech Cheney asserted that Russia has used its natural resources for 'intimidation and blackmail'. In response, Putin implied (although he did not directly say) that the United States is a 'wolf' who 'eats without listening', a reference from a Russian fable. This perception of America's behaviour as that of an international troublemaker paved the way for the most ambitious modernization programme of Russia's armed forces offered by Putin.

According to Putin, contrary to the more or less stable 1990s, the world is changing rapidly and a large number of new problems have arisen. What is new about these threats is that they are less predictable than before and just how dangerous they are has not yet been fully gauged and realized. The general conclusion was 'that conflict zones are expanding in the world and, what is especially dangerous is that they are spreading into the area of our vital interests'. Besides the terrorist threat, Putin mentioned local conflicts that remain a fertile breeding ground for terrorists, a source of their arms and a field upon which they can test their strength in practice. The third traditional security issue is the proliferation of weapons of mass destruction that might fall into the hands of terrorists. Other security risks mentioned by Putin stemmed from the United States, although America was not mentioned specifically by name. Being afraid of involvement in a devastating arms race which once ruined the Soviet economy, Putin referred to the disarmament issue and called for an end to the arms race as an important part of international politics that has existed for decades. Major concerns on the Russian side were not only so-called destabilizing weapons, but also plans to deploy weapons, including nuclear weapons, in outer space. These developments, along with plans to expand NATO eastward, for example onto the territory of some states of the CIS, demand the modernization of Russia's armed forces. To make this point even more convincing, Putin invoked history by pointing out that one of the biggest lessons of the Second World War is the importance of maintaining the combat readiness of the armed forces.

Does this pose a turning point in Russia's security thinking or this is just return to normality, as it was viewed by George Kennan in his famous long memo? As Putin's argument goes, it is clear that he does not want to be labelled a militarist. Putin made a point that Russia's defence spending as a share of GDP is comparable or slightly less than in the other nuclear powers, for example France and the UK. In terms of absolute figures, Russia's defence spending is half that of France and the UK, and bears no comparison at all with the defence spending figures of the United States. Their defence budget in absolute figures is almost 25 times larger than Russia's. As Putin said:

> The bottom line for Russia's military spending is not to repeat the mistakes of the Soviet Union, the mistakes of the cold war era, either in politics or in defence strategy. Keeping to the line of 1993 consensus, Putin argued that Russia must not resolve her defence issues at the expense of economic and social development. This is a dead end road that ultimately leaves a country's reserves exhausted. There is no future in it.

Another important argument in favour of a widened approach to security is Putin's belief that the world has reached a point where the entire global security architecture is indeed undergoing modernization. 'If we let old views and approaches continue to hold sway, the world will be doomed to further futile confrontation. We need to reverse these dangerous trends and this requires new ideas and approaches.'

It is remarkable that, given the severity of Vice President Cheney's accusations, the Russian president's response was brief and calm. Also of rhetorical interest is the fact that Putin chose a quote from former president Franklin D. Roosevelt to introduce the main topic of his speech. Putin was careful to show that while he disagrees with the current US administration, he has respect for the United States as a country. What Putin did not say in his address more explicitly, but obviously wanted to say, was his negative attitude toward NATO, which has became a sort of a magnet for some CIS states. Ideally, modernization of the global security architecture meant and means for Russia, first and foremost, replacement of NATO by 'something else, more general, more political, less American'.[27] For Russia, the ideal organization would be the United Nations. Contrary to the situation in the cold war era, when the discipline of blocs, political expediency, and the interests of saving ideological 'face' prevailed, after the end of the cold war the organization could fully reveal its potential. As Russian Foreign Minister Lavrov has indicated, 'If the UN managed to serve the interests of the world community in the worst of times, it is even more capable of doing it effectively today, given the good will of all the states.'[28]

In order to prove this point, Sergei Lavrov recalled that in the era of globalization threats are becoming global. This suggests only one conclusion: the new challenges and threats to security and sustainable development can only be effectively opposed together, through the collective efforts of the whole international community. The fact that security and prosperity are indivisible gives us no sensible alternative. In turn, it requires a common denominator to enable us to distinguish practical policies based on legitimate interests of states and a commitment to values whose interpretations inevitably differ.

Meanwhile, Russia made an effort to revitalize a collective security system within the CIS. It seems that Russia feels quite lonely in meeting her security challenges, and for this reason does not risk challenging openly her mighty counterparts in the West. In such a situation, looking for common ground with the West in the security area serves not only the domestic interests of Russia, but feeds the security dialogue between the sides. Indeed, the priorities of the Collective Security Organization (CSO) of the CIS are very broad and range from non-proliferation to illegal trade in light arms in the area of the CSO mandate. On the eve of the 15th anniversary of this regional organization, the Russian president made it clear that he regards it as a central element of the security architecture in the region and one of the major driving forces of integration within the CIS,[29] but the reality is that the CSO lacks a shared perception of secur-ity and in addition the resources to deal with new challenges.

Rotating leadership in the G-8 as a factor of the security identity of Russia

Another important factor that effects the Russian perception of security was her rotating presidency in the G-8 in 2006. It gave Russia a chance to promote her own vision of leadership in the modern world, and promote a new formula of leadership in the modern world. As was expected, Russia fell a victim of sharp criticism from many members of the club that were not ready to accept Russia's return to proactive foreign and security policy.

Russia began speaking of joining the G-7 in Gorbachev's time. Westerners in turn began talking of bringing in Russia during the last years of the Gorbachev era. In the subsequent decade, Russia gradually was in fact brought in, first as an observer or guest, then as a participant in a 'G-7 plus 1', then as a part of the 'political G-8'. Nowadays it is usually described simply as 'a member of the G-8'. Today, the G-8 is the one transatlantic institution in which Russia is a clear-cut member; in all the others, Russia is still in a process of joining or still left out.

Few people might recall today that the current Russia's rotating presidency in the G-8 was a result of a compromise between Boris Yeltsin and Bill Clinton over NATO expansion. This compromise took place in Helsinki in 1997. The Finnish capital inspired the US president to make a deal with the stubborn Yeltsin and to bargain NATO expansion eastward for getting Russia in the G-7 and the World Trade Organization. According to Clinton:

> (I) told Yeltsin that if he would agree to NATO expansion and the NATO-Russia partnership, I would make a commitment not to station troops or missiles in the new member countries prematurely, and to support Russian membership in the new G-8, the World Trade Organization, and other international organizations. We had a deal.[30]

For Clinton, the original idea of getting Russia in was to symbolize Russia's importance to the future and to strengthen Yeltsin at home. President Clinton and Prime Minister Blair were among those who pushed for Russian membership. They saw it as a way to reward then President Yeltsin for his bold reform path and induce him to stay the course. Ten years later, while Yeltsin has been leading a quiet life in his dacha near Moscow, his successor Vladimir Putin hosted the G-8 summit for the first time. This fact means *de jure* a return of Russia to the concert of powers that is a long-awaited step from the periphery to the centre of world politics.

It is common wisdom that post-Soviet Russia has never lost its hope to regain the status of a great power, and in an ideal world Russia as the pre-eminent Eurasian power belongs in the leaders' group. But neither the world nor Russia is ideal. Putin's critics argue that what started as a clever tactic to leverage the prestige of membership has turned into a rather dubious strategy. In the past few years, Russia has quietly but steadily moved in a non-G7 direction, that is, away from being a modern democracy.[31] Under sharp criticism for turning Russia into a non-free country under his presidency, Putin nevertheless, has been doing his best to play the role of a leader, although only a 'leader for an hour'. Putin's reply to his critics at his January 2006 press conference was also quite strong. 'The dogs bark, and the caravan passes', he said. As for democracy as such, Russian leaders have a sceptical attitude to it, considering democratic slogans a cover for concrete and usually self-interested goals.

Thus, having started with membership in the G-8 with a mere goal of socializing Russia into the community of developed nations, in 2006 Russia has ended up with a formal responsibility to set an agenda for the G-8, which is one of the most important features of leadership. Indeed, there is a ready list of characteristics to fit the status of an ideal leader in world politics. Besides traditional features such as ability, ambition, and hard power, there are some new facets that are labelled today as soft power, for example, attractiveness for those who are supposed to be led. A leader has to be able to persuade others to go with him in order to solve the most acute issues of world politics. Another important qualification is vision. In the words of the Russian writer Leo Tolstoi, 'power, from the standpoint of experience, is merely the relationship that exits between the expression of someone's will and the execution of what that will by others'. And finally, leadership means responsibility. This last facet of leadership has been advanced and elaborated by the Russian Foreign Minister Sergei Lavrov, who defined responsible leadership as the ability to form common approaches with all the leading powers and to strengthen multilateral, collective principles of world policy. The same principles must apply for meeting international security challenges. Russia declared that her criteria for cooperation in international affairs are uniform for all of her partners, including the CIS nations, China and India, the United States and Europe and other leading states of the world. They are complete equality and mutual engagement from the very beginning; that is, the joint analysis of threats, the joint elaboration of decisions and also their joint implementation. Respectively, those who are not able or not willing to do so, do not qualify for leadership. And this idea was not Lavrov's invention at all.[32]

As for particular spheres of her leadership, Russia has chosen energy security. The increased significance of the energy factor in global politics is obvious. Those who have got used to thinking in terms of geopolitics even assume that such a development changes the equation formula of strategic stability, reducing the specific weight of nuclear deterrence. Anyway, all agree with the validity of Russia's choice of the theme of energy security as a priority of Moscow's G-8 presidency. All in all, the underlying principles of Russian foreign policy are threefold – pragmatism, the so-called multivectorness, and finally, a consistent promotion of national interests, but without sliding into confrontation.[33] Moreover, in the new economic situation, Russia declared that she is not a status-quo country and is against any attempts by certain of our partners to secure their dominance in any new world order. Such an approach was labelled by the Russian Foreign Minister Sergei Lavrov as 'anti-historic, simply a utopia' predicated on one of the myths, of which a multitude arose immediately after the end of the cold war, including that of 'victors and vanquished'.

By identifying Russia as a multicultural society and referring to Russia's history, geography, and the multifaith character of her society, Sergei Lavrov argued that Russia cannot take anybody's side in a clash of civilizations. Neither does Russia intend to take the position of a detached onlooker. The only admissible approach for Russia is to pursue a foreign policy strategy directed at the maintenance of international stability and the reduction of tension for the sake of reaching lasting negotiated settlement options acceptable to all. Russia is ready to play that role, one of a 'bridge'. Throughout its existence Russia has practically been this kind of cultural and civilizational bridge. Invoking lessons of early twentieth-century history, Russian leaders made it clear that they will not repeat mistakes of their predecessors when Russia allowed itself to be drawn into the confrontationist logic of European politics that led to the tragedy of the First World War and a national catastrophe for Russia itself. Not surprisingly the most quoted Russian leaders of the past are Chancellor Gorchakov and Prime Minister Stolypin, who became famous, among other things, for promoting the idea of self-interest for Russia which meant in their times to keep Russia out of any wars both internal and external. The whole experience of the past century showed that it is a sacred duty of each state to think for itself, not entrust its destiny to an uncontrolled development of events.

In search of a new enemy?

We have already noted that one of the most important tenets of Putin's speeches about world politics is constant existence of America as Russia's *other*. In many cases the rhetoric about this *other* is so articulated that it gives the impression of building this other into the enemy. What is behind this trend? Why does Russia need such an enemy?

As Samuel Huntington pointed out, by depriving America of an enemy, the Soviet leaders deprived themselves of an enemy, and the Soviet Union needed an enemy more than the United States. Lacking the struggle with world capitalism, the Soviet Union had no identity, and quickly dissolved into 15 states. Without the cold war, what's the point of being a Russian?

Wars and enemies have a tremendous impact on identity formation. 'It is war which turns a people into a nation', Heinrich von Treitscheke said. This is certainly true for Russia, too. The October Revolution produced the Soviet people, the Civil War the Soviet Nation, and the Great Patriotic War promoted Russia's return to the club of great powers. It also stimulated civic engagement, as well as a broader sense of national unity and commitment to the nation. Not surprisingly, Victory Day of 9 May is the main holiday in contemporary Russia, too.

The second war in Chechnya has made Putin what he is now for the majority of Russians, the savior of the state, the father of the nation. If war may contribute to the building of identity, does peace challenge it? In the situation of a more or less stable Caucasus, the Russian leaders face the problem that Huntington described in his last book devoted to the debates over American identity. He pointed out that sociological theory and historical evidence suggest that the absence of an external enemy, or *other*, encourages internal disunity. In the absence of an external enemy, individual self-interest trumps national commitment.[34] Perhaps with a failure to offer the country a clear positive national idea (joining the EU, for instance) the Russian leadership, which mostly consists of *siloviki*, might be interested in constructing such an enemy to keep the diverse peoples of the vast country together. To serve as a sort of common denominator, this threat should be universal for all citizens of Russia, both in terms of the country's historical tradition and of her cultural and religious dimensions – that is, it might be understood by the main ethnic and religious groups of the country, and first of all by the Orthodox Russians and by the nationalities representing Islam.

It seems that America, too, has been interested in finding an enemy. With the collapse of communism, democracy was left without a significant secular ideological rival, and some scholars even argued about the end of history.[35] The United States was left without a peer competitor. In the words of Samuel Huntington, the absence of an ideological threat produced an absence of purpose. 'Nations need enemies', he quotes Charles Krauthammer. 'Take away one, and they find another.' The ideal enemy for America would be ideologically hostile, racially and culturally different, and militarily strong enough to pose a credible threat to American security.[36] In many ways, Russia fits this portrait perfectly. More to the point, America also goes well as Russia's other, although it seems that the Russian leader understands the limits of selling America as a full-fledged foe. Not surprisingly, Putin made it clear on the eve of the July 2006 G-8 summit in St Petersburg that he rules out a perspective of confrontation with the United States in the future, not just because Russia cannot stand such a confrontation, but for a set of common security challenges to meet, and first of all non-proliferation and disarmament.[37] In an interactive webcast in which Putin answered Russian and foreign Internet users' questions, he made it clear that cooperation in both areas is in the interest of the United States, first and foremost. He also stressed that Russia's role in world politics is not the same as during the Soviet Union, when Russian leadership wanted to provide a counterbalance to the United States. 'We won't get into that position again', Putin said, 'even if somebody wants us'.[38] Nevertheless, there is a clear anti-American trend both in public statements made by Putin in 2006 and in public perceptions of the United States in Russia.

Public opinion under Putin: America as Russia's other

As Hans Rogger suggested almost twenty years ago, Russian and Soviet perceptions of the United States from the early nineteenth century until perestroika, were quite stable on the Russian–Soviet side. He concluded by saying that 'Russian and Soviet, official as well as unofficial, perceptions of America are made up, in shifting proportions, of affinities and contrasts, of memories of friendship and hostility, of realism and dogmatism, of bright and dark colours. Future generations', he continued, 'as have previous ones, will select those that need and preference, politics and prejudice dictate.'[39]

As public polls show, from 1998 on there has been a shift in the perception of major security threats in Russia (see Table 1).

Who are those potential invaders? A quarter of respondents believe that the United States might attack Russia, while only 7 per cent suggested that Russia might fall victim to Islamic states. Roughly the same number of respondents sees Chechnya, which is a part of Russia, as the major 'external' threat for the country. As for China, for instance, just 3 per cent of respondents believe that this state might attack Russia in the future.[40] At the same time, only 7 per cent of Russians believe that the Unites States is Russia's friend. In this respect, America is far behind such countries as Germany, France, and Belarus. Even contemporary Ukraine, led by the orange coalition, is viewed by the Russians more positively than America.[41] In general, there is a drift in public perceptions in Russia in favour of countries of the so-called near abroad and China, while the West (and first of all, the United States) is losing its attractiveness for the Russians.[42]

According to polls conducted in April 2006 by the Russian Levada Center and the World Association for Public Opinion Research, in cooperation with Knowledge Network, only 25 per cent of Russians believe that United States foreign policy has a positive impact on the world affairs, while 61 per cent believe the opposite. About three quarters of Russians regard

Table 1: Public opinion in Russia on potential foreign adversaries that might attack Russia

Russia has foreign adversary	August 1998	April 1999	November 2001	October 2004
yes	44	73	61	68
no	35	15	27	18

the use of force or threat to use force by America as negative or very negative for international relations. And only 13 per cent of Russians support
America in this respect.[43]

The same negative image prevails among the Russians for NATO. This
alliance is still viewed by the people of Russia as one of the most important US foreign and security policy instruments. In June 2006, about
50 per cent of Russians believe that NATO poses a threat to Russia, while
only 25 per cent of respondents disagree with this statement.[44]

Conclusion

Russia's search for her security identity is not over yet. During the past
two years we have seen a quite remarkable change in security perceptions in the Kremlin. International instability and fast economic growth
alongside a chance to 'run the world' as a G-8 president have stimulated
Russia's drift in the direction of the great power behaviour in the area of
security. Not everyone was ready to see Russia begin to restore its economic health and its position on the international stage so rapidly. Some
countries still see Russia through the prism of past prejudices and see a
strong and reinvigorated Russia as a threat and are ready to accuse Russia
of reviving neo-imperialist ambitions or of energy blackmail. At the same
time, recent developments in Aids/HIV programmes in Russia demonstrate
a new approach to one of the most crying soft-security issues almost neglected during the Yeltsin tenure. Which way Russia pursues in the future
in the security field – the traditional focus on hard security issues or a
broader perspective that includes soft security concerns – will depend on
many factors, for example the international situation (and first, the Iran
nuclear programme), world prices of major Russian commodities, perceptions about Russia in major centres of power, etc. It seems that at the
moment Putin considers that both scenarios are probable. Closer to the
2008 elections, he will have to make a choice about his successor between
traditionalists, now represented by First Prime Minister Segei Ivanov,
and wideners, whose front man is another First Vice Prime Minister,
Dmitry Medvedev. This will be a symbolic moment that will reflect
debates inside the Kremlin about Russia's security identity.

Notes

1   Of all great European states, only Germany has had a comparable instability
    in respect with its identity: Germany has gone from a monarchy to a republic,

to a Reich, to partition between communism and capitalism and finally to reunification.

2 According to Winston Churchill, after the October Revolution of 1917 Russia had changed her identity. 'We saw a state without nation, an army without a country, a religion without a God. The Government ... had denounced the faith in treaties; it had made a separate peace; it had released a million Germans fro the final onslaught in the West .... It had repudiated alike all that Russia owed and all that was owing to her. Just when the worst was over, when victory was in sight, when the fruits of measureless sacrifice were at hand, the old Russia had been dragged dawn, and in her place there ruled "the nameless beast" so long foretold in Russian legend. Thus the Russian people were deprived of Victory, Honor, Freedom, Peace and Bread': Winston S. Churchill. 'The Nameless Beast', in Robert A. Goldwin and Marvin Zetterbaum (eds), *Readings in Russian Foreign Policy* (New York: Oxford University Press, 1959), vol. 1, pp. 93–4.

3 Robert Jervis, 'Cooperation under the security dilemma', *World Politics* (January 1978), pp. 167–214.

4 James Sperling and Emil Kirchner, 'Economic security and the problem of cooperation in post-Cold War Europe', *Review of International Studies*, 24/2, (1998), p. 226.

5 Samuel P. Huntington, *Who are we? America's Great Debate* (New York: Free Press, 2004), p. 263.

6 For a detailed analysis of how the security agenda has expanded away from the narrow military focus generated by the cold war, see Barry Buzan, 'Rethinking Security after the Cold War', *Cooperation and Conflict*, 32/1 (March 1997), pp. 5–28.

7 William D. Jackson, *Imagining Russia in Western International Relations Theory*, at <http://casnov1.cas.muohio.edu/havighurstcenter/papers/Jackson.pdf>.

8 Huntington, as note 5 above, p. 266.

9 Igor Ivanov, 'The new Russian Identity: Innovation and continuity in Russian foreign policy', *Washington Quarterly* (summer 2001), p. 10.

10 *Basic Provisions of the Russian Federation's Foreign Policy Concept were approved by order of the Russian President Boris Yeltsin on April 23, 1993. See The Current Digest of the Soviet Press* (29 April 1993), XLV 17, pp. 13–15.

11 See Dmitry Trenin and Bobo Lo, The Landscape of Russian Foreign Policy Decision-Making. Moscow, 2005, p. 14, at <www.carnegie.ru> For a historical account on Russian national interests see Ivo J. Lederer (ed.), *Russian Foreign Policy. Essays in Historical Perspective* (New Haven and London: Yale University Press, 1962); Alvin Z. Rubinstein. *Soviet Foreign Policy Since World War II. Imperial and Global* (New York: Scott, Foresman, 1989); Alfred Rieber, 'Persistent Factors in Russian Foreign Policy: An Interpretive Essay', in Hugh Ragsdale (ed.), *Imperial Russian Foreign Policy* (New York: Woodrow Wilson Center Press and Cambridge University Press, 1993), pp. 315–59.

12 *Diplomaticheskii vestnik*, 1–2, 1993; Spetsvypusk, S. 22.

13 *Diplomaticheskii vestnik*, 2, 1998; S. 3–18.

14 The broadening of the concept of national security to include non-military issues has been under way for some time. The recognition that the stability and security of nations is shaped by multidimensional factors has led political scientists to argue for an expanded definition of security. According to the

American political scientist Richard H. Ullman, 'a threat to national security is an action or sequence of events that (1) threatens drastically and over a relatively brief span of time to degrade the quality of life for the inhabitants of a state (states); or (2) threatens significantly to narrow the range of policy choices available to the government of a state (states) or to private, non-governmental entities (persons, groups, corporations) within a state (states)'. Richard H. Ullman, 'Redefining Security', *International Security* 8/1, (Summer 1983), p. 133. Brian R. Shaw, 'When are Environmental Issues Security Issues?', *Environmental Change and Security Project Report*, The Woodrow Wilson Center, issue 2 (spring 1996), p. 40.

15 *Official Journal of the European Communities*, 24 June 1999, pp. 2–3.

16 Cf. *Johnson's Russia List* (Center for Defense Information), 7028, 22 January 2003, at <www.cdi.org>.

17 See, for instance, Geir Hønneland, and Anne-Kristin Jørgensen, 'Implementing Russia's International Environmental Commitments: Federal Prerogative or Regional Concern?', *Europe–Asia Studies*, 54/8 (2002), pp. 1223–40

18 According to Russian official data, the number of people infected by HIV/Aids has been growing very rapidly, from 196 persons in 1996 or 1 person in every 100,000 tested, to 231.5 infected persons out of 100,000 tested in 2000. About 40 per cent of all those infected are resident in Moscow, St Petersburg, the Moscow region and other large cities.

19 World Bank report data, 22 September 2003 (RFE/RL).

20 Nikita Lomagin, 'Forming a new security identity in modern Russia', in Jakob Hedenskog, Vilhelm Konnander, Bertyl Nygren, Ingmar Oldberg and Christer Pursianen (eds), *Russia as a Great Power. Dimensions of Security under Putin* (London and New York: Routledge, 2005), pp. 265–6.

21 Alexander Rahr, 'Russia-European Union-Germany After September 11 and Iraq', in Alexander J. Motyl, Blair A. Ruble and Lilia Shevtsova (eds), *Russia's Engagement with the West: Transformation and Integration in the Twenty-first Century* (Armonck, NY: M.E. Sharp, 2005), pp. 226–7.

22 Ibid., p. 227.

23 Vladimir Putin, Address to the Federal Assembly, 2004, at <www.kremlin.ru/text/appears/2004/html>.

24 C. Wallander, 'The Challenge of Russia for U.S. Policy', Testimony before the Committee on Foreign Relations United States Senate, 21 June 2005, at <www.csis.org>.

25 Vystuplenie ministra zdravookhanenia i socialnogo razvitia M.Surabovi na Konferencii po voprosam HIV v Vostochnoi Evrope i Centralnoi Asii, Moscow, 15 May 2006 (Russian Healthcare and Social Development Minister Address to the Conference on Issuers of Aids/HIV in Eastern Europe and Central Asia), at <www.mid.ru/brp_4.nsf>.

26 BBC News. Excerpts from Putin's address, at <www.news.bbc.co.uk/go/pr/fr//2/hi/europe/3627878stm>.

27 Paul Kennedy' *Preparing for the Twenty-first Century* (New York: Vintage Books, 1993), p. 270.

28 Sergei Lavrov, '60 let Fultona: Uroki kholodnoi voiny i sovremernnost' (60 Years of Fulton: Lessons of the Cold War and Our Time), *Rossiiskaya Gazeta*, 6 March 2005.

29 Vladimir Putin, Statement at a meeting of the Council for Collective Security Organization at Minsk, 23 June 2006, at <www.kremlin.ru/text/appears/2006/06/107693.shtml>.

30 Bill Clinton, *My Life* (New York: Alfred A. Knopf, 2004), p. 750.

31 Mark Medish, *Russia Odd Man Out in the G-8*, Theglobalist.com, 24 Feb. 2006.

32 See, for instance, Richard N. Haass, 'The Opportunity. America's Moment to Alter History's Course', *Public Affairs* (2005), pp. 16–32.

33 Sergei Lavrov, 'Rossia v globalnoi politike' (Russia in Global Politics), *Moskovkiye Novosti*, 3 March 2006.

34 Samuel P. Huntington, *Who Are We? America's Great Debate* (New York: Free Press, 2004), p. 264.

35 Francis Fukuyama, 'The End of History?' *The National Interest* (Summer 1989).

36 Huntington. as note 34 above, p. 266.

37 *Kommersant*, 7 July 2006, pp. 1, 6.

38 See <www.kremlin.ru/eng/speeches/2006/07/06/shtml>.

39 Mark Garrison and Abbot Gleason (eds), *Shared Destiny. Fifty Tears of Soviet-American Relations* (Boston: Beacon Press, 1985), p. 140.

40 Fond Obshestvennoe mnenie, at <www.bd.fom.ru/report/cat/frontier/rossiya_i_stran_mira/vragy/>.

41 Ibid.

42 At <www.levada.ru/press/2006050600.html>.

43 At <www.levada.ru/press/2006060202.html>.

44 At <www.bd.fom.ru/report/cat/frontier/blocks/NATO/tb062311/printable>.

3
Choices for Russia: Preserving Inherited Geopolitics Through Emergent Global and European Realities

Vladimir Rukavishnikov

Introduction

The world has been changing faster in the past few years than perhaps at any time in the past. The most salient examples of these changes were the enlargement of the European Union and NATO eastward and the US-led 'global war against terrorism' that started after the tragic events of 11 September 2001 in the United States.

The public perception of threats and challenges has also changed and this fact was registered by opinion polls across Europe. Each nation steps into the future carrying the heritage of its own past. This past leaves its mark on the development of society and on the way people perceive the present and foresee the future, including the way politicians, journalists and the military staff think. For instance, quite recently regarding NATO's intention to accept new members, the Russians described the process as 'NATO expansion', while the Americans and the Europeans tended to refer to the process as 'joining NATO' or simply as 'NATO enlargement'. The terms 'expansion' and 'enlargement' are virtually identical terms in English, but not in the Russian language, where they have different meanings: 'expansion' has a distinctly aggressive connotation. But, of course, not only historical experience equips minds for making military-political 'calculations'. The link between the current domestic political cleavage, on the one hand, and the official foreign and security policy of the state, on the other hand, is equally important in each country in this regard.

Russian national interests, security and foreign policy goals, and the military policy during the first years of post-communist development under President Boris Yeltsin (1992–99) were poorly articulated and vaguely formulated. In December 1999, President Boris Yeltsin resigned and was succeeded by Vladimir Putin, who, as Prime Minister, had launched the second Chechen war in August 1999 and was elected President in his own right in March 2000.

Since the 2000 presidential election, and particularly after the American tragedy of 9/11, there were many debates about how to 'frame' Russia's foreign and security policy, in order to make it congruent with many emergent geopolitical conditions. The task was to dispel the *real* security threats, both immediate and longer term, and to recommend possible paths and methods for countering them. The discussion that shaped Russia's political future and international standing was about preserving Russian security interests through the first quarter of the twenty-first century within the new European realities and a new set of global and local threats and challenges. The questions to ask were these: Which threats and challenges? And how broadly and deeply will our defence and security politics be redefined? How much can the Russian Federation influence the nature of the evolution of change in the international political-military configuration? Which policy choices are likely to be most critical in exercising that influence? Is it possible for an interstate war to break out somewhere, and if so, between whom and by whom is it to be undertaken? The debates focused on the implications of the rapid geopolitical change and economic globalization accompanied by the impact of the scientific-technological revolution on the security sector, on new missions of the armed forces, their organizational structure, maintenance and training, and Russia's rather limited financial resources.

Putin's electoral rhetoric in the winter/spring 2000 campaign and during his first presidential term was focused almost exclusively on four issues: to eliminate separatist militants in Chechnya at any cost and as soon as possible; to strengthen the Russian state; to introduce a 'dictatorship of the law', in order to fight crime and corruption; and to modernize the armed forces and to revive Russia's influence in world affairs. All of these objectives were to be pursued while continuing the liberal economic policy launched by his predecessor's administration.[1] None of these tasks suggested strong support for democratic reforms; none of these aims have been completely fulfilled by the time of writing. During Putin's second presidential term, which started in 2004, both the President's entourage, on the one hand, and the opposition fractions of various kinds, on the other hand, have been searching, some would say desperately, for the right 'narrative', the right answers on the above mentioned questions, to get electoral success at the next national voting and new presidential elections in 2008.[2]

On the issues of national security, the right-wing opposition has always argued that the safety of the Russian Federation mostly depends on the credibility of its relations with the West, while the left-wing opposition has argued that the Russian Federation must rely only on its own military might, primarily on its strategic nuclear forces. They advocate bringing 'near abroad' countries into Russian-led security alliances. The pro-Western right-wing of the political spectrum raises concerns about Putin's respect for the Soviet Past, despite the numerous presidential 'reverences' to the United States made before and immediately after 9/11.[3] The left-wing political groupings, for their part, are dissatisfied with the shift towards the West in Russian foreign policy, but may be even more upset with the successful exploitation by Putin's team for their own political aims of the widespread feeling of nostalgia for the USSR's international position within society and among the military. The opposition forces, both from the left and right flanks, have not offered new ideas and a fresh agenda so far, in fact they are trying to sell politics based a mix of old myths, phobias and interest group demands, and – partly – ideology.[4]

In this chapter, I will neither discuss the political metamorphosis in Russia in detail, nor comment on the rhetoric of politicians. The conclusions in this chapter are mainly drawn from official statements, documents, and speeches of the president and his ministers of defence and foreign affairs. Three kinds of strategic documents are most important in this regard: the National Security Concept, the Military Doctrine and the Foreign Policy Concept of the Russian Federation.[5] I pay special attention to a revision of earlier approved strategic documents made after 2004.

The Russian reaction to emergent realities

Pragmatism is the guiding light of Putin's security and foreign policies. Therefore, I start with a short review of the principal factors that underline Russia's external policies at present, as well as the limits within which Russian policies are likely to operate in the foreseeable future. To be specific, I select several areas in which Russia should make or had made policy's choice.

The first issue is terrorism. This issue dominates in President Putin's rhetoric. Perhaps, it is the only theme with which the former KGB officer himself feels really comfortable. Since Putin's coming to power in the autumn of 1999, the Kremlin has portrayed the second war in Chechnya as a struggle against foreign mercenaries – with international terrorists, Islamic fanatics, responsible for the instability on Russia's southern borders.

There is a national consensus that the ongoing war in Chechnya represents a key internal threat to Russian state security, although the tiny group of pro-Western liberals argue that Russia will never take its due place in the international community nor will it have a truly 'attractive business climate' while the war in Chechnya continues.

Putin's non-compromise line in the Northern Caucasus is an inherited policy with deep roots. It might be drawn from the experiences of both Tsarist Russia, which had conquered that area by force in the nineteenth century, and Stalin's policies. The Soviet Union had shown no mercy to the nationalists underground or to militants fighting against Soviet troops in Western Ukraine and the Baltic republics after the end of the Second World War. In spring 2002, President Putin stated that the 'military phase of the counter-terrorist operation in Chechnya may be considered closed'. But the military victory in Chechnya had already been claimed many times before, since the last capture of Grozny, the capital of the region, in 2000.[6] In fact, the guerrilla war in Northern Caucasus is continuing, and the ultimate victory of the federal power is still far away.[7]

September 11 emotionally shocked Russia to much the same degree as it did other nations. Russia's President was the first foreign leader to express his condolences to the American people over the tragedy that had befallen the residents of New York, Washington and the whole American people. Russia proceeds from the assumption that the challenge of international terrorism has been thrown down not only to the Americans, but also to all of humanity. Therefore, Russia's support for Americans is rooted in what Moscow perceives as a common cause: the fight against Islamic radicalism.[8] Moscow uncovered links between the Chechen separatist formations and international terrorist circles because Chechen rebels get financial support from abroad and foreign mercenaries are taking part in clashes with Russian troops. Putin's entourage emphasized the alleged links between Osama bin Laden's Al-qaeda and Chechen insurgents.

The second issue to be mentioned is Iraq and the continuation of the global war on terrorism. This point is connected to the previous policy issue. The Iraq conflict has fuelled Muslim extremism all over the world. The recent terrorist incidents in Europe (bombings in Madrid and London) have revived fears of 9/11 and ignited talks about the global terrorist network of Islamic extremists. In response to these incidents, President Putin has again emphasized the necessity of international cooperation for the joint struggle against this new global threat.[9]

The 9/11 tragedy was a *casus belli* for the war against Iraq because the attack on Iraq had been planned by the White House before 11 September 2001. While many Americans insist that humankind is entering a new epoch of war and that the twenty-first century will be the American century, Russians argue that America's 'global war on terrorism' ignores lessons from the past. An increased traffic of narcotics from Afghanistan after the liberation from the Taliban regime has become a real national security threat for Russia,[10] the solution of which has not yet been found. For many in Moscow the 'export of democracy' on American bayonets is unacceptable. Russians see no concrete benefits that justify the costs and risks of US 'global leadership' (a euphemism for 'world policeman'), but insist that there are several alternatives to US global leadership, including greater reliance on the UN and regional security organizations.

Russia was a strong opponent of the US-led action that toppled Saddam Hussein, because, first, it had maintained close economic relations with Baghdad for years. Moreover, the US-British military action was not sanctioned by the UN Security Council. The post-Saddam development did not catch Russia unprepared. The increasing resistance against the occupation forces as the aftermath of US action had been predicted in Moscow. Russians remain sceptical with respect to the ultimate US goals in Iraq and in the entire Middle Asia region.[11] Craig Murray, the British ambassador to Uzbekistan in 2002–04, wrote on the occasion of the popular unrest in Uzbekistan (May 2005) that was suppressed by the authorities:

> The airbase opened by the US at Khanabad is not essential to operations in Afghanistan, its claimed *raison d'être*. It has a more crucial role as the easternmost of Donald Rumsfeld's 'lily pads' – air bases surrounding the 'wider Middle East', by which the Pentagon means the belt of oil and gas fields stretching from the Middle East through the Caucasus and Central Asia. A key component of this strategic jigsaw fell into place this spring when US firms were contracted to build a pipeline to bring Central Asia's hydrocarbons out through Afghanistan to the Arabian seas. That strategic interest explains the recent signature of the US–Afghan strategic partnership agreement, as well as Bush's strong support for Karimov.[12]

Relations between Washington and the government in Tashkent had been badly strained by US criticism of the Andijan crackdown, which human rights activists said left hundreds of civilians dead. While the US authorities warned the Uzbek government, one of the most authoritarian in the Islamic world, to open up politically – or risk the kind of upheavals witnessed recently in Ukraine, Georgia and Kyrgyzstan, the Uzbek authorities said in return that 'Uzbekistan does not wish to indulge the USA in conducting "coloured revolutions" in Central Asia'.

We should note that Uzbek President I. Karimov is viewed as a dictator in the Western media, but the Russian authorities shut their eyes to the absence of democracy and freedom. He got Putin's support after the brutal action against insurgents. Then, in late July 2005, Karimov decided to remove the US base from his country.[13] Most likely the Uzbek president had thought that Russia and China, his Shanghai Cooperation Organization partners, would not leave his country face to face with the United States.[14]

The likely outcome of the US–Russia disagreement concerning developments in the Middle East is unclear. Misunderstanding between the United States and the Russian Federation concerning the Iranian nuclear programme should be mentioned while on the subject. One may try to trace the present-day Russian diplomatic activity back to the past, that is Soviet policy in Middle East. This means there are clouds on the horizon: resulting from Russia's nostalgia for its former superpower status and from the European ambition for participating in the Middle East game. Some suggest that China as the potential superpower of the twenty-first century could be a third competitor. In combination with one another and with Islamic fundamentalism and the widespread anti-American mood in the Muslim world that feeds terrorist networks, such a grand alliance against US hegemony could pose a serious geostrategic threat to American interests in the post-Bush world, which Russia might use for its inherited geopolitical aims.

The third point is a long-drawn-out problem of proliferation of the weapons of mass destruction. With the end of the nuclear stand-off between the Soviet Union/Russia and the United States, nuclear weapons lost much of their relevance for international security. But that is not true when national security of nuclear states is considered. Until now, the military in these countries considered the nuclear deterrent as the ultimate mean of defence, and weapons of mass destruction are still around in very large numbers. The world has undoubtedly gained from the reduction of the scale of this deadly threat, but the number of member states of the 'nuclear club' is growing despite the efforts of the international community to stop the process of proliferation of weapons of mass destruction.[15] The 'leaks' of information about the nuclear ambitions of North Korea and Iran constantly fire public interest in this theme.

This enduring issue has many dimensions. The dimension that cannot be avoided is the following. The Russian Federation has a huge arsenal of nuclear weapons and intercontinental missiles and long-range bombers. After the US withdrawal from the 1972 ABM Treaty, it became clear in Moscow that Russia's strategic arsenal should be renovated, despite the signing in 2002 of the US–Russia treaty on the limitation of the strategic arsenals of the two sides. And the deterrent value of its nuclear arsenal remained the cornerstone of Russia's defence. Even more, it is a basic determinant of Russia's weight in world affairs today and in the future. Put simply, without nuclear weapons, economically poor Russia would not be regarded as a regional superpower, its political influence on neighbours would be insignificant, and a non-nuclear post-Soviet Russia would surely not have become a member of the G-8. That is why President Vladimir Putin again and again tells the military top brass that, although the armed forces must continue to modernize, post-Soviet Russia still commanded a nuclear arsenal of 'unparalleled' strike power.

Putin's team is trying to push ahead military reform by increasing defence spending and the wages of military officers. The point to be stressed here concerns the dynamics of defence spending. After the end of cold war, the defence expenditures of the major powers fell significantly.[16] Today, the tendency is the opposite – defence spending is increasing essentially, not only in the United States,[17] but also in the EU, China, India, and the like; the pace of growth of expenses on security accelerated after the conflict in Kosovo in 1999 and the 11 September 2001 events. While in 1999 Russia planned to spend on defence only about 93 billion roubles, in 2005 it was 526 billion roubles (or about US$18.8 billion); that is, double the 1999 amount, if one accounts for the inflation rate. In the 2006 financial year, the military budget will be about 20–25 per cent higher than that of the previous year.

The quick rise of defence spending in Russia is only partly the reaction to the NATO action against former Yugoslavia in 1999; basically, it has been caused by the reform of the armed forces in general. The military always attempt to exploit advanced technology, even though the cost of the modern high-tech weaponry tends to be very high. The age-old 'projectile vs. amour' problem lives on. The revolution in military affairs and the onset of information warfare and operations is silent but it creates a truly strategic gap between the countries, which benefit from its advantages, and those, which cannot afford to renovate their armaments. What is important in this regard is that new types of *weaponry for inter-state wars*, not for local low-intensity conflicts or fighting against terrorists, are currently on Russian production lines, covered under president's talks about the international terrorist threat to Russia.[18]

The last, but not the least, important point to mention concerns recent changes in Russia's 'near abroad' landscape due to the so-called 'coloured revolutions' in Georgia, Ukraine and Kyrgyzstan, that brought to power leaders whom Russia did not initially support. In our view, the coloured revolutions have narrowed the 'window of opportunity' for Russian foreign policy in the near abroad; they have set certain limitations for Russia's plans for the future. These changes have provoked heated debates over the growing problem of relations with neighbouring countries. The Russian authorities now must insist that, whatever the political changes in its neighbourhood could be, they should never obstruct the country's path to more effective future cooperation with all ex-Soviet countries.

As important as the above-mentioned issues are, the longer-term demographic and environmental challenges have not gone away. Global demographic trends should be mentioned ahead of other challenges. The entire world rather soon will be older and far less Caucasian and Christian than it is today. This shift will demand an appropriate reaction on national, regional and international levels. Thus, demographic factors will serve as catalysts and shapers of political instability and conflicts inside and among nations. It is always hard to know where the fire hazard could be. But there is a fear that we are facing a problem that could actually be dangerous for present-day great nations.[19] In 1950, Europe and Russia comprised 22 per cent of the global population; at the beginning of the twenty-first century this share is now about 10–13 per cent and by 2050 it will fall to about 7–8 per cent. In short, the population of the largest part of the world that served as the locus for most twentieth-century history will shrink dramatically in relative terms.[20] The mentioned demographic change raises a question concerning the far-reaching consequences for the key elements of national power – economic, military, and political – and for each great nation's weight within the international community.

As for Russia, an aging and declining population – especially among working-age native Russian males – can impact economic growth and military capacities,[21] if not domestic stability, and create vulnerabilities that internal political forces (ultranationalists, to be named first) and/or external forces may seek to exploit. Declining fertility and rising mortality have resulted in annual losses of about 700,000–1,000,000 persons during the past decade. The decline in Russian healthcare, the wide range of pollutants, the decline in the quality of diet, extensive damage to the natural environment, a rise in infectious diseases, alcohol consumption and drug addiction have combined to reduce the overall health of the population and to increase premature deaths. Life expectancy has dropped below 60 years for men and below 72 years for women. According to demographic projections, the Russian population is expected to contract further in the next five decade to somewhere near 118–120 million people, the level of 1960.

Russia's Far East region is suffering the most sizeable population reduction according to the results of the last Russian census. The same is true for Russia's northern territories. The economic recovery of the Russian Far East and Siberia will require the import of labour from the neighbouring ex-Soviet republics and some Asian states, notably China.[22] However, such labour migration is already creating social tensions.

Although the Russian leadership is aware that multiple negative demographic trends complicate the governmental ability to manage other issues, including foreign relations, labour productivity and economic growth, it is difficult to say how effective will be a new immigration law,[23] because the entire migration policy is rather poorly articulated and managed. The unpleasant reality of the beginning of the twenty-first century is the fact that large-scale illegal immigration and the illegal trafficking of people to the Russian Federation, which ultimately increase the profits of organized crime despite all efforts to fight it. A concentration of such people in certain areas creates social tension which in its turn jeopardizes inner stability.

Global ecological trends are hard to ignore as well. Global warming is a security problem that is still underestimated, although the EU pressed Russia to ratify the Kyoto Treaty.[24] In fact, it was the political decision made by President Putin, who chose a cleaner world over oil and gas interests.[25] Russia's economic growth, about which so much has been said for most of the years of Putin's reign, is a product of high world oil prices to a large extent.[26] This cannot be considered an achievement of the incumbent president, but rather a stroke of luck or good fortune that cannot be relied upon to endure. The low inflation rates and the relative stability of the national currency should also be considered as the corollary of high world oil prices: as an oil currency, the rouble could almost be said to be the dollar's twin. It is a common knowledge that, if the present high price of a barrel of oil were to drop even slightly – say, by one US dollar – then Russia would lose over one billion dollars. Russia's economy would falter in the event of a significant decrease of the price of oil. This means that Russia's profits depend upon US oil prices and European natural gas consumption policy.

To be precise, the Russian Federation and the European Union are now economically more dependent upon each other than ever before. For the first time in history, energy imports from Russia have become vital for the European economy, and this importance will continue growing in the foreseeable future. At the recent summits, Vladimir Putin emphasized the idea of the Russia–EU strategic partnership. He has also drawn the attention of his counterparts to the negative consequences caused by attempts to separate from Russia after the EU enlargement by the new kinds of economic and bureaucratic barriers – a lack of visa-free regime between the Russian Federation and the EU, etc. Russian foreign policy toward Europe is not trapped by the EU and NATO enlargement. As the emergent realities make traditional Europolitics an increasing anachronism, Russians understand that the only way to eliminate new threats and to cope with challenges is to work together with Europeans. United Europe and Russia are the two most important actors who can talk across the Atlantic as equals about how to make the world a more peaceful place.[27] Once that happens, the United Nations can be developed to work more effectively.[28]

The changes in strategic doctrine

Historically, the major attention in state politics has been directed to the military aspects of national security and relations with nations, that may poses external security threats. Today, the world leaders understand that lasting peace requires a broader vision or the so-called idea of *comprehensive security*, which includes the people-centred concept of *human security*. Human security is complimentary to *state security*.

The concept of comprehensive security encompasses not only the safeguarding of the integrity of the sovereign territorial state by arms, but also the security of individual citizens, who must be protected in all aspects of their life, namely in their human dignity and their worth as a human being. Specifically, human security addresses the issue of the enormous amounts of national wealth and human resources devoted to armaments and armed forces, while countries fail to protect their citizens from the chronic insecurities of hunger, thirst, decease, inadequate shelter, crime, unemployment, social conflict and environmental hazard.[29]

Because of limitations of space we will examine only briefly how the aforementioned concepts are reflected in the Russian strategic concepts and doctrines issued after 2000, focusing mainly on a comparison of US and Russian grand strategies. It is premature, in our view, to talk about the EU grand strategy as a directive for actions.[30] In view of the intimate interaction between the Russian Federation and the EU, this cannot be done in any case without special assumptions about common European defence and security policy that are beyond the area of our consideration.

The years 1999–2000 marked a watershed in Russian security thinking analogous to what occurred in the United States in 1998, when the bipartisan Hard-Redman Commission (National Commission on National Security in the 21st Century – Hart-Redman Commission) was formed. The Hard-Redman Commission reconsidered the main principles of the US grand strategy in the 1990s, and specified international terrorism as the new global threat. Reports and hearings of the Commission rendered assistance to the architects of security and foreign policy of the President G.W. Bush administration.[31]

The shift in the perception of risk against which the nation ought to be guarded by the armed forces, is associated with the second Russian president coming to power. At that time, the revised editions of the National Security Concept of Russia, the Military Doctrine and of the Foreign Policy Concept of the Russian Federation were published.[32] Although quite recently all of these documents have been reworked and adjusted again to the new security environment at the beginning of the second presidential term of Mr Putin in 2004, the principal positions presented in 1999–2000 have not been radically changed, despite the turn in foreign affairs towards closer cooperation with the West made by the Putin administration after 9/11.

When state officials use the term 'security', they always imply that some specific issues, to which it points, could ultimately threaten its sovereignty. Sovereignty is 'the name of the game for survival of the state', and therefore it is mentioned as a referent in various security areas (political, military, economic, environmental, food and energy supplies, etc.) where the state sees a threat.[33] President Vladimir Putin repeats time and again that there are no *external enemies* for Russia today. This position is echoed in the official strategic documents.[34] For Russian decision-makers, Russia's key threat is *internal*. It is associated with terrorism and instability in the Northern Caucasus, the immediate consequence of the recent revolt in Chechnya that to a large extent challenged the country's territorial integrity in the 1990s. The safeguarding of the state's integrity directly refers to *state security* (the national security concept in its traditional conception). The bulk of other internal problems defined as threats in Russian strategic documents and the annual presidential state-of-the-nation addresses refer to *human security*.[35] It is correct to say that the pillars of state security and human security are interrelated in this country's grand strategy.[36]

However, the NATO operation against Yugoslavia during the days of the Kosovo crisis in 1999, triggered among the Russian military staff, politicians and the public at large the growth of anxiety concerning the *potential external enemies*. The Russian military thought that the expansion of the North Atlantic Alliance to the east of Europe in opposition to Russia's objections added to the challenge to Russian military security. Analysing Russian military doctrine and national security and foreign policy concepts, one may easily come to the conclusion that the General Staff and the government have adopted a viewpoint that magnifies both the internal threats and the external challenges to Russia and that they regard those threats and challenges as growing in both number and saliency.[37] They serve as an orientation for military and intelligence activity and foreign policy actions.

Russian security experts consider the current unipolar world order with US dominance unacceptable for Russia (although it has not been openly mentioned as an external threat to Russia's security); for this reason, Russia always says that the role of the UN must be strengthened. Perceived foreign threats also include military build-ups that change the balance near the borders of Russia and its allies, anti-Russian policies of certain neighbouring governments, and the US withdrawal from the 1972 ABM Treaty announced by the George W. Bush Administration.[38]

The documented threat assessments are clearly the culmination to date of a long-standing process by which the Russian military and government have forsaken the optimistic Westernizing postures and visions of the initial post-Soviet years and returned in many respects to assessments and demands for specific policies that evoke the Soviet mentality. But there is a significant difference: despite the fact that *global ambitions* are declared in the Russian Federation foreign policy concept as in the 'good old (Soviet) days', in reality national interests and goals of post-Soviet Russia have no global character.[39]

There is no definition of *internal threats* in the US strategic documents issued by Democrats and Republicans since at least 1991. The Bush administration, as its predecessor the Clinton administration, sees only *external* threats for America. Most prominent among these threats are: (1) International terrorism; (2) 'rogue states' hostile to US interests; (3) the proliferation of WMD (threats by potential adversaries and terrorists to acquire or use nuclear, chemical, or biological weapons and their means of delivery); (4) threats to democracy elsewhere, including the former Soviet Union successor states; (5) regional instability and humanitarian problems: local internal political conflicts that undermine friendly governments, and clashes between ethnic, national, religious, or tribal groups that produce forced mass migration, threaten innocent lives, and undermine internal stability and international order; attempts by regional powers hostile to US interests to gain hegemony in their regions (through aggression or intimidation, subversion and lawlessness, etc.); and (6) threats to US prosperity and economic growth that can come from a variety of sources (global environmental degradation, the illegal drug trade, international crime and illegal immigration, etc.).

State security depends upon the (in)security of a society on which it is based. Societal security is relevant in itself and not only as an integral element of state and human security concepts. This is true for both US and Russian grand strategies. But referring to the US strategic documents it is necessary to underline that the US government's accentuation of external threats leads to specific policies in such areas as immigration control, protection of trade, domestic production, etc., and implies pre-emptive military operations abroad.

In both the US and Russian strategic documents, international terrorism is viewed as the newly emerged threat, which challenges both global and domestic security. All in all, this allows us to speak about certain signs of similarity of attitude between the Americans and the Russians towards the terrorist threat. However, President Putin, who initially came out in favour of Russia's joining the international counter-terrorism coalition led by the United States after 9/11, today is not very enthusiastic concerning its future.

As their American counterparts, Russia's president and his minister of defence had warned that 'Russia cannot absolutely rule out even the pre-emptive use of force if the interests of Russia and obligations to its allies require it'.[40] That warning showed that the Bush principle of pre-emption had being noted and exploited in Putin's rhetoric, though not in action.[41]

There is a resemblance of Russian and US views on the problem of weapons of mass destruction (WMD) as a strategic risk. The immediate threat of global nuclear war has significantly declined in recent decades, thanks to the efforts of many states, above all Russia and the United States. However, the nature of the nuclear threat has fundamentally changed, and now varies from the possibility of a large-scale attack against Russia by its possible enemies (the central point of view on this issue in Russia) to the possible use of one or a few devices by a so-called 'rogue nation' or subnational terrorist groups against the United States or one of its allies (a popular version in the West). Countering the proliferation of nuclear weapons – by slowing the spread of nuclear capabilities among states, assuring that nuclear devices do not get into the hands of terrorist groups, and protecting existing stockpiles – has, thus, become as high a priority for the two leading nuclear powers as deterring major nuclear attacks.

Russia's inherited strategic worldview is fundamentally at odds with the American view, and, perhaps, with American perspectives on international security. For George W. Bush the United States must, first of all, remain engaged in exporting democracy and must exert leadership abroad in order to shape the international security environment in ways that protect and advance US interests. If the United States chooses not to lead in the post-cold war world, it will become less able to secure the basic objectives outlined above. The Bush administration is disappointed with the UN and convinced that without active US leadership and engagement abroad, threats to US security will worsen and the window of opportunities will narrow.

The fundamental national interest of the Russian Federation is to preserve and develop good relations, if not strategic alliances, with the United States to cope with challenges of the twenty-first century, but not at the expense of national sovereignty and pride. The disagreements concerning the deployment of American national missile defence system (NMD), international control over Iran's nuclear activity, and Iraqi reconciliation policy, to take just a few examples, form the atmosphere in which this line of behaviour is implemented.

For the Russians, US global dominance jeopardizes world stability. The Russians disagree with the view that, as 'the nineteenth century belonged to Europe', the twenty-first century will belong to the United States. The basic reason for this is the US share in global economy.[42] In fact, US military might and political influence in the world does not match its share of the global economy, which will likely continue to shrink in the foreseeable future.

In conclusion, it is not clear whether the similarity of viewpoints on two main strategic risks – international terrorism and WMD – have formed a *sufficient* base for a US–Russia partnership to provide genuine security for the entire world in a dynamic international context of the twenty-first century or not.

Chilly winds

In our view there are grounds to refer to the current historical period as a 'cold peace'.[43] To support this thesis, let us go back to 9 May 2005, as Russia and other nations celebrated the 60th anniversary of Victory in Europe, the anniversary of the victory of the Allies over fascism in the Second World War. Russian President Vladimir Putin collected about 60 presidents and heads of governments in Moscow on that day. Such an assembly should have been, according to the intention of the Russian authority, a display of successful foreign policy, although it was never so stated explicitly. However, very soon it became clear for both Russian and foreign observers that around the Day of Victory political debates began, there were exchanges of charges and accusations.

First, there were immediate disagreements between Russia and its nearest neighbours, the Baltic States and Poland, concerning the interpretation of the results of the Second World War, the Yalta division of Europe, and particularly the Molotov–von Ribbentrop Pact. These disagreements disclosed how different are the visions of history that the Russians and their neighbours hold today. The post-communist leaderships of the Baltic States regard their countries as victims of the Soviet occupation that emerged after the German–Soviet Treaty and the agreements of the Yalta Conference, which sketched the post-Second World War map of Europe.[44] This perception of pre- and postwar history has echoed in Poland (see, for instance, the really confrontational article of Maciej Letowski in the Polish popular newspaper *Rzeczpospolita* on 16 May 2005).[45] From the Russian point of view, the Nazi–Soviet pact was already officially condemned in the USSR in the late 1980s, the entire issue is closed, and new calls on Russia to apologize for the 'illegal annexation' and 'nearly a half-century of Soviet occupation of the Baltic states' are purely provocative.

Second, US President George W. Bush openly supported the Baltic States before his appearance in Moscow,[46] and in that situation it was a very serious collision as the American media noted. The initial concern was expressed in very plain words:

> What should be clear after Bush angered Russians by speaking of the Soviet 'occupation' of the Baltic states – rather than the 'liberation' Russia's President Vladimir Putin has evoked – is that one's reading of history can have a great bearing on the present and the future. And though Bush said some things in the Latvian capital of Riga and in Moscow that needed to be said, he was speaking as a leader who has demonstrated an unfortunate insensitivity to the lessons his predecessors learned from the inferno of World War II.[47]

Bush shelved his anti-Russian rhetoric when he met with Putin, but no sooner did he visit Georgia than he resumed. And immediately after that, the US media sarcastically asked, 'Does anyone really want to see US or British soldiers fighting to preserve a security guarantee to Georgia? What's more, the West needs Russia as a friend, not an enemy. Bush should be working to gain Putin's cooperation.'[48]

Politization of the *holy holiday* – for the bulk of Russians, at least – has demonstrated the weight of historically rooted problems that the former allies are facing today. History is not always a remembrance of the past; in fact, it is deeply imprinted in the present-day security and foreign policy of the Russian Federation, the United States, the EU, and the West as a whole. During his visit to Georgia after the Moscow celebration, President Bush welcomed the possible admission of Georgia and Ukraine into NATO in the future. For his part, Putin warned that, if Ukraine were to enter NATO, it 'could have problems, to say this frankly',[49] the Russian commentators noted that the same would hold true for Georgia. All of this leads to the question of what is hidden behind friendly smiles and cheers of the American and European leaders today, sixty years after the Second World War.

In Russia, historical consciousness is traditionally very strong. The terrorist attack against the United States on 9/11 altered many things. It influenced the shift in the US–Russia and NATO–Russia relationships. But even for Putin it was not an event akin to the collapse of the Soviet Union.[50] Vladimir Putin's remark that the dissolution of the Soviet Union was 'the greatest geopolitical catastrophe of the 20th century', which was made before the Victory Day, met an angry retort in the Western media. Columnist Martin Wolf wrote in *The Financial Times*, 'The greatest catastrophe of the 20th century was not, in fact, the dissol-ution of the Soviet Union, but its creation. The Soviet party-state was the organ-isational model and negative inspiration for Hitler's National Socialism.'[51] The implications of this statement are self-explanatory.

There was nothing wrong with Bush's declaring in Riga: 'Stable, prosperous democracies are good neighbours, trading in freedom and posing no threat to anyone.' That goes without saying. But Bush did not consider that, from the Russian perspective, he had actually given anti-Russian forces in the Baltics, Ukraine and Georgia a diplomatic boost.

We have to say that, all in all, the disagreements and criticism of summer 2005 meant that the inherited views are still largely in force. On the occasion of Victory Day, Russians read in the Western media about the new 'iron curtain' like the one that has already been and gone, separating Russia from the rest of Europe,[52] about 'old imperial tendencies that are trendy once again in Putin's Russia',[53] and, even about 'the beginning of the new "cold war" that will be colder than the previous one'[54] In Russia this was all considered evidence that the others' view of the Russians as infernal foes and their distrust and misinterpretations based on fears rooted in the past are still widespread in the West.

Conclusion

Perhaps, we may say, Russia's basic post-cold war national security objectives have crystallized in the period of Putin's presidency. The key idea reiterated annually in the president's addresses to the Federal Assembly is to preserve Russia as a great nation and to cope with challenges of the twenty-first century. This goal includes security, political and economic interests. Interests are driving forces of politics. The national interest is not something that shifts back and forth from administration to administration or from crisis to crisis. And Putin's pragmatic twist after 9/11 should be considered first of all as a part of inherited geopolitics, not a break with the past.

Contemporary Russia is a pseudo-democracy. Since 2000, Russia's political regime has turned into the soft cult of personality of the incumbent president.[55] President Vladimir Putin is no communist, but he has brought back the dream about the strong Russian central state and his regime is developing by means that some democrats fear. The specificity of the current political situation in Russia consists in the implementation of Putin's strategy that stresses security, enhanced struggle against terrorists and extremists, as well as centralization and consolidation of power along with pragmatism in interstate relations. On these points, the visions of the ruling clique and the right-wing opposition political parties are at odds with each other, thereby weakening Russia's economic capabilities. This appears to have compelled the Putin leadership to accept the fact that its foreign and security policy objectives should be correspondingly modest.

Nevertheless, at the present moment Russia utilizes various approaches towards advertising of its re-emergence as a great power. Feeling that Russia's public finance is rapidly improving Putin's entourage turns their eyes to South Africa, Latin America and other remote territories as in the 'good old (Soviet) times'. And it is just one example.

Overall, the recent changes in oil prices and current development of Russia–EU relations will require, in my opinion, a more profound adjustment in Russia's strategy from the Kremlin, with due regard to the increased regional differences in the field of interstate relations. *Inter alia*, there are ample signs of giddiness caused by the growing governmental oil revenues, one of which should be mentioned. The ruling clique is using frictions with the pro-Western Georgian and Ukrainian leaderships to raise a wave of nationalist feelings and to mobilize the nation around the flag again, as they did in 1999 when Mr Putin entered the national political scene. Of course, the next parliamentary and president elections to be held respectively in 2007 and 2008 are in sight and the Kremlin's speculators are trying to re-enforce the position of Putin's United Russia party, but such a shift of Russian official rhetoric in the area of foreign affairs is potentially dangerous.

Today's world is at the end of the transitional stage from the East–West confrontation that formed the model of international relations in much of the twentieth century to a new pattern of international relationships, creating a huge opportunity for constructive cooperation and the settlement of conflicts by political means, dialogue, and compromise. The official strategic documents of the United States and the Russian Federation admit that both nations need to secure the cooperation of a number of groups, nations, and international organizations to protect themselves from traditional and newly emerged threats. There is a common understanding that new global challenges (demographic, ecological, social, etc.) can only be tackled at the global level. One nation, even one as powerful as the United States, cannot keep the lid on this boiling pot of global problems. Alas, neither Russophobia in the West nor NATO-phobia in Russia have completely disappeared since the cold war and, as experts say, 'not much new thinking has penetrated the facilities of "nuclear theology" of old in the light of what is new', at least in the present-day strategic military-political calculations.

Finally, the distinguishing feature of the beginning of the twenty-first century is not the great power competition that Tocqueville foresaw between the United States and Russia, but a new world order profoundly different from that of 1990s and the 1980s. It is no surprise that Russia is in a quest for its role in the post-cold war world order. History is accelerating. Russia has a great past, but will she have a great future? While many people in the West are pessimistic in this regard, Russian optimists say that one of the interpretations of the Chinese hieroglyph, that means Russia, is the country of surprise.

Notes

1   Putin's first state of the nation speech in 2000 contained plenty of talk about 'patriotism' and 'strengthening of state', but later his rhetoric employed words of liberal economic reforming, not returning to a state economy. Therefore the concerns about the likely return to the Soviet past should be interpreted as the alarm that pluralistic democracy has became a victim of consolidating of enormous personal power.

2   The anti-Western leftists and nationalists and pro-Western right-and right-centre political formations could not enter the parliament at the past national elections. They can be ultimately ruined at the coming parliamentary and presidential voting. Needless to say, the potential losers are not in favour of the opening perspective.

3   V. Rukavishnikov. 'The Russian Perception of the American "War on Terror" ', *Central European Political Science Review*, 39 (Fall 2002), pp. 92–139.

4   Language is clearly important in politics, but in my view the message remains more important than the messaging. Because the President's party has captured the language of patriotism and the nation's revival, the opposition has also being asking how to 'take back former Russia's influence in world affairs', and what they are for and what they are against. But that means far more than throwing a few nationalist-like slogans into political discussions, or blaming the US policy, the army reform and government's politics in Northern Caucasus.

5 The National Security Concept represents formally adopted general political goals on protecting the citizens, society and state against external and internal threats of any nature, taking into account the available resources, and conforming to the level of guarantees which provide the global and regional security system. This document defines the security objectives and reviews the risk factors that currently threaten the security of Russia. The Military Doctrine presents a system of strategic views, principles and approaches to ensure national security in military-political and military terms. The doctrine explores the military-strategic environment, and defines defense policy priorities and directions of employment, build-up and development of the armed forces in the interest of national security and promotion of peace and stability in the region and the world as a whole. The Foreign Policy Concept is a system of views on the content and main areas in the foreign policy activities of Russia. The legal basis of these documents consists of the Constitution of the state and other legislative acts that regulate the activity of certain bodies of state power in foreign and security policy, generally recognized principles and norms of international law, and international treaties signed by the name of the given state.

6 In August 2005, Chechnya's State Council Head, Taus Dzhabrailov, named the total official and civilian casualties in the breakaway republic for the first time – revealing that up to 160,000 people have been killed in the two military campaigns since December 1994. Most of those killed were ethnic Russian civilians, who had no place to hide and had to stay in war-torn cities, while ethnic Chechens stayed with their relatives in villages. Only 30,000–40,000 among those killed were ethnic Chechens. The number that Dzabrailov made public included also Russian, policemen, and rebel militants. The Russian Defence Ministry, in turn, in mid-August announced that more than 3,450 Russian federal troops had been killed in Chechnya since federal forces re-entered that region six years previously. And, according to the General Staff of the Russian Armed Forces, 3,826 troops were killed and 17,882 were wounded during the first Chechen campaign, which started in 1994 and ended in 1996, 1,906 are missing. The total losses of Internal Affairs Ministry, Federal Security Service and other federal forces have not been released so far. However, independent experts doubt the accuracy of the official figures. Independent rights groups, for instance, have issued civilian death tolls in the past, estimating that anywhere from 60,000 to 100,000 civilians were killed only during the second military campaign launched in autumn 1999 (*Moscow News*, No. 31, 17–23 Aug. 2005, p. 2).

7 What became more or less clear from the Russian domestic experience is that to counter terrorism, the government must coordinate justice and home and foreign affairs to good effect. Prevention, not military operations, should be at the heart of any counter-terrorist strategy, and its primary instrument is intelligence operations. The state and/or the international community must react to the terrorist threat, but avoid overreaction.

8 Although the events of 9/11 exposed a new and dangerous form of terrorist action, the US global war against terror is by its very nature a war with no simple conclusion.

9 Whatever the official statements say, terror is not a new phenomenon. But up to the day of writing, the UN has not agreed on what is terrorism, because the discrepancy concerning the issue of definition of terrorism between various countries exists. In this regard, we have to note that for the first time in the European

history 'international terrorism is considered to be a strategic threat' as it has been stated in the European Security Strategy.

10 The rise of the flow of drugs through the Afghan–Tajikistan border emerged after the fall of the Taliban regime. It is an indicator that neither the new central government, nor the US-led peacekeeping forces, control the situation in Afghan provinces.

11 Some time ago, Russian President Vladimir Putin said that Russia, like its partners in the anti-terrorist coalition, including the United States, want to improve the situation as quickly as possible. Answering a question, Putin insisted Russian contracts agreed during the rule of Saddam Hussein had to be honoured. The Kremlin leader was far gentler in tone than UN Secretary-General Kofi Annan who, in blunt criticism of Washington, said earlier the world body could not play a proper political role in Iraq under Washington's terms.

12 Craig Murray, 'What drives support for this torturer?' *The Guardian*, 16 May 2005.

13 However, US Defense Secretary Donald Rumsfeld said in response to such an initiative that American bases were not leaving anywhere. Kyrgyz President Kurmanbek Bakiyev had agreed that the US base in Manas, Kyrgyzstan, would continue its existence.

14 'The Uzbek authorities took an absolutely pragmatic and logical step', Sergei Mironov, the speaker of Russia's upper house of parliament, the most senior Russian figure to comment on the surprise Uzbek decision, said (see at <http://www.rusnet.nl/news/2005/08/02/currentaffairs03.shtm>). The popular explanation of the Uzbek decision distributed by electronic media states: 'The USA supported Osama bin Laden in the 1980s in the war against the USSR in Afghanistan. The enemy's enemy did not prove to be a friend. Hardly had the previous adversary left Afghanistan, when Al-qaeda set about the former sponsor. It brings up the idea that Uzbek Islamists, the majority of which have ties with Bin Laden, are not likely to do something different. The USA is digging its own grave, as it tries to harm Russia and China' (posted 29 Aug. 2005 on the web site ForumWarfare.ru).

15 In a world community totalling nearly 195 member states of the UNO, seven have declared their possession of nuclear weapons in the past century, and only one of them – South Africa – has cancelled its nuclear arms programme; North Korea and Israel are also believed to possess such weapons, even if undeclared. Twenty or more states have chemical weapons, ten or more possess biological weapons, and a dozen or more have operational ballistic missiles. The number of states in each category threatens to grow as expertise and technical capability grow with each passing year.

16 The Clinton administration in the mid-1990s followed faithfully in the footsteps of its predecessor President George Bush senior in fixing the need of American manpower at about 1.5 million people on active duty and defence spending in the range of about $250 billion a year. For instance, in spring 1996, US Secretary of Defense William J. Perry had asked Congress for $242.6 billion in spending authority for fiscal year 1997. The mentioned US military spending were minimal in the first post-cold war decade, although its size exceeded that of Russia and the major powers of Western Europe combined. Russia's military spending of that time was less than one tenth of US defence spending.

17 It is likely that in fiscal year 2005, the US defence budget will be double that of the mid-1990s.

18 For instance, the anti-missile and anti-satellite weapons, that are being developed in the United States together with the new Russian warheads, which are capable of going through the American anti-missile shield, are difficult to classify as anti-terrorist weapons.

19 Almost all population growth will occur in developing nations. Population growth and global poverty pressures will generate more emigration from poorer to richer areas and deplete resources further.

20 The European Union and the Russian Federation are entering an unprecedented crisis of ageing with an expected climax in the mid-2020s (source: European Commission).

21 For Russia, with its basically conscript army, an ageing and declining population – especially among native Russian males – might impact military capacities that its potential foes may seek to exploit, some strategists say.

22 Nationalists have argued that Chinese's infiltration into Russian cities, towns and villages in Siberia and Far East may dramatically change the demographic balance of these regions. They share a gloomy prognosis that by the mid-century or even earlier, Russia might lose its eastern part without a defeat in war with its eastern neighbor (source: Author's review of Russian media).

23 Fighting illegal immigration, as much as in Europe, Russia welcomes highly educated migrants, ethnic Russians and Russian-speaking, especially young and those born in Russia, from the near abroad.

24 Some scientists at the World Climate Change Conference in Moscow (2003) said that global warming could slash Russia's grain harvests, while others were more optimistic. In fact, despite the common understanding of validity of the problem there was no agreement of opinion concerning the effects of global warming and measures to smooth them. While the EU and Russia ratified the treaty, the United States refused to join them (source: Reports and private communications at World Climate Change Conference in Moscow (2003)).

25 Currently, Russia is in second place on the list of countries exporting oil (after Saudi Arabia). The Russian government welcomes foreign investments in the oil and gas sector of economy. Russian oil tycoons often say, in their opinion, oil reserves in the Russian Federation have been 'underestimated', and in reality they account for no less than 150 billion barrels, but the adopted figure is 50 billion barrels. But there is an alarming forecast which we could not avoid in our analysis: some experts say, if Russia continues to export raw oil in the coming years in the same amount as today, then its huge oil resources may be depleted by the year of 2050. How close to reality is this forecast, only the future will show (source: Ministry of Natural Resources of the RF).

26 While in last decade of the past century American and European GNP rose, Russia's GDP took a downward trend due to the collapse of the USSR. This tendency has been reversed under Putin, and since 2000 Russia's economy has been growing at annual rates of near 5–7 per cent. However, although things are as they are, it is just a start (sources: Annual official statistical reports of the Government of the Russian Federation).

27 Economically, post-communist Russia does not resemble the former Soviet Union, which it replaced in the United Nations Organization and other international bodies. Today Russia's economic strength is much smaller than

that of the United States or the EU (in 2000 its real GDP was about $1.2 billion – roughly about 2.6 per cent of the world GDP). And the basic objective of Russia is to narrow this gap (source: UN statistics).

28 There was a presumption that the US global leadership would be indefinitely sustained because the traditional US allies in Europe 'automatically' followed the United States. It was true for the cold war period when the European allies were frightened of the Soviet Union. It was true for the 1990s when Europeans were scared of occurrences in the Balkans. Now they are not. Preparing for the war against Iraqi President Saddam Hussein, the US President was no longer choosing between war and no war, but rather war alone or war with allies. Germany and France voiced protest against the 'pre-emptive' war against Iraq without a UN sanction. Russia, the US partner in 'the global war on terror', also was against that war.

29 The materials of the UN organized discussion on this issue may be found in *State and Human Security in the 'Age of Terrorism'* (2004).

30 The concept of grand strategy had emerged from the work of military analyst Basil H. Liddell Hart, published in 1967; its roots may be found in the ideas of Carl von Clausewitz. The grand strategy involves the country's ability to mobilize all its resources – military, economic, political, cultural – in aspiring toward a principal political aim. Generally, in the United States, there is a perceptive distinction between the grand strategy (or the national security doctrine) with an emphasis on principal and long-term defence and foreign policy goals (geopolitical aims), the security strategy at large, oriented to the elimination of threats to the very existing of the state or stability of society, or diminishing them to the rational level of risk, and the military strategy with its concrete tasks, limits and means of obtaining precisely formulated aims. In Russia such a distinction between three levels of strategy traditionally is not so evident. In fact, the essence of post-Soviet Russia's grand strategy may be drawn, first of all, from the annual presidential messages to the Federal Assembly, and the national security doctrine approved by the president. But when the military doctrine is considered the Russian military analysts often underline its 'comprehensive and normative character', exaggerating its virtues, in our view. See Basil H. Liddell Hart, *Strategy* (London: Faber and Faber, 1967).

31 Office of the President, *National Security Strategy of the United States* (Sept. 2002).

32 The National Security Concept of the Russian Federation was approved by the National Security Council on 5 Oct. 1999. The Russian Federation Military Doctrine was approved by presidential decree of 21 April 2000. President Putin approved the new foreign policy concept on 28 June 2000. This Foreign Policy Concept replaces the previous published in 1993, which was felt no longer to correspond to the changing realities of the contemporary international system (source: National Security Council of the Russian Federation).

33 In this regard, the Soviet period of Russia's history was characterized by comprehensive securitization of *almost all aspects* of state politics.

34 There is nothing new in the Putin statements, because the previous (Yeltsin's) national security doctrine, which was published in December 1997, clearly stated that no foreign country posed a threat to Russia's security.

35 Due to diversification of the content of security, a large list of risks is presented in Russian strategic documents. We cannot analyse this array in further depth for a lack of space.

36 In our view, post-Soviet Russia's grand strategy is committed to a broad (comprehensive) approach to security, which recognizes the importance of and interplay between political, economic, social, informational, demographic and environmental security risks in addition to the traditional vision of internal and external threats.

37 Clearly, these are largely political concerns about possible threats that would reduce and even potentially marginalize Russia's role in European and even Eurasian security processes. The last are not, for the most part, military threats against Russia or its vital strategic interests. The large-scale external threats to Russia are basically hypothetical in nature. They can and must be neutralized by political means with reliance on the state's military might, and first and foremost on combat-ready strategic nuclear forces and general-purpose forces with precisely functioning command and control, communications, intelligence, and early-warning systems.

38 Contrary to Yeltsin's politics, Putin intensifies military reform and each fiscal year asks the parliament to increase defence expenses (source: President's Addresses to the Federal Assembly, of the RF, Putin's speeches to the military brass and the National Security Council, Annual Budgets of the Russian Federation, 2000–05).

39 While Africa and Latin America traditionally occupied an essential part of the text of the US foreign policy documents, where the reader may discover that the United States has its (distinctly articulated) national interests and aims in almost all parts of the world, only a few sentences were devoted to the Russian activity on these continents in the RF foreign policy concept issued in 2000. Perhaps the most significant feature of that concept was the emphasis it placed on Russia's foreign policy capabilities. It noted 'the limited resource support for the foreign policy of the Russian Federation, making it difficult to uphold its foreign economic interests and narrowing down the framework of its information and cultural influence abroad'. Elsewhere, the concept argued that a 'successful foreign policy ... must be based on maintaining a reasonable balance between its objectives and possibilities for attaining these objectives. Concentration of diplomatic, military, economic, financial and other means on resolving foreign political tasks must be commensurate with their real significance for Russia's national interests' (source: Ministry of Foreign Affairs of the Russian Federation).

40 Cited in Steven Lee Myers, 'Putin Vows Hunt for Terror Cells', *New York Times*, 29 Oct. 2002.

41 The first time Putin's Russia used the threat of air strikes against the Taliban forces at the Afghan–Tadjik border in 2001, Moscow wanted to support its allies in Central Asia. Since the mid-1990s, Russia has blamed Georgia for providing a shelter for Chechen militants. At the end of 2001, Georgia for its past had complained bitterly about the alleged Russian air raids inside its territory. Most ordinary Russians do not consider the war in Chechnya as a part of the *global* war against *international* terrorism, because for them it is primarily Russia's backyard affair in which a few foreigners are involved. When they blame Georgia for providing a shelter for Chechen militants or Saudi Arabia for financial support of wahhabites, they do not regard these countries as enemies that should be punished by pre-emptive strikes with 'accidental' but unavoidable collateral killings of innocent civilians.

42 The EU, after the enlargement in 2004, is comparable with the United States in terms of GDP, population, a share in world economy, etc. It is important to learn that the US share of world output today is almost identical to its share in the mid-1960s and – not accidentally we suspect – the same as it was before the Second World War. In 2000, US real GDP totalled near $10 billion (roughly 21 per cent of the world GDP), that of the European Union $9.7 billion (nearly 20 per cent of the world GNP) (source: European Commission).

43 V. Rukavishnikov *Kholodnaya Voina, Kholodniy Mir (Cold War, Cold Peace: public opinion in the USA and Europe toward the USSR/Russia, foreign policy and security of the West)* (Moscow: Academichesky Project, 2005).

44 The presidents of Estonia and Lithuania were invited, but did not go to Moscow. Although the Latvian president attended the Moscow festivities, she persistently interpreted May 1945 as a mark of the end of the Second World War but also the beginning of Soviet occupation, thus rejecting historical truth, in Russian eyes. This viewpoint has an impact on everyday practice. For instance, the anti-fascists and aged veterans of the Soviet army who liberated this country from the German troops, are humiliated, while ex-Nazis parade with the wholehearted support of the Latvian authorities. The EU looks at this shaming politics, saying, 'it is necessary to focus on the future, instead of on the past' (source: Review of international media reports).

45 The President of Poland also spent about a month justifying his decision to celebrate this particular anniversary in Moscow. He was under fire from local Russophobes. They were angry that ex-General Wojciech Jaruzelski, the former communist leader of Poland in the 1980s, who liberated his country together with Soviet soldiers, would go to the event along with other honoured as guests. According to their opinion, Poland suffered after Germany was defeated and Europe liberated, and it continued until the late 1980s when the country became free of its postwar Soviet/Russian oppressors and their local communist supporters. With Poland's centuries-long grudge against Russia, as well as the Russian empire's history of clampdowns on Polish uprisings in the nineteenth century, such an interpretation of post-Second World War Polish history does not look poised to abate soon.

46 In April 2005, a resolution was presented in the US Congress by Rep. John M. Shimkus (R-Ill.), which supported the opinion about the 'illegal annexation of the Baltic republics by the USSR'. All three Baltic States are now members of the EU and NATO and therefore US allies.

47 'WWII lessons for Bush', *Boston Globe* editorial, 10 May 2005.

48 'Poking the Russian Bear', *Los Angeles Times* editorial, 11 May 2005.

49 The interview was given on French television on 7 May 2005.

50 In fact, this is not surprising. Putin, as almost all today's political elite in Russia, has exclusively Soviet roots, and the way in which he perceives history is related to the collective identity of the Russians.

51 Martin Wolf, 'Russia Needs Help to be "Normal"', *The Financial Times*, 2005 May 10.

52 This theme initially was discussed in a connection with the EU and NATO eastward enlargement. Then the very idea of a 'new iron curtain' was set up again in days of the 'orange revolution' in Ukraine ('The New Iron Curtian', *Washington Post*, 24 Nov. 2004). Analysts say a new iron curtain may be formed between the EU and the RF unless trade and investment picks up

markedly between East and West. Russia is not going to erect a new iron curtain, while the West would like to see Russia as a partner instead of an unpre-
dictable opponent.

53 The author agrees with Dr Dmitri Trenin from Moscow Carnegie Center who
wrote that 'today' s Russia is not so much neo-imperialist as post-imperialist –
the residual rhetoric of its politicians notwithstanding' (see at <http://
www.cer.org.uk/pdf/essay_russia_trenin_sept05.pdf>).

54 This 'final diagnosis' was presented by Giulietto Chiesa in the Italian newspaper *Il Manifesto*, 10 May 2005.

55 Today, the parliament is under almost total control of *United Russia*, the pro-
president fraction. The federal powers control the mainstream media, and
primarily national television channels, directly or indirectly. Putin's supporters say, he is simply answering a popular longing to have a 'strong hand'
national leader, and they emphasize the majority approves how he is handing
his job. But critics of the ruling regime charge that something far more sinister
is at hand: the gradual demolition of democracy, which is Yeltsin's legacy.
The direction of domestic policy toward what was named 'managed democracy'
or/and so-called 'sovereign democracy' (the most recent pseudo-ideological
product of inventors from the Kremlin), in which emasculated democratic
institutions and procedures serve the president and the ruling clique,
remains unchanged under Putin's presidency.

Part II
Russia, the CIS, and the World Beyond

4
Russia's Transdniestria Policy: Means, Ends and Great Power Trajectories

Graeme P. Herd

Introduction

This chapter explores the nature of Russian policy towards a separatist Transdniestria – or *Pridnestrovskaya Moldavskaya Respublika'* (PMR) – that emerged on the territory of Moldova in 1990. The evolution of Russian policy towards PMR signposts changes in Russia foreign policy in the post-Soviet period. The ad hoc, reactive and directionless foreign policy of the Yeltsin era, which lacked the consensus, approach and resources to implement, gave way to a more pragmatic active diplomacy of Putin's first term. Russian state consolidation and the high price of energy allow President Putin now to prioritize political security concerns within Russian foreign policy. As a result, Russia has the means and political will actively to implement geopolitical concepts that had informed, but not defined Russian foreign policy in the 1990s through lack of resources to implement them effectively – including the balance of power, spheres of influence, and zero-sum politics.

Moscow's current policy towards breakaway republics in both Moldova and Georgia strongly suggests a concerted effort to reassert Russian power within the Commonwealth of Independent State (CIS), thereby both buttressing domestic elite continuity within Russia and providing a more stable platform for its projection of Russian identity as a 'centre of global power'. PMR has been largely sustained through a combination of direct official Russian state policy and indirect and unofficial state and state-structure-related support for the separatist regime in PMR.[1] The distinction between what is official and unofficial, formal state policy and unstated objectives can be hard to untangle, making the study of Russia–PMR relations an examination into the opaque heart of the Russian policy-making process towards its near neighbours. Official Russian support has included a direct military-security presence in PMR as peacekeepers, and FSB training and support to the home-grown militia and security forces in PMR. In the political sphere, Russia has officially had a diplomatic role in the conflict resolution process, most notably its tabling of a plan to federalize Moldova in late 2003 (the Kozak Plan). Although at least hitherto not formally as part of Russian state policy towards PMR, the Russian State Duma and various Duma committee chairs have issued statements in support of PMR independence and this can be construed as psychological support. Economic support includes subsidized Russian energy exports to PMR, investment in PMR privatizations by Russian transnational financial industrial groups that operate in the CIS, as well as Russia acting as a market for PMR goods, particularly the purchase of weapons and other items from its military-industrial complex. In addition, Russian official diplomatic and media support has buttressed the power of the PMR regime.

To what end this influence is exerted has also been contested, though it is generally accepted that Russia has sought to use its support for breakaway states within post-Soviet space (a vital Russian sphere of influence) as a strategic instrument. The preservation of PMR as an unresolved 'frozen conflict' strengthens Russia, while weakening the presence and influence of other external actors: PMR poses serious 'credibility traps' for the Organization for Security and Co-operation In Europe (OSCE) or EU and failure to negotiate a conflict settlement undermines their credibility, legitimacy and integrity. Russia now seeks to use such influence as a bargaining chip in diplomacy with Western institutions, looking for a quid pro quo in return for supporting either a negotiated conflict settlement or for adopting a more muscular approach to PMR – for example, by cutting subsidies, collecting debts, enforcing visa restrictions, withdrawing FSB direction – to pressure the PMR regime to capitulate. Following the Orange Revolution of November 2004 and in the build-up to the March 2008 Russian presidential elections, this option is less likely for PMR is beginning to exert a role in Russian domestic politics and becomes as much a means to an end as an end in itself.

The Soviet legacy

The preconditions and roots of Russia's post-Soviet relations with PMR were grounded in the manner in which the Soviet Union expanded in the context of the Great Patriotic War (1941–45). The history of Moldova is one of constant change and contestation of territory and, thus, of identities and loyalties. Following the October 1917 Russian revolution, Bessarabia declared independence (January 1918) and its parliament called for union with Romania in March 1918. The Treaty of Paris (1920) recognized the union of Bessarabia with Romania, but the Bolsheviks did not, establishing in 1924 the Moldavian Autonomous Soviet Socialist Republic (MASSR) on the territory east of the Dniester River within Ukraine – a showcase republic designed to act as an attractive ideological magnet to lure and orientate Moldavians in Bessarabia towards the Soviet sphere. The Molotov–Ribbentrop Pact of 1939 resulted in Romania's carve-up between Germany and the USSR, with Bessarabia incorporated through annexation into the USSR and combined with most of the MASSR to form the Moldavian Soviet Socialist Republic (MSSR). During 1941–44 the Moldavian SSR was ruled directly from Bucharest but such rule was severed shortly before the end of the war when the USSR regained control.

In the post-1945 period during the Sovietization (largely 'Russification') of Moldova, Transdniestria became the centre of heavy industry and the military industrial complex in the Moldavian SSR (40 per cent of industry with only 14 per cent of the population), while Western Moldova was developed as a centre of agriculture. It was also a strategic communications hub for the republic, generating the political and economic elites (pro-Moscow-orientated factory managers or 'Red Directors') who were either Russians or Russified Moldovans. Indeed, under state-directed Soviet migration policy, Soviet immigrants doubled their share of the Transdniestria population during this period. The headquarters of the 14th Army in PMR (with 8,000–10,000 troops deployed), the proximity of PMR to the Black Sea and Odessa (and so its relative attractiveness as a retirement location), as well as need for workers in the military industrial sector, all combined as pull factors for migrants. Although Moldovans remained the largest ethnic group in Transdniestria in 1989 with 39.3 per cent of the population, 28.3 per cent were Ukrainians and 25.5 per cent Russians.[2] The Soviet 14th Army, consisting of troops that were mostly native to the region was located on its territory. In short, Transdniestria was the centre of military and economic gravity of the entire republic.

By the second half of the twentieth century, both sides of the river had developed divergent values, ideologies and undergone different historical experiences – this, more than ethnicity and ethnic difference, fuelled the conflict. The unofficial status of the Moldavian SSR as 'fruit-basket and vineyard' of the Soviet Union was to be sharply contrasted with the post-Soviet experience after 1991: Moldovan links with the Soviet command-control economic system were shattered and the independent Moldova emerged as an unstable, marginal and peripheral entity.

In the late 1980s, a resurgence of the Moldovan national revival movement took hold and fed into a nationalist sentiment unleashed by the era of glasnost and perestroika. This period witnessed the gradual Mold-ovanization (de-Russification) of power structures in the SSR and in August 1991, Moldova declared its independence and in December 1991 joined the CIS along with many other republics on the periphery of the Soviet Union. The Gagauz, a minority of Christianized Turks who had emi-grated to the south of Bessabaraibia in the early eighteenth century (cur-rently 3 per cent of Moldova's population) declared their independence, followed by the Transdniestria region. Although the central power in Chisinau annulled these declarations, elections were held nonetheless in these localities. On 2 September 1990, PMR declared its existence and on 2 September 1991 voted to remain within the Soviet Union. By 1991, as the Soviet Union collapsed, Moldova's declaration of independence was accepted and it joined the CIS.

The Moldova–PMR conflict was most violent in June 1992, with over 1,000 casualties, and particularly heavy fighting in the towns of Dubasari and Bender on the Dniester River and around 100,000 refugees. The Russian 14th Army under General Lebed was deployed as a peacekeeping force, but it rapidly became unclear to what extent Moscow controlled Lebed and to what extent Lebed was able to exercise control over sub-units during this period.[3] This caveat aside, Lebed did denounce the Chisinau leadership as 'war criminals' fronting a 'fascist state'.[4] On 21 July 1992, presidents Snegur of Moldova and Yeltsin of Russia signed a ceasefire, and a tripartite peacekeeping force came into being.

In the post-Soviet period, the Russian Federation successfully disentangled itself from the Baltic States and Western Ukraine, but it is still embroiled in PMR and so remains central to shaping Moldovan security politics. In many ways, PMR might be considered as the 'Kaliningrad of the Black Sea region' to the extent that tensions between Russia's geopolitical and geo-economic interests are apparent in its approach to the region. It is also to suggest that a political settlement to this frozen conflict might serve as a litmus test (or, in the Putin–Kaliningrad formulation, 'a pilot project') that demonstrates and showcases the capacity for cooperation between Russia and the EU. Only EU–Russian cooperation can facilitate the rein-tegration of PMR into a stable and sovereign Moldova. Such a negotiated reintegration process might also then serve as a template for the reinte-gration of South Ossetia, and Abkhazia into a sovereign Georgia.

Anatomy of a super-presidential PMR

On 27 April 1993, the OSCE opened a long-term mission in Chisinau and provided a framework for a comprehensive conflict settlement.

On 24 November 1994, a new Constitution proclaimed Moldova's neutrality. The Constitution granted a special autonomy status to PMR and the Gagauz region and declared Moldovan to be the official language. Through the 1990s, it became clear that the Tiraspol elites preferred upholding the status quo to achieving a settlement of the conflict. The OSCE-based approaches to political settlement, the pace and scope of whose activity Russia controlled, facilitated the emergence of a *de facto* independent PMR. In this period, it also became apparent to the international community that Russian links to PMR were not just or even primarily military-based, put included economic, political and psychological support.

The Tiraspol elite under the control of 'President' Igor Smirnov, who holds a diplomatic passport issued by the Russian Federation, prefers the continuation of the status quo to settlement, and is using state-type institutions to consolidate power. He has advanced PMR's corporate interests 'through lobbying, economic opportunism, political posturing and creative negotiating'.[5] Grigori Marakutsa, Speaker of the Supreme Soviet in Tiraspol, stated on 26 December 2003: 'Every year we are getting closer to our international recognition.'[6] PMR has all of the symbolic and many of the actual attributes of an independent state: a Constitution, President, national bank and currency judiciary, army, police and militia, strong internal security services, national anthem, coat of arms, and a flag and even a 'national' football stadium. It also exhibits foreign policy pretensions.

Smirnov has stated that PMR 'is historically geared to the priority of ties with Russia and Ukraine'.[7] At the same time it has maintained permanent contacts with leaders of the breakaway republics of South Ossetia and Abkhazia in Georgia. In mid-May 2004, for example, Igor Smirnov announced: 'We [the Dniester region, Abkhazia Nagorno-Karabakh and South Ossetia] have signed a treaty on mutual help in difficult times. If there is an act of aggression, we will not stand aside, we will provide our brothers with all-round help, including military help.' Commenting on the situation in South Ossetia following the 'Rose Revolution' of November 2003, Smirnov stated that he saw it 'as nothing other but preparations for an act of aggression by Tbilisi'.[8]

On 4 October 2004, the three 'foreign ministers' of Abkhazia, South Ossetia and PMR accused the governments in Chisinau and Tbilisi of 'violation of the existing security and stability system'. They argued that only the CIS could negotiate a resolution to the conflicts between Chisinau and Tiraspol, and between Tbilisi and Sukhumi and Tzchinvali.[9] According to Grigory Marakutsa, in 2005 PMR would open diplomatic representations in Moscow and Kiev and $250,000 has been earmarked in PMR's budget for this purpose.[10] After the Orange Revolution this did not occur.

PMR can be considered a 'super-presidential republic', in that all polit-ical power resides with the presidency. The President appoints and dismisses all heads of administration and ministers to the Cabinet of Ministers (which replaced the office of Prime Minister, and is chaired by the President), and an indeterminate legal environment is maintained.[11] The PMR Minister of National Security is Vladimir Antyufeyev, who formerly headed an OMON unit in Latvia during the 'January events' of 1991 and is currently wanted by Interpol for the murder of Latvian journalists during this period. He restored and reformed the Cossack forces in PMR, and is believed to be under the control of and in permanent consultation with Russian FSB personnel and is perceived to be the right hand of the Smirnov clan.

PMR–Russian relations: Interlocking pillars of support

The relationship between Russia and PMR is difficult to characterize pre-cisely. As one report noted: 'At its most mischievous, the Kremlin's strategy may view Transdniestria as a second version of Kaliningrad, the Russian enclave near Poland – in other words, a trouble-making outpost on the borders of NATO.'[12] President Voronin has concluded that Russia's role is complete and decisive in shaping policy-making with PMR. After the experience of the Kozak Memorandum process (see below) of late 2003, Voronin concluded that President Putin has opportunity and capacity to influence the Tiraspol regime: 'I am convinced that, if Russia wants it, this Smirnov will not stay even two hours longer in Tiraspol.'[13] This is perhaps to overstate the case, although Russian influence is undoubt-edly strong, underwritten as it is by $50 million paid annually in energy subsidies, which are now calculated from the early 1990s to the present to be the equivalent of $1 billion with interest.[14]

Material aid for the Smirnov regime from the Russian government is reinforced by acts of symbolic support by government officials. To take one example, on 2 September 2004, PMR marked the 13th anniversary of secession from Moldova with Soviet songs, self-praise and a military parade in Tiraspol. The parade featured 'regular troops', 'border guards', militiamen, rapid reaction forces, and Russian Cossacks. A visiting Russian delegation, led by the Deputy Chairman of the State Duma, Sergey Baburin, told Olvia-Press (PMR's press service) that 'one genuine reality must be accepted: Moldova is today made of two states – the Moldovan Transdniestrian Republic and the Republic of Moldova, while the Trans-dniestrians have fully demonstrated their right to choose their fate alone'.[15]

Political and military levers of control in PMR are buttressed by a man-aged economic order, both legal and illegal. Sheriff Company, whose director-general is a former investigator at the Dniester region interior ministry, Ilya Kazmaly, is PMR's largest private corporation, holding a monopoly of telephone communications (both fixed and mobile), Internet provision and a near monopoly on television receivers (90 per cent), trade in oil products (some estimates suggest 90 per cent of the oil market). It owns the television channel TSV (Television of Free Choice/[Televideniye Svobodnogo Vybora]) and a radio station.[16] The Russian firm ITERA controls the majority of shares in the Moldovan Metallurgical Plant, which generates two-thirds of the region's tax revenues, and the Cuciurgan power station and KVINT brandy factory also provide the PMR with 'state' revenues. Smirnov has stated that PMR has a \$53 million positive trade balance with the United States, Germany, Poland and the Czech Republic, and that: 'Trade with CIS member countries totalled 639 million dollars in the first 11 months of 2004, of which import made up 440 million dollars.' Italy, the United States, Portugal, Germany, Greece and Poland are among PMR's main trade partners in the West: Russia, Ukraine and Belarus in the CIS. In 2004, 'imports' from Moldova fell by 20 per cent and 'exports' by 15 per cent after economic sanctions were imposed in August (see below), according to Smirnov.[17] Just over 50 per cent of PMR's officially registered exports are directed towards two key markets – Russia and Russian companies registered in North Cyprus.[18]

The illegal economy is widely perceived to be dominant and is fostered by PMR's indeterminate legal status. Romanian Foreign Minister Mircea Geoana characterized the PMR as 'a black hole of trans-border organized crime, including drug smuggling, human trafficking, and arms smuggling'.[19] Trafficked humans, particularly women and children, are transported primarily to the Balkans, UAE, Turkey, and Western European 'markets'. President Voronin himself noted that 'foreign specialists' and analysts have 'calculated that about 2–3 billion dollars are being laundered in this black Dniestr zone annually'.[20]

Elements of the Soviet-era military-industrial complex are still active. Some arms factories, such as the Elektromah and Tochlitmash works produce weapons for the Russian military. However, since the conclusion of the civil war in 1992, there has been a steady stream of allegations that the PMR 'defence ministry' sells the products of secret military production lines and surplus materials on the black market to countries involved in regional conflicts or even terrorist organizations, including Chechen rebels and the Abkhaz regime, which are well positioned to purchase such weapons.[21] The airport in Tiraspol is not part of the 'security zone' and so OSCE and other foreign observers are unable to monitor exports. The chairman of the Moldovan parliamentary committee for national security, Iurie Stoicov, has stated that he had: 'information from foreign secret services that certain criminal groups in the Dniester region are selling weapons. Any activities in the Dniester region related to selling armaments abroad are illegal. Any weapons being sold without a strict record may fall into the hands of terrorists, criminal groups or other structures.' However, the OSCE mission spokesman, Claus Neukirch, cautioned: 'There is often talk about the sale of armaments from the Dniester region, but there is no convincing evidence.'[22] Most recently, *The Sunday Times* reported that three radioactive (strontium and caesium) Alazan rockets capable of contaminating a city centre were offered for sale for $500,000 (£263,000).[23]

The status and role of PMR in shaping Moldova's internal security politics and those of the wider region – particularly its relationship with Abkhazia and South Ossetia and associated informal criminal networks – has implications for economic and political elites in Ukraine. Not only does Ukraine share 460 kilometres of the PMR segment of the Moldovan–Ukrainian border (which is widely considered to be porous), but there are also currently approximately 300,000 ethnic Ukrainians resident in PMR. Russian and Ukrainian oligarchs have taken part in the PMR privatization process, profiting from and contributing to both the legal and illegal political economy. The five-sided conflict resolution format[24] ideally suits the business interests of these companies as it effectively freezes the conflict and upholds the profitable status quo and according to one analyst: 'With Moscow's open support, the Dniester region has fulfilled no agreements signed at the five-party talks since 1999.'[25]

Political track: Istanbul to the 'Kozak Memorandum'

The 1999 OSCE Istanbul Summit agreed that the deadline for the withdrawal of Russian troops and ammunition from PMR was 2002. However, PMR halted the withdrawal of Russian military hardware, which had been proceeding in accordance with international agreements. In December 2002, at the OSCE Porto Ministerial, the deadline for the withdrawal of Russian weapons from PMR was extended until the end of 2003, and then subsequently further extended into 2004. Russia declared its 'intention' to do this, 'provided the necessary conditions are in place', so serving, in the eyes of many observers to the process, to underscore the ineffectiveness of the five-sided OSCE-sponsored conflict resolution format.

The 14th Army has been perceived as a Russian lever of control over PMR, and therefore over the strategic orientation of Moldova proper. However, it is increasingly clear to Moscow that new political levers of control need to be developed and the OSCE Porto Summit appears to have signalled that the West was less interested in Moldova, and that Russia was free to take the lead. This provided the opportunity to switch from military to primarily political levers of control in the shape of Russian-sponsored federalization plans. After a visit to Moscow during 7–9 February 2003 by President Voronin, the 'Voronin Initiative' appeared on 11 February 2003. The 'Kozak Memorandum' was presented on 17 November 2003, and can be understood as the Russian political response to the diminishing utility of military levers of control in PMR. Dmitry Kozak, First Deputy Head of the Russian Presidential Administration (that is, deputy chief-of-staff), was considered a personal representative of President Putin and he introduced a 'Memorandum on the Basic Principles of the State Structure of a United State'. This suggested a 'federation on a contractual basis' that would allow the right of PMR secession and recognition of PMR independence, and the 'two equal subjects/two unit federation' formula allowed the possibility of a PMR veto of all federal laws.[26]

On 5 November 2003, President Voronin met with OSCE chairman Jaap de Hoop Scheffer and began to reconsider his position on federalization plans. Although Voronin had initialled each page of the Kozak Memorandum, he had not actually signed it, allowing him to disavow it on 24 November 2003. At the OSCE summit in Maastricht on 1–3 December, it became clear that Western OCSE states did not consider Moscow's approach constructive. The United States, EU and European NATO states subsequently rejected the Kozak Memorandum. The US Secretary of State, Colin Powell, praised the OSCE's 'constructive multilateralism', and President Voronin highlighted the necessity of Moldovan integration into 'Western' Europe as a policy priority.

As a result, President Voronin and his ruling Communist Party then came under pressure as Moscow began to more openly support the candidacy of Serafim Uruchean, the Mayor of Chisinau. Voronin was facing an implicit choice: Moscow would back or threaten to back an opposition candidate and party in the spring 2005 parliamentary elections, unless Voronin supported the logic of the Kozak Memorandum. Voronin's choice was to cooperate with Moscow or run the risk of being replaced by an alternative Moscow-supported candidate. On 17 February 2004, without any publicity, the Moldovan Minister of Reintegration presented OSCE mediators with the 'Chisinau view' – the Moldovan government's comments on the OSCE document that was the basis of the negotiations. However, as the 'Chisinau view' was 'Kozak II' in all but name, Voronin appeared to accept this implicit deal.[27]

Moldova, or more accurately Voronin, was caught trying to balance stronger tendencies toward European integration with continued Russian influence (as embodied in the 'Kozak Memo II'). In essence, Voronin faced the task of managing to uphold Moldova's national interest while at the same time maintaining his personal political viability and hold on power. By early to mid-2004, in the absence of a clear EU policy, even an optimist might well have concluded that Moldova's national interest would only be upheld as an unintended by-product of the political infighting between Voronin and opposition parties (that the President alleged were Russian-supported). Reorientation towards the West might well have occurred, but only by default rather than by design.

Post-Kozak strategic reorientation Westwards: Russia's response

However, by 2004 a number of factors merged to tip the balance towards a strategic reorientation Westwards. First, Voronin was not prepared to be president while Smirov (and so Moscow) had a veto over Moldova's foreign and security policy-making – the Kozak Memo made it clear that this outcome was one that Moscow sought. Second, strategic reorientation was facilitated by the emergence in 2004 of more determinedly pro-Western regimes in Ukraine and Romania. Third, the prospect of Romanian and Bulgarian EU integration in 2007 increased EU focus and the resources it was prepared to deploy in the region, so providing Voronin with a more viable and effective partner. As a result, the ongoing low-intensity 'frozen conflict' between Chisinau and Tiraspol began to heat up as 2004 unfolded. In February 2004, the foreign ministers of EU member states decided to extend the one-year travel ban imposed in February 2003 on 17 senior PMR leaders, including Igor Smirnov and his two sons. The ministers said the stance of the separatist leadership, which they say remains unwilling to engage in full efforts to reach a peaceful and comprehensive solution to the conflict with Moldova, is 'unacceptable'.[28]

The regime of visa sanctions against the PMR leadership was intensified in July 2004 in reaction to Tiraspol's harassment of six Moldovan-language schools (i.e., schools that use the Latin rather than the Cyrillic alphabet) after the refusal of the boards of these schools to register with the PMR authorities.[29] In response to the schools crisis, on 1 August 2004, the Moldovan customs authorities suspended the customs service to PMR businesses not registered in Moldova (i.e., did not pay taxes to Moldova), the Chamber of Commerce and Industry ceased issuing certificates of origin and Moldovan Railways withdrew the provision of carriages for companies based in PMR. All government privileges to PMR companies were suspended. An 'emergency meeting' of the security council of PMR on 30 July stated: 'This will completely destabilize the Moldovan economy and, coupled with suspension of power and gas supply, will spell disaster for the state.'[30] Both Igor Smirnov and the Russian Foreign Ministry have described the measure as economic blockade.[31]

On 12 October 2004, at a conference dedicated to the 80th anniversary of the Moldavian Autonomous Soviet Socialist Republic, Igor Smirnov announced that PMR would hold a referendum to 'to prove the legitimacy' of its independence. The results of the referendum would become law and force the international community to acknowledge the PMR people's will.[32] Smirnov had previously argued in August 2004 that holding separate referendums in Moldova and PMR to settle the PMR–Moldovan conflict was a possibility. Such action would be in accordance with the Cyprus settlement model of conflict resolution, and would afford the people of PMR 'the right to self-determination'.[33]

These proposed actions point to the emergence of a more concrete PMR strategy aimed at moving beyond the status quo of frozen conflict to outright independence. Smirnov has attempted to manipulate events in order to confront Russia and Ukraine with a dilemma: to choose between a renewed war between Tiraspol and Chisinau or avoid war by recognizing PMR as an independent and sovereign state. In either case, Moldova is rendered a weak and unstable entity, unable either to assimilate PMR or to contain the spillover of instability. Ultimately this would allow for the realization of the 'Belkovskiy plan': independence of PMR and the integration of Moldova into Romania.[34]

Smirnov will not entertain the prospect of the integration of PMR into Moldova proper yet PMR integration into Moldova is a necessary precondition for the integration of Moldova into the EU. Thus, PMR integration into Moldova would spell the end of his power base and raise the prospect of legal prosecution. Currently, a 'soft landing' option that would provide immunity from personal prosecution and the opportunity to export capital to some third destination does not appear to be in the offing.

Chisinau and the West lack the means and capacity to force the Smirnov regime to comply. Following the 'Orange Revolution' in Ukraine, Russia has begun to assert its national state interest even more strongly where it can as compensation and, thus, it is likely to strengthen not weaken or severe ties with PMR. As Gleb Pavlovsky, an adviser to President Putin, announced: 'Russia is currently revising its policy in the post-Soviet space and the mechanisms of its implementation.' As a general principle, 'any country [that would] promote the doctrine of Russia's rollback will certainly create a conflict in the relations with this country. This must be clearly understood.'[35]

President Voronin's willingness to compromise Moldova's sovereignty so apparent in late 2003 was reversed through 2004, and this reversal continued through to 2006, mainly as a result of frustration at Tiraspol's intransigence and unwillingness to fulfil commitments and a strategic reorientation Westwards that appears to pay dividends. Coincidently – Smirnov argues that this was the primary purpose – such actions also had the effect of accruing political capital ahead of the parliamentary election in spring of 2005. In September and October 2004, Voronin stated that his administration would no longer negotiate with the Transdniestrian administration and noted that the idea of federalization was now to be considered outdated, confirming that other conflict resolution methods would be applied. He argued that a multinational peace mission should replace the Russian peacekeepers in PMR: 'instead of respecting the treaty and helping Moldova settle this conflict, Russian forces support Smirnov and his regime'. Current negotiations had produced little by way of substantive results and 'Smirnov and the Russian and Ukrainian authorities are seeking to freeze the conflict and let the Transdniestrian cement their independence'.[36] Voronin dismissed such talks as: 'fruitless and counter-productive. We have analyzed the situation and found out the sides have already signed 99 documents. Moldova abides by 99 per cent of them, and Transdniestria – 1 per cent.'[37] This echoed an earlier statement in which he stressed: 'All these years, the Transdniestrian regime has been and will remain a puppet regime, because it is ruled from the capitals of Russia and Ukraine. A lasting settlement of the Transdniestrian conflict depends in fact entirely on the Russian Federation's position. We want to clarify this position to the very end.'[38] His statements were surprisingly vociferous and colourful, identifying a litany of abuse and corrupt practice, attacking Tiraspol's 'aggressive militarism', 'secret police repression', 'intimidation of the population', 'linguistic cleansing' and 'brutality towards children'. Indeed, not to mince words, PMR's leadership represented a 'totalitarian regime of a fascist type' led by 'a handful of adventurers who had robbed 700,000 people of the right to enter the 21st century'.[39]

From President Voronin's perspective, in terms of moving the conflict resolution agenda to a format and process better suited to Chisinau's objectives, 2003–04 can be understood as a success. The status and implications of PMR are no longer viewed as an internal Moldovan security issue, but rather, in the words of one Moldovan newspaper: 'If so far Europe viewed the Dniester conflict as a scandal between two villages located on different banks of the Dniester river, now the international community admits that this conflict threatens regional and even continental security.' Moldova's reintegration will increasingly be supported by the EU and United States and so included in their working agendas, as well as the OSCE.[40]

There are compelling reasons why the PMR frozen conflict should be considered an issue of rising strategic importance. First, by 2007 Romania will be an EU member state and the 'soft security' threats that emanate from PMR will have become more obvious and less easy to dismiss – particularly as similar 'soft security' threats in the Balkans hopefully diminish as Balkan reintegration into the Euro-Atlantic security order gathers pace. Second, as EU third-echelon enlargement in the Black Sea region (Moldova, Ukraine, Georgia) will be unlikely, EU contributions to the unification and thus state consolidation of Moldova can be presented as a compensatory alternative to membership. Third, as the Balkans stabilizes and the ESDP gains operational confidence and strength, it will become harder to avoid the logic of the deployment of civilian and/or military instruments in PMR to tackle transnational threats of illegal migration, human trafficking and organized crime on EU borders. Fourth, a failure to uphold the credibility of the EU's wider partnership policies, in particular the European Neighbourhood Policy and the Partnership and Cooperation Agreement (PCA) with Moldova, will be exposed by inaction. In addition, Moldova has few options given the September 2003 decision by Russia, Belarus, Ukraine and Kazakhstan to sign an agreement to form their own common market before 2010, so undermining the utility of the CIS.

At the same time, Moldovan officials at the OSCE Permanent Council in Vienna have invited the United States and EU to become more actively involved in the settlement of the conflict in PMR.[41] They also called on Russia, Ukraine and Romania to support the declaration of stability and security for Moldova in order for Moldova to enter the Stability Pact during the OSCE Council of Ministers in Sofia, on 6–7 December 2004. In response, the deputy head of the CIS states department at the Russian Foreign Ministry, Nikolay Fomin, stated: 'Russia will not sign the declaration on stability and security for Moldova. In the basic political accord Russia admitted the territorial integrity, sovereignty and independence of Moldova. This is enough for the development of the relations between our states and it meets mutual interests.'[42]

According to OSCE sources, the draft declaration reiterated the obligation for the Russian Federation to respect its commitments assumed at the 1999 Istanbul summit regarding the complete and unconditional withdrawal of troops and ammunition from Moldova. The former US

Secretary of State, Colin Powell, stated that the United States will makes its ratification of the Conventional Forces in Europe (CFE) Adapted Treaty conditional upon the willingness of the Russian Federation to fulfil its commitments on unconditional withdrawal of all troops and ammunition from Moldova and Georgia, assumed at the Istanbul summit. Moldovan Foreign Minister Andrei Stratan stated 'the presence of Russian troops in Moldova is illegitimate, because it violates Moldovan laws and international treaties'.[43]

In late January 2005, following a meeting at the inauguration ceremony of President Yushchenko, Ukraine and Moldova resumed talks on enhancing control at the border between the two countries.[44] The newly appointed Ukrainian Minister of Foreign Affairs Boris Tarasiuk identified the Transdniestria settlement efforts as: 'one of the important-most tasks of the Ukraine's national security'. In a very strongly worded statement he noted that Ukraine regards Transdniestia as 'Europe's black hole, where very few get fabulously rich while hundreds of thousand eke out hand-to-mouth existence. I am convinced that the existence of the Transdniestrian and other puppet regimes, impeding the building of a unified Europe, are strategically disadvantageous for the Russian Federation as well'. He went on to declare: 'We must recognize also that the illegitimate, corrupt regimes of self-styled republics have nothing in common with the legitimate rights of the people living in such territories'. Signalling a new approach to PMR and a more active and independent role within the OSCE sponsored five sided format, he stated: 'Terms such as 'sanitary cordons', 'red lines', 'spheres of influence' and the like ought to be withdrawn from European diplomats' vocabulary. Ukraine is not an exercise ground for geopolitical battles between the European Union, United States, and Russian Federation.'[45] The prospects for the creation of effective Ukrainian–Moldovan border monitoring and agreement on customs stamps and exports from PMR are much higher.[46]

The results of the presidential elections in Romania in December 2004 have also reinforced the pressure for Moldova to consolidate its strategic reorientation westwards. Romania's new President, Traian Basescu, declared Romania's willingness to participate in the negotiation process on the settlement of the Transdniestrian conflict during a press conference in Moscow in mid-February 2005: 'no matter what would be the final variant of the Transdniestrian settlement, it must be based on the respect for the Republic of Moldova's sovereignty, independence and territorial integrity'. He also underscored Romania's support for the process of the Moldovan European integration: 'The European partnership with Moldova is not only a project, but a priority. In the first place, we shall support

Chisinau's steps, aimed at the implementation of the RM–EU Plan of Actions.'[47]

It is also clear that President Voronin of Moldova has hardened his attacks against Smirnov and Russian support for PMR and appears much more willing to entertain closer EU integration efforts. In late January 2005, Voronin prevented Russian and Ukrainian ambassadors from entering Tiraspol, leading Smirnov to respond: 'Moldovan authorities' decision to ban the entrance to the Dniester region by Russian and Ukrainian diplomats, Nikolai Ryabov and Pyotr Chkalov, pursues far-reaching aims.' In his view, 'attempts are made to put an end to Russia's presence in the Dniester region and replace Russian peacekeepers with foreign ones. In addition, this is made to change the format of the talks – with the involvement of the United States, the EU and Romania. Moldova is trying to exclude the Dniester region as a participant in the talks.'[48]

The re-election of President Voronin on 4 April 2005, as a result of the Communist Party receiving 44 per cent of the vote at the 6 March 2005 election, maintained stability and predictability in Moldova security politics, and the trends that characterised the post-2003 era are being consolidated, albeit within a changing strategic context. Continuity is maintained by the persistence of the same issues which block conflict resolution; namely, the federal structure of the state and the division of competencies between local and federal authorities; as well as Russia's failure to fulfil the Istanbul commitments of 1999 (withdrawal of military forces, bases and munitions) and the linkage of this to order.

Change is introduced through the process of strategic reorientation and engagement westwards, which President Voronin has pursued into 2006. On 7 June 2005, Voronin made an address to the North Atlantic Council. He asked that Moldova advance its PfP commitments to include an Individual Partnership Action Plan.[49] The EU appointed its special representative in Moldova in March 2005 and the European Commission delegation was established in autumn 2005. An EU-established Border Assistance Mission (EUBAM) on 1 December 2005 and a new 'five plus two' negotiation format have increased the visibility and presence of the EU in Moldovan security politics. While the May 2005 Russia–EU Moscow Summit produced agreement on the *Road Map for the Common Space on External Security*, the continued deterioration in Russia–Moldova relations point to the obstacles that any potential EU–Russia brokered agreement would have first to overcome.[50] At the same time, a number of resurrected settlement plans have been proposed – in April, Ukraine's National Security and Defence Council advocated the 'Towards settlement – through democracy' so-called 'Yushchenko Plan', and in July the OSCE and Russian Federation advanced a Yushchenko-Kozak hybrid variant settlement proposal.[51] Each of these variants essentially stick to the traditional five-sided format and if adopted would limit the foreign and security policy-making ability of a central authority based in Chisinau.[52] In July 2005, the mediators delivered a proposal to Moldova/PMR entitled 'Arms Control – Confidence and Security Building Measures in Moldova' – but this appeared largely rhetorical.

By 2006, many Russian commentators and politicians were noting with some alarm events in the Western Balkans and making direct comparisons with PMR. The final status of Kosovo will also be decided in 2007, with a decision by the international community that the status quo is not sustainable. It is highly likely that by the end of 2007, some sort of qualified sovereignty will have been agreed, with the international community in an EU supervisory role for the next 10–15 years. Will independence for Kosovo and now Montenegro break the log jam by overcoming the expectation, development and integration gaps in the Western Balkans? Will the international community be able to guarantee viable autonomy for minorities, or will such an outcome reinforce the current trend of indirect ethnic cleansing in the province, and serve as a precedent to other secessionist movements in the region, not least PMR and Abkhazia and South Ossetia in Georgia. Panacea or Pandora's box: either outcome will affect stability in Serbia, Montenegro, Kosovo and Macedonia and relations between the EU and Russia at least until the centenary of the assassination of the Archduke Franz Ferdinand, at Sarajevo, in summer1914.

Russia–PMR policy 2006–08: Recognize sovereignty, facilitate reintegration?

The 2003 OSCE–Russia–Ukraine moves to federalize Moldova, thereby giving greater legitimacy to PMR, would not have been in the longer-term interests of the EU or Moldova. However, while there are compelling reasons why the EU and NATO should focus on Moldova, it is not clear whether this process can occur in a decisive manner. The PMR elite remains intransigent and the EU is 60 per cent energy dependent on the Russian Federation and has much higher priorities in its agenda than conflict settlement and resolution in PMR. Indeed, the expectation that after the 'Orange Revolution', Russia might accept a reduction in its ability to manage its sphere of influence remains slim. The EU may well become a key external actor, but Russia will maintain its block on conflict resolution. In the words of Mikhail Margelov, chair of the Foreign Relations

Committee in Russia's Federation Council: 'Given Moscow's influence on the region and the degree to which the Moldovan economy depends on it at the present time, any unilateral settlement attempt in Transdniestria in circumvention of Moscow is doomed.'[53]

On 20 June 2005, Modest Kolerov, the head of the newly created Division for Inter-Regional and Cultural Relations with Foreign Countries within the Russian Presidential Administration, stated that Russia is deeply interested in the security and success – including political and economic – of PMR. As in Russia, the main task of PMR and its 'compatriots', he suggested, was to preserve its sovereignty. This indicated a willingness to extend quasi-recognition of PMR sovereignty by a high-ranking Russian official.[54] In June 2005, President Putin also appointed Vladimir Titov to be a special representative on PMR under Kolerov within the Presidential Administration. Both moves suggested a hardening of Russia's support to PMR, which in policy terms might be understood as a calibrated attempt to balance increasing EU presence in the region.

Indeed, following the renewed Russian and PMR allegations of economic blockade of PMR in response to the imposition of a customs regime on the 460 kilometres-long PMR–Ukraine border in early 2006, PMR authorities threatened to leave the negotiation process, demanded that only Russia play the role of conflict resolution negotiator, blocked rail transit, and organized a coordinated 'defence of Transdniestria' with the Russian State Duma.[55] The EU Border Assistance Mission was instrumental in pushing for such monitoring to begin on 3 March 2006, which is a sign of greater EU involvement in the region, an involvement that threatens Moscow's post-Soviet model of conflict resolution.[56] Russia's Ambassador to Moldova, Nikolai Ryabov, explicitly challenged EU involvement when on 20 March 2006 he claimed special rights for Russia in Moldova and the 'post-Soviet space' generally:

> Russia by virtue of its great-power status has legitimate, indisputable interests in the post-Soviet space as guarantor of stability. Russia has a legitimate right to reassert these interests and to demand through any means that they be observed. The intervention of the EU or the United States in support of Moldovan–Ukrainian actions on the border cannot cause Russia to renounce its interests and its foreign policy. The new customs regime on that border infringes directly on Russia's legitimate interests. The economic blockade is a planned political action by Chisinau and Kyiv and some Western policymakers ... Chisinau and the West are trying to revise the agreements signed earlier during the negotiating process.[57]

Modest Kolerov is also assumed to be responsible for the introduction in June 2005 of a new actor into PMR politics – the International Youth Corporation 'Proryv' ('Breakthrough'). Although Dimitri Soin, head of the PMR branch of the Council for National Strategy of Russia, is its main ideologist,[58] 'Proryv' is funded by the Russian Presidential Administration.[59] As such it is the only foreign funded non-governmental organization (NGO) pursuing political goals able to operate in PMR (with branches created in Crimea and Odessa) and received this dispensation directly from Smirnov. Its ostensible purpose is to represent a cadre of pro-Smirnov loyalists who oppose Western-imposed 'Colour Revolutions' in PMR,[60] as well as to 'overthrow [Moldova's President] Voronin's regime and export democracy from Transdniestria to Moldova'.[61] By appropriating public space it is able to fill and occupy any political vacuum by mimicking an independent civil-society grouping and by bridging the gap between civil society such as it exists in PMR and political parties. 'Proryv' has the potential to be a much more useful and flexible instrument of Russian power than this Potemkin-democracy structure suggests. It could become the key ideological mechanism through which Russia facilitates a post-Smirnov era in PMR, allowing for a soft landing and providing the new cadre of post-post-Soviet leadership that is much more sensitive and loyal to Moscow. Kolerov has stated that PMR could become an important source of skilled personnel for Russian politics and this has led some observers to conclude that 'Proryv' may officially join the pro-Putin 'Nashi' movement as its legitimate Transdniestrian branch. Such action would provide additional indirect evidence that the Kremlin contemplates recognizing PMR independence.[62] In addition, we might surmise that 'Proryv' is also able to monitor more closely other key players in PMR that might be tempted to accept as negotiated solution to the frozen conflict, and so reduce Russian influence in the region.

These actors would include Sheriff, a company that balances its interests in PMR with those in Moscow and Kyiv, and could be tempted to accept a change in PMR status should the EU offer business guarantees and safeguards for its position in a post-Smirnov PMR. In early 2005, Sheriff developed its own political movement 'Renewal' and on 18 March 2005, 34 of 43 Dniester region MPs approved the amendments to the Dniester constitution that would turn PMR from presidential to parliamentary republic and so undercut the Smirnov power-base and with it Russian influence. Under executive pressure this move was defeated.[63] With the deputy parliament speaker (and former deputy head of the Ribnitsa Sheriff branch) Yevgeniy Shevchuk as its leader,

'Renewal' ran in the 11 December 2005 PMR parliamentary elections, with the aim of again gaining a majority, pushing through constitutional amendments and forcing Smirnov from power. 'Renewal' gained 23 (up from 17) out of the 43 seats in the Supreme Soviet during the 11 December 2005 Parliamentary elections, and on 29 December 2005 Shevchuk was elected speaker, succeeding Smirnov's long-time ally Grigoriy Marakutsa – 'apparently as a result of a deal between the "old guard" and the new business elite'.[64] On 2 June 2006, 'Renewal' declared its intention to become a political party, led by Shevchuk. One of its leaders stated: 'we would like to be the promoters of new political society in the Dniester region'.[65]

The hardening of Russian policy towards PMR has been evident throughout 2006. For example, on 5 May 2006, Smirnov was received officially in Moscow by Russian Foreign Minister Sergei Lavrov, at a meeting where Russian and PMR flags and other symbols of statehood were on display – 'Those in the know say that the Foreign Ministry doesn't change its protocol for no reason.'[66] On 23–24 May 2006, Smirnov attended a public reception in Moscow with a Russian deputy PM, where he signed a Protocol on International Cooperation in which an MFA press release referred to him not as the 'leader' of PMR but, for the first time, as the 'president'. As President Voronin commented:

And here something unacceptable in relations between states starts, that is, on the one hand to condemn separatism and, on the other, openly and clearly to support separatists in the Dniester. And when [Russian] First Deputy Prime Minister Zhukov signs an agreement in which for the first time in Russian official documents the Dniester leader is called president this speaks volumes.[67]

Tiraspol promised a referendum on independence (followed by accession to Russia), and the harmonization of the PMR laws with those of the Russian Federation.

A PMR referendum held on 17 September 2006 saw 97 per cent of those who took part (78.6 per cent of the electorate) vote for independent status followed by joining the Russian Federation. Sergei Lavrov characterized the vote as 'democratic and transparent'.[68] It has been reported that the Russian Foreign Ministry is now discussing whether to recognize the referendum and unification with South Ossetia and Abkhazia (after unification referendum in these self-declared republics) within the framework of the Russia–Belarus union.[69] Russian officials have throughout

2006 publicly stated that should Kosovo become independent via referendum, then it would move to recognize PMR, as well as Abkhazia and South Ossetia.[70] Such a tit-for tat approach suggests that Moscow views PMR as a bargaining chip on the Eurasia geopolitical chessboard. Moldova's foreign minister acknowledged as much in September 2006 when he stated: 'The Transdniestrian conflict is most and foremost a "product" of the geopolitical interests and designs.'[71] Should this occur, such an event could well be presented by Lavrov and Smirnov as a Colour Revolution, reflecting the 'will of the people'. Such a Colour Revolution would achieve Russian geostrategic goals in its near neighbourhood, and, in a distorted symmetry of mirror imaging, Proryv-FSB will have assumed the perceived role of SOROS-CIA.[72]

Conclusions: PMR and Russian great power status?

How might we characterize Russia's policy into the near term? PMR can be understood as a Soviet legacy issue, as well as a current tool of Russia's Moldova policy, a means to increases its geopolitical influence in the Black Sea region and ultimately a strategic lever in Russian–Euro–Atlantic relations. It is clear that overt military instruments of control – a characteristic of the early 1990s when the 14th Russian Army and 40,000 tonnes of military material were in evidence – has been replaced by economic and political influence exercised in PMR and, to a lesser extent, Moldova proper. Indeed, by 2003, 'only' 20,000 tonnes remained and the 14th Army had been reduced to light regiment strength. The military instrument has not died, but political and economic levers of influence are paying higher dividends for Russia, and Russian state consolidation under Putin, and the high price of energy, has given Russia the political will and economic resources to utilise these instruments in support of Russian strategic influence. The policy end remains the same; the means to that end have evolved.

Hitherto, the Russian policy framework has had two key components – the official one, which is advanced by the MFA through rhetoric and diplomatic negotiation stances, and the unofficial, which is pursued using covert means and under FSB direction. The Presidential Administration has a bridging role, attempting to play both roles with poor results as the Kozak debacle indicated. Officially and symbolically, Russia has sought to preserve the territorial integrity of the republic of Moldova, while at the same time providing guarantees for the special status of PMR. The necessity of preserving Russia's geopolitical interests in the region undercut this largely rhetorical framework, and concrete and practical Russian policies have supported primarily PMR rather than both parties. The tensions generated by such dualism have become more explicit in the new century and appear to have broken in 2006.

This escalation of Russian policy towards recognition of PMR statehood in 2006 may also represent the opening salvos in what might be termed the 'new Kremlin Project' – an attempt to devise an electoral strategy to allow for elite continuity after the March 2008 Russian presidential election. Rather than the 'loans for shares' Faustian pact of 1996, or the initiation of a second Chechen campaign in 1999 ahead of the 2000 election, March 2008 could well be characterized by the creation of a new supernational Russian idea – a unifying strategic rationale on par with the 'Third Rome' ideology of the medieval and early modern period and 'Third International' of the Soviet era. Such a discourse is founded on the contention that Russia faces a host of implacable state, structural and systemic enemies, both domestic and foreign. The demographic crisis, Chechnya and the dangers of fundamentalist Islamist spillover into Dagestan, the rise of organized crime, NATO encirclement and US military bases in Central Asia, the Western-backed 'colour revolutions' and the worsening plight of 'compatriots' living in post-Soviet space are the likely contenders. Collectively, they create the spectre of multiple threats, which the opposition parties and potential presidential candidates may well be able to identify, but that only the incumbents can defeat. 'Sovereign democracy' – a phrase that Vladislav Surkov, the deputy head of the Presidential Administration test drove earlier in 2005 – will become the watchword of such a policy, its *raison d'être* and the sunlit uplands to which only Putin's (s)elected successor can lead the Russian people. The very existence of the Russian state is at threat: existential survival can only be guaranteed by elite continuity.

If creating a psychological environment characterised by fear and xenophobia (an enduring feature of Russian political culture) to promote incumbent power is the chosen electoral strategy of Kremlin strategists and political technologists, it will be extremely interesting to see how exactly PMR is utilized instrumentally to this end – the securing of domestic political power and buttressing Russia's great power status. Under such conditions, Russian policy towards PMR will begin to be driven as much by the desire to extend Russian foreign policy influence as by the necessity to consolidate domestic political power around a Putin–FSB nexus within the Russian state. As a result, PMR rises in strategic importance for Russia and a study of Russian policy towards PMR tells analysts as much about Russian foreign policy as it does about domestic political constellations and the continuity and exercise of power by the president within

Russia itself. A longer-term policy challenge for Russia will be to square the circle of applying geopolitical principles to its near neighbourhood while on the global stage promoting the importance of sovereignty and territorial integrity.

Such thoughts are speculative and at best represent only one possible trend that may yet be discarded. Nevertheless, a study of Russian policy towards PMR through the prism of domestic Russian politics may well prove rewarding. Given the near irrelevance of political parties and the rubber stamp nature of the legislature in Russia, such a study would focus on executive power and politics within the Presidential Administration. As the key concern of the Presidential Administration is to manage the March 2008 presidential election to ensure Russia remains a 'sovereign democracy', a pertinent research question presents itself: 'To what ends and by what means is PMR a factor in the Russian presidential election, March 2008?'

Notes

1 Moldovan state officials, not least President Voronin, refer to this territory as the Dniester region rather than PMR.
2 Marius Vahl and Michael Emerson, 'Moldova and the Transdniestrian Conflict', in Bruno Coppieters, Michael Emerson and Michel Huysseune (eds), *Europeanization and Conflict Resolution: Case Studies from the European Periphery* (Ghent: Academic Press, 2004), p. 4.
3 Moscow threatened to bomb Chisinau's airfield in retaliation for a successful raid by Moldova on PMR positions. Author's confidential source.
4 Trevor Waters, 'Security Concerns in Post-Soviet Moldova', *Occasional Paper*, Conflict Studies Research Center (April 2001), pp. 5 and 8.
5 Nicolas Whyte, 'Moldova: Regional Tensions over Transdniestria', International Crisis Group, 17 June 2004. Nicholas Whyte is Director of ICG's Europe Programme.
6 *No End in Sight*, IWPR'S Balkan Crisis Report, No. 524 (5 November 2004).
7 *Rossiyskaya Gazeta*, Moscow, in Russian, 31 March 2004.
8 'Moldovan Breakaway Region Pledges To Help South Ossetia In Dispute With Georgia', *Interfax news agency*, Moscow, in Russian, 2 June 2004.
9 'Transdniestria, Abkhazia and South Ossetia Claim that Moldova and Georgia Would Like to Use Force', BASA-PRESS, 5 Oct. 2004.
10 Infotag News Agency, Chisinau, in Russian, 21 Dec. 2004.
11 'Residents of Transdniestria cannot elect their leaders democratically, and they are also unable to participate freely in Moldovan elections.' See Freedom House Report on Transdniestria for 2004, at <http://www.freedomhouse.org/research/freeworld/2004/countryratings/moldova-transnistria.htm>. See also 'Severe Violations of Human Rights in the Transdniestrian Region of Moldova', Statement by the International Helsinki Federation for Human

Rights (IHF) and the Moldovan Helsinki Committee, 11 Aug. 2004, at <http://www.ihf-hr.org/documents/doc_summary.php?sec_id=3&d_id= 3955>.

12 'The hazards of a long, hard freeze', *The Economist*, 19 Aug. 2004, at <http:// www.economist.com/world/europe/displaystory.cfm?story_id = 3110979>.

13 ProTV, Chisinau, in Moldovan, 1 Dec. 2004.

14 Tod Lindberg, 'Turmoil in Transdniestria', *Washington Times*, 1 June 2004.

15 'Transdniestria Marks 13th Anniversary of Secession from Moldova with Military Parade in Tiraspol', *BASA-PRESS*, 2 Sept. 2004.

16 Vadim Solokhin, 'On whom does Voronin wager?', *Pridnestrovye*, Tiraspol, in Russian, 25 Nov. 2005, p. 2.

17 Infotag News Agency, Chisinau, in Russian, 28 Dec. 2004: 'In August–September 2004 alone, the losses from exports totalled 41.38 m dollars, while another 32 m dollars' worth of products failed to be exported'.

18 Vladimir Socor, 'Western Diplomacy Unmoved by "Linguistic Cleansing" in TransDniestr', *Eurasia Daily Monitor*, 3 Aug. 2004.

19 George Jahn, 'Soviet weapons cache, arms dealing, dirty bomb cause concern in Moldova's separatist enclave', AP Investigations, 12 Jan. 2004.

20 ProTV, Chisinau, in Moldovan, 1 Dec. 2004.

21 In 1993, seven Grad (rocket) units assembled in Tiraspol from Russian parts were sent to Abkhazia, according to an expert analyst Oazu Nantoi: 'Most probably, the equipment was loaded onto railway carriages and taken to [the Ukrainian cities of] Odessa, Ilychivsk and Mykolayiv, from where they were shipped to Abkhazia. This means that this is an international gunrunning network.' In 1998, V. Nemkov (a Lt.Col. in the PMR armed forces), admitted that he had sold Igla air-to-surface rockets from the Cobasna arms depot in 1996–97. In autumn 2000, Vasilyok mortars, which are manufactured only by factories located in PMR, were seized by the Russian armed forces from Chechen rebels. More recently, in May 2004, three rocket launchers were allegedly sold to Chechen rebels for $150,000. Dumitru Lazur, 'Tiraspol rockets for Chechens', *Jurnal de Chisinau*, Chisinau, in Moldovan, 28 May 2004.

22 Ibid.

23 Brian Johnson Thomas and Mark Franchetti, 'Radiation rockets on sale to "terrorists"', *The Sunday Times*, 8 May 2005, at <http://www.timesonline.co.uk/ article/0,,2087-1602963,00.html>.

24 A five-sided (3 + 2) format was developed, with Ukraine, Russia and the OSCE on the one side and the Republic of Moldova and PMR on the other.

25 Corneliu Mihalache, 'Government Paper Defends Moldova's "Pro-Western" Stance', *Moldova Suverana*, Chisinau, 21 Oct. 2004, p. 1.

26 'Forum of Moldovan Non-governmental Organizations Not Warming Present Federalization Project', 20 Nov. 2003: *BASA-PRESS*, <http://www.azi.md/ news?ID = 26740>; Vladimir Socor, "Pro-Western Moldovan Groups Resisting Russian-Controlled 'Federalization', *IASPS Policy Briefings: Geostrategic Perspectives on Eurasia*, 26 Nov. 2003.

27 Author's confidential interview, Chisinau, Spring 2004.

28 *World of Information Moldova Country Report*, 18 May 2004, p. 1.

29 The OSCE High Commissioner on National Minorities, Rolf Ekeus, characterized the closure as 'linguistic cleansing' and on 22 July the OSCE Permanent Council described the PMR actions as 'irresponsible and provocative'. Europe

Information Service European Report, 31 July 2004. Up to eight schools in PMR are said to use the Latin script to teach Moldovan students. The Moldovan language is virtually identical to Romanian. PMR authorities claim that Moldovan is only an official language of the region when written in Cyrillic script. Five thousand pupils have been studying the language in the Latin script for over ten years.

30   Moldova received 60 per cent of its power supply from the Cuciurgan power station (located in PMR) and imports Russian gas via a pipeline that transits PMR. According to a decree by President Igor Smirnov, imports from Moldova into the Dniester region are subject to a 100 per cent duty. Infotag news agency, Chisinau, in Russian, 2 Aug. 2004.

31   Nicholas Whyte, 'In Search of a Solution', *IWPR'S Balkan Crisis Report*, 524, 5 Nov. 2004; 'Moldovan-Dniester Railway War Enters Second Day', ProTV, Chisinau, in Moldovan, 3 Aug. 2004.

32   Olvia-Press web site, Tiraspol, in Russian, 12 Oct. 2004. An opinion poll published on 11 Oct. said that two-thirds of respondents back a referendum on independence (see Olvia-Press News Agency web site, Tiraspol, in Russian, 11 Oct. 2004).

33   Olvia-Press web site, Tiraspol, in Russian, 31 Aug. 2004.

34   Petru Bogatu, 'Regional Dniester conflict becomes international', *Flux*, Chisinau, in Moldovan, 5 Aug. 2004, p. 1. The article argues that Russian political scientist Stanislav Belkovsiy works in the security ministry of PMR and is a confidante of President Putin.

35   Vladimir Socor, 'Kremlin Redefining Policy In "Post-Soviet Space"', *Eurasia Daily Monitor*, 2/27, The Jamestown Foundation, 8 Feb. 2005.

36   'Transdniestria, Abkhazia and South Ossetia Claim that Moldova and Georgia Would Like to Use Force', BASA-PRESS, 5 Oct. 2004; 'Socor Considers that Voronin is Right', *OSCE News Digest: OSCE Mission to Moldova*, 6 Sept. 2004.

37   'Voronin Confirms Refusal to Speak to Current Tiraspol Leaders, and Grows Cool to Federalization Idea', INFOTAG, 30 Sept. 2004, at <http://www.azi.md/news?ID=31084>.

38   'President Voronin Says Moldova Refuses to Speak with Tiraspol in Previous Manner', INFOTAG, 3 Sept. 2004, at <http://www.azi.md/news?ID=30689>.

39   Vladimir Socor, 'Moldova President Criticises International Appeasement of Tiraspol', *Eurasia Daily Monitor*, 31 Aug. 2004.

40   *Moldova Suverana*, Chisinau, in Moldovan, 21 Oct. 2004: 'During his recent visit to Chisinau, the US State Department special negotiator for Eurasian conflicts, Steven Mann, said the USA accepted the pact and Chisinau's actions aimed at solving the Dniester conflict in accordance with the principles of sovereignty and territorial integrity.'

41   'Moldova wants to alter format of Transdniestria settlement talks', 12 Nov. 2004, at <http://www.interfax.com/com?item=Mold&pg=0&id=5769803&req=>.

42   Infotag News Agency, Chisinau, in Russian, 6 Dec. 2004.

43   'OSCE Ministerial Council Closes, No Document Adopted', 7 Dec. 2004

44   Valery Demidetsky, 'Moldova to resume talks to enhance border control', ITAR-TASS News Agency, Chisinau, 26 Jan. 2005.

45   'New Ukrainian Foreign Minster Speaks on Transdniestria', INFOTAG, 14 Feb. 2005, at <www.azi.md/news?ID=33033>.

46 George Dura, 'Prospects for the establishment of an international monitoring mission on the Ukraine-Moldova border', *Eurojournal.org*, April 2005.

47 'Romania is Ready to Participate in the Negotiation Process on the Settlement of the Transdniestrian Conflict', 15 Feb. 2005, at <http://www.azi.md/news? ID=33053>.

48 Yelena Volkova and Andrei Popov, 'Chisinau actions show probable final break-up with Tiraspol', ITAR-TASS News Agency, Moscow, 26 Jan. 2005; Olvia-Press web site, Tiraspol, in Russian, 24 Jan. 2005.

49 Vladimir Socor, 'Voronin at NATO says farewell top post-Soviet Space', *Eurasia Daily Monitor*, 2/112, 9 June 2005.

50 Dov Lynch, 'EU-Russia: Prospects for the Common Space', *Eurojournal.org*, June 2005.

51 Vladimir Socor, 'Kozak Plan resurfaces under OSCE Colors', *Eurasia Daily Monitor*, 2/136, 14 July 2005; Vladimir Socor, 'Moldova Elegantly Disposes of the Poroshenko-Yushchenko Plan', *Eurasia Daily Monitor*, 2/120, 21 June 2005.

52 For Moldovan reaction See Declaration of the [Moldovan] Foreign Policy Association regarding the 'Settlement Plan for the Transdniestrian problem' proposed by Ukraine on 16 May 2005; Roman Petrenko, 'Ukraine, Moldova at the Crossroads', *Eurojournal.org*, 31 May 2005, at <http://eurojournal.org/ more.php?id=184_0_1_0_M>; Nicu Popescu, 'The Ukrianian plan on Transdniestria will succeed if it is accompanied by concrete actions on the border', interview with the newspaper *Vremea*, at <http://www.vremea.net>, Chisinau, 27 May 2005 (in Russian).

53 *RIA Novosti*, 8 June 2005. See also 'Statement by Alexander Yakovenko, the Spokesman of Russia's Ministry of Foreign Affairs, Regarding the Recent Decisions of the Parliament of the Republic of Moldova', 11 July 2005, at <http://www.ln.mid.ru/brp_4.nsf/e78a48070f128a7b43256999005bcbb3/ 7015979b7d7>.

54 'Kremlin to Force Dnestr', *Kommersant*, 23 June 2005.

55 Igor Botan, 'The Hostages of the Transdniestrian Regime', *Igor Botan. E-Journal*, 4/68, 14 March 2006.

56 Interfax-Ukraine, Channel Five TV, Moldpres, 20–23 March 2006.

57 'Russia-West Standoff in Transdniestria: Overall Post-Soviet Order at Stake', Jamestown.Org., 24 March 2006.

58 *VolgaInform*, 6 June 2005, at <http://www.volgainform.ru/allnews/465946/>.

59 'Proryv' replicates the Kolerov/Kremlin-created youth movement 'Nashi'.

60 Nicu Popescu, 'The EU in Moldova – settling conflicts in the neighborhood' *European Institute for Security Studies*, Oct. 2005, at <http://www.iss-eu.org/ occasion/occ60.pdf>.

61 'Five blows of Russian President's adviser Modest Kolerov to Putin's policies' ('Piat' udarov govetnika prezidenta Russia modesta kolorova 'p pditike Vladima Putina'), *Nezavisimaya Moldova,* 22 June 2005; 'Transdniestrian idols'; *Dnestrovskiy Kur'er* (translated from *Der Spiegel*), 11 Jan. 2006.

62 'Five blows ...', ibid.

63 Vadim Solokhin, 'On whom does Voronin wager?', *Pridnestrovye*, Tiraspol, in Russian, 25 Nov. 2005, p. 2.

64 'Profile Of Moldova's Dniester Parliament Speaker Shevchuk', BBC Monitoring International Reports, 28 Feb. 2006.

65 Olvia-Press website, Tiraspol, in Russian, 2 June 2006.

66   Ruslan Gorevoi, 'Our Fair Union', *Versiya*, 37, 25 Sept.–Oct. 1 2006, p. 9; Svetlana Gamova, 'Abkhazia and Trans-Dniester will replace Georgia and Ukraine in the CIS; Bagapsh and Smirnov are knocking on every door in Moscow to gain admission into the CIS', *Nezavisimaya Gazeta*, 12 May 2006, pp. 1, 5.
67   Ekho Moscovy radio, Moscow, in Russian, 21 July 2006.
68   Valery Demidetsky, 'Tiraspol to announce final results of independence referendum', ITAR-TASS News Agency, Moscow, 26 Sept. 2006.
69   Gorevoi, as note 67 above, p. 9.
70   Arkady Dubnov, 'Trans-Dneister Leader Brings An Argument to Moscow: an argument against sovereignty of Kosovo', *Vremya Novostei*, 19 Sept. 2006, pp. 1–2.
71   'Foreign Minister Andrei Stratan Addressing the Sixty First Session of the UN General Assembly. Un.org. 26.06.2006', *Transdniestrian Digest*, 31/41, 5 Oct. 2006.
72   Luke March and Graeme P. Herd, 'Moldova between Europe and Russia: inoculating against the colored contagion?', *Post-Soviet Affairs* forthcoming.

5
Putin's Attempts to Subjugate Georgia: From Sabre-Rattling to the Power of the Purse

Bertil Nygren

Introduction

Since the demise of the USSR, the South Caucasus has been the most un-stable part of Russia's immediate neighbourhood, and Georgia has been the most unstable of the 'weak states' in that neighbourhood.[1] As a result, 'hard security' issues are intrinsically linked with 'softer' security issues, all of which tend to be linked to the chase for hydrocarbon resources in the Caspian/Caucasus area.

The situation in Georgia has never been fully normalized since 1992. After the civil war in Abkhazia in 1993–94, some one hundred thousand refugees fled the region. While Russian forces supported the separatists dur-ing the civil war, since then they have been a necessary stabilizing factor. In South Ossetia, another breakaway region of Georgia, the situation was similar. President Eduard Shevardnadze was never able to unite Georgia, and was highly dependent on Russia.

The ouster of Shevardnadze in November 2003 in itself displayed President Vladimir Putin in a new role – that of mediator in Georgian internal affairs. Since then, Putin began to use economic instruments instead of the sabre-rattling policies he had pursued toward Georgia since 1999. Such economic instruments have been found appropriate in Russia's relations also with other former Soviet republics (especially with Armenia and Kyrgyzstan). Putin has exchanged his previous 'sabre-rattling' methods towards Georgia for softer 'purse' policies based on increasing control of crucial elements of Georgia's economy.[2]

Putin's foreign policies in the South Caucasus are part of his more gen-eral foreign policy approach, of an 'economization' of foreign relations (i.e., a greater reliance on economic means).[3] This can be seen in the attempts at economic re-integration of former Soviet space, most evident in the acquisition or control of energy sources and transfer, especially in Kyrgyzstan, Armenia, Ukraine, Belarus and Moldova. This foreign policy approach is based on the notion of Russia as the (only) great regional power in the Russia-led regional security complex, a great power with particular responsibility for the security (and well-being) of the CIS states. From Moscow's horizon, Russia is the 'natural' security provider in the CIS region and the 'natural' economic engine around which the other CIS states may develop. Traditional instruments of power politics should be avoided to the extent possible, but at the same time, Russian national interests are always the top priority. This mix of 'new' EU-like thinking on economic integration on the one hand, and traditional great power security thinking, on the other, is the hallmark of Putin's version of re-establishing Russia as a regional great power. To the weakest CIS States, this re-integration might seem more enforced than voluntary. To Russia, it is the fate of her great power mission.

The 'softer' Putin touch

Putin's reactions to the 'Rose Revolution' in late 2003, the Adjaria crisis in spring 2004 and to the Abkhazia crisis in autumn 2004, bear witness to a 'softer' Russian voice, to less of a sour reaction to events that are not going Russia's way. At the same time, there has been some evidence also of 'purse policies', especially the activities of the Russian state-controlled Unified Energy Systems and Gazprom. Both of these innovations indicate, in my view, a re-orientation of Putin's foreign policy towards Georgia.

The 'Rose Revolution' in Georgia in autumn 2003

The 'Rose Revolution' broke the stalemate in Russian–Georgian relations, and when new President Mikhail Saakashvili began to assert his powers over the two separatist regions, Abkhazia and South Ossetia, he was bound to meet resistance. Chronologically, these encounters between the Georgian centre and the peripheries took place first in Adjaria, then in South Ossetia and last in Abkhazia, all in 2004, and the general issue was 'who is to govern'. From the point of view of Russian foreign policy, the outcome of the encounters in Adjaria and Abkhazia was the most interesting, and unexpected.[4]

The Russian reaction to the 'Rose Revolution' in itself showed a new and unexpected side of Putin. In the upcoming Georgian parliamentary elections, there was one pro-presidential (or pro-Shevardnadze) party and one major opposition (Burdjanadze-Democrats) bloc. Warnings of 'chaos' were frequent prior to the elections, and the government was accused of forging voting lists.[5] A few days before the elections, railroads and roads around Tbilisi were blocked by demonstrators. By the time the final voting lists were published by the Central Election Commission (CEC), the number of eligible voters was far above the figures that the opposition accepted.[6] On election day, the CEC gave in to the opposition and ruled that anyone who could identify him/herself would be given the right to vote. While Shevardnadze called the election 'the fairest and most transparent election ever held in Georgia', OSCE and Council of Europe observations described the voting as falling short of many international standards.[7] Thousands took to the streets in Georgia to protest voting falsification, and the National Movement leader Mikhail Saakashvili threatened that Shevardnadze would face 'a revolution'. The events that followed could have taken just about any direction: while Saakashvili talked to several thousand supporters in Tbilisi, Adjar Supreme Council Chairman Aslan Abashidze sent his supporters to Tbilisi to stand up for Shevardnadze. Despite a meeting between Shevardnadze and the opposition leaders Mikhail Saakashvili, Nino Burdjanadze and Zurab Zhvania, no solution was found.[8] Saakashvili began to collect signatures to demand the resignation of Shevardnadze, who, in turn, appealed for calm on national television.[9] Mass demonstrations became the standard feature of street life in Tbilisi, and in Southern Georgia, there were violent clashes between supporters and opponents to Shevardnadze. Shevardnadze had a telephone discussion on the situation with Putin and others.[10] When the final results of the parliamentary election were announced on 20 November, they pointed in favour of the pro-Shevardnadze bloc.[11] Saakashvili appealed for mass demonstrations on 22 November, and up to 30,000 people marched to the government and parliament buildings, storming the latter. Shevardnadze declared a state of emergency to 'restore order'.[12]

The same day, Russian Foreign Minister Igor Ivanov went to Tbilisi and met with Shevardnadze and opposition leaders. Later in the afternoon Saakashvili threatened to have his supporters storm the presidential residence, but instead met with Shevardnadze in talks mediated by Ivanov. The brief meeting ended with the resignation of Shevardnadze. The role of Russia was restricted to formal mediation, and Saakashvili himself praised Ivanov's role: 'I simply did not expect it of him. He just arrived and turned the whole situation around, appearing at a meeting of the opposition and expressing support for us'.[13] The behaviour of Ivanov corresponded to the interests of the Georgian people, even more than it did to Russia's (short-term) geopolitical interest, since it was generally believed that Saakashvili was not a pro-Russian candidate.[14]

A couple of days later the three opposition leaders jointly announced the nomination of Saakashvili for the presidential election and, on 4 January,

Saakashvili was elected new Georgian President. The new Georgian leadership soon ran into problems with respect to the repeat parliamentary elections that were to follow on 28 March, the gravest in Adjaria. Saakashvili swore to restore Georgia's unity and territorial integrity.[15] This was the beginning of the next crisis in Georgia, with an equally unexpected ending.

The Adjaria conflict in spring 2004

The Adjarian leader, Aslan Abashidze, had ruled the Adjarian republic as his own feudal estate since 1991. Abashidze supported Shevardnadze during the 'Rose Revolution' and threatened to boycott the new presidential elections in January 2004. He gave in, though, after talks among acting Georgian President Nino Burdjanadze, the Russian Foreign Minister Igor Ivanov, Russian Defence Minister Sergey Ivanov and Putin. The conflict deepened, however, when the (anti-Abashidze) Democratic Adjaria movement was founded in Tbilisi with the explicit aim of replacing Abashidze. In Batumi (Adjaria), armed supporters of Abashidze took to the streets, and the new Georgian president threatened to use force to subjugate him. In late February, street fighting occurred in Adjaria between supporters and opponents of Abashidze. In mid-March, there was a virtual standoff between Abashidze and Saakashvili, when the latter was halted on the border between Adjaria and the rest of Georgia. Saakashvili issued an ultimatum to Abashidze to give him free passage in his own country, ordered the closing of the Batumi airport, inspection of all cargo entering Batumi and the closing of the border with Turkey. Abashidze militia forces began to group along the internal border between Adjaria and the rest of Georgia. At this stage first Burdjanadze, then Saakashvili went to see Abashidze, exacting a promise that voting for the Georgian parliament would be allowed also in Adjaria.[16]

The parliamentary elections did also take place in Adjaria. Saakashvili then threatened to prosecute all 'illegal armed groups' and asked for Abashidze's paramilitary groups to lay down arms, or for Abashidze to resign. A Georgian general took the side of Abashidze, and this was followed by Georgian military exercises close to Adjaria. Abashidze urged his troops to respond, which they did by blowing up two bridges that linked Adjaria to the rest of Georgia.[17]

In Batumi, several thousand anti-Abashidze demonstrators ignored a curfew after clashes with the local police and remained encamped on the streets overnight. Many local policemen joined the demonstrators who were growing in number and soon amounted to some 15,000.[18]

At this juncture, the Russian security adviser (and former Foreign Minister) Igor Ivanov flew to Batumi to persuade Abashidze to resign and to offer him a safe haven in Moscow. Abashidze accepted the offer and returned with Ivanov to Moscow. The next day, Saakashvili flew to Batumi and was met by cheering demonstrators.[19]

The Russian assistance in resolving a situation that threatened to become dangerous to Georgian statehood was, of course, highly appreciated in Tbilisi, but did not pass unnoticed in Abkhazia and South Ossetia, the two self-proclaimed independent regions that traditionally enjoyed strong Russian assistance. The fact is that Putin chose to support central Georgian power to the detriment of Russia's traditional allies and its own short-term geo-political interests. Truly something strange was going on, and speculations abounded about the kind of 'deal' that had been struck between Ivanov and Abashidze.[20]

The Abkhazia conflict in autumn 2004

The pre-history of the crisis in Abkhazia that developed in autumn 2004 goes back to the civil war in the early 1990s. In 1994, Russia and Georgia signed a friendship treaty, which guaranteed Georgia's territorial integrity, and in 1997 then Russian Foreign Minister Yevgenii Primakov organized direct negotiations between Abkhazia and Georgia that resulted in a cease-fire agreement, which was never signed. Putin reopened discussions on a new friendship treaty in 2000, but because of the tensions that followed in the aftermath of 11 September, nothing came of it until Putin and Shevardnadze agreed (in March 2003) to the return of Georgian refugees who had fled during the civil war – one of the major stumbling blocs of the treaty. The separatist Abkhazian government was worried about the implications of the rapprochement between Russia and Georgia.

In April 2003, the Abkhazian government resigned after mass protests by the opposition movement, and President Vladislav Ardzhinba named Defence Minister Raul Khadjimba to head the new Abkhaz government.[21] The situation remained tense, however, and he refused to give in to opposition demands to step down before his presidential term that was to expire in October 2004.[22]

When Saakashvili decided to unite Georgia in January 2004, tension in Abkhazia rose again.[23] In May, there was some new turbulence after attempts to exclude candidates for the upcoming presidential elections. In June, an opposition leader was murdered, and several ministers in the Khadjimba government resigned in protest.

In August, outgoing President Ardzhinba asked voters to elect Prime Minister Raul Khadjimba to succeed him in the elections scheduled for 3 October. In late August, Putin and Khadjimba met in Sochi, which was generally regarded as a sign of support. The Georgian parliament condemned the meeting and accused Putin of actually recognizing the illegal elections in Abkhazia. There were also other strange things going on, such as excluding candidates by an Abkhazian language test.[24]

On 3 October, the Abkhazian presidential elections were held.[25] The election reporting went totally wrong and triggered a crisis. At first, the Abkhazian Central Election Commission (CEC) suggested that Khadjimba had won with 53 per cent of the vote, followed by Bagapsh with 34 per cent. Soon afterwards these results were retracted. Immediate protests against voting irregularities followed from both candidates. The next day, the CEC announced that none of the candidates had received the necessary 50 per cent, but that Bagapsh had a strong lead. One week after the first announcement of the election results, the CEC declared Bagapsh the winner, now with 'some' 50.08 per cent of the vote. Members of the CEC resigned in protest, and Ardzhinba – the outgoing president – criticized the CEC decision as 'illegal and absurd' and instead suggested that Bagapsh had received only 49.9 per cent of the vote (which Bagapsh in turn dismissed as 'utter nonsense'). The next day more than 5,000 Bagapsh supporters took to the streets of Sukhum, while some 4,000 people demonstrated in support of Khadjimba.[26]

In late October, the Abkhaz Supreme Court declared Bagapsh the winner of the 3 October election. In reaction to the announcement, Khadjimba supporters stormed the Supreme Court, which then reversed its decision and announced that a new election would be held in two months. New protests followed, and Bagapsh supporters surrounded the television building (but were later dispersed by police). Khadjimba supporters surrounded the government building and prevented a parliamentary debate on the Supreme Court decision. At this stage both Bagapsh and Khadjimba went to Moscow for support. They were not received by Putin, but by the Security Council Secretary Igor Ivanov and the Federal Security Service head Nikolai Patushev.[27]

The two contestants now began bilateral talks to resolve the issue, but without success. Again, they convened their supporters, while Ardzhinba appealed for restraint.[28] Bagapsh supporters occupied the government building and tried physically to oust Ardzhinba and Khadjimba. Russia warned that if 'illegal' actions continued, Russia would 'take steps to protect its interests', which in turn immediately resulted in Georgian formal diplomatic protests asking Russia to 'refrain from interfering in the internal affairs ... within a foreign state'. Russia seemed confused concerning its response to the Abkhazian crisis: support Ardzhinba's favourite Khadjimba, or support his opponent Bagapsh. A repetition of the Russian involvement in Tbilisi one year earlier and in Adjaria half a year earlier (to assist in the ousting of the person in power) seemed impossible. There were no points to be won from Tbilisi either, whatever the Russian action was and whomever it was directed against.[29]

The solution to the deadlock came some ten days later, when the Abkhaz Council of Elders met in Sukhum and decided that Bapagsh was the winner of the 3 October election, but also demanded that Khadjimba should occupy a leading post on Bagapsh's team. The Abkhaz parliament appealed to Ardzhinba to 'respect the will of the people' and recognize the CEC decision on 11 October that declared Bagapsh the winner.

By now, Russia threatened to close its borders to Abkhazia if further 'unconstitutional actions' were launched by Bagapsh and the 'criminal elements' with the help of whom he had tried to seize power by force.[30] But at the same time Russia sent the Deputy Prosecutor-General to mediate between Bagapsh and Khadjimba, and it was soon agreed that the two contestants should run on a single ticket in a new round of presidential elections (where Bagapsh would seek to become President and Khadjimba to be his Vice-President). The Abkhazian parliament then passed a law to that effect and decided to hold new elections on 12 January 2005.[31] Bagapsh obviously had to repair his reputation in Moscow and stressed that Russia had 'helped Abkhazia to resolve problems peacefully'. Putin realized that he had bet on the wrong horse, Khadjimba instead of Bagapsh and on 23 December, for the first time, he qualified a statement of support for Georgia's territorial integrity, saying that 'we stand for the territorial integrity of Georgia, but only if the interests of all the people living on this territory are observed'.[32] The repeat elections took place on 12 January, and Bagapsh won. Tbilisi declared the elections illegal, of course, and new bomb explosions killing several policemen followed in southern Abkhazia, while the Abkhazian prime minister survived an assassination attempt.[33]

How is one to understand the fact that Russia did so little to support 'its' candidate, Khadjimba? Except for some verbal barrages against Bagapsh' 'street democracy' (which incidentally was of the same nature as the 'Rose Revolution' in Tbilisi), Russia did little. One way to explain Putin's low-key profile during the crisis is to argue that he had already decided that Abkhazia would not stand in the way of his more general objectives with respect to Georgia, and that Russia would not be held hostage to narrow separatist interests.

The Russian 'purse policy' towards Georgia – the 'geo-economic' touch

The other element of Putin's new policy *vis-à-vis* Georgia since the ouster of Shevardnadze is his 'purse policy', that is, a policy where Russian capital is employed in an attempt to secure future influence over a state – or

what Anatoly Chubais referred to as building a 'liberal empire' by monop-
olizing energy resources and their transportation systems. This attempt
at 'liberal imperialism' need not have a direct connection to specific
political issues, but political implications are hard to avoid. Putin's
're-imperialization' attempt is based on the fact that the Russian government is formally or informally in control of the giant Russian energy
companies (Gazprom, Rosneft, Lukoil, Transneft, UES) that operate in
the former Soviet space – they are either state-owned or controlled by
state interests. Together with some loyal oligarchs, Putin has created an
'alliance' that soon will be in a position to control the energy sector in
much of the former Soviet space. The 'liberal empire' is already extending
its reach to most of Caucasus and Central Asia.[34]

Some of the former Soviet republics are already trapped in this dependency. In Moldova, Russian energy companies have monopolized gas and
electricity markets, including pipelines and grids. Russian capital has
been most active also in Ukraine, and the energy dependency was distinctly felt by the new political leadership in December 2005.[35] Belarus
experienced a similar 'gas war' in winter 2004, when the gas pumps were
used to show political will.[36] Some of the states in Central Asian and
Caucasus have found it extremely difficult to circumvent the fate of their
geographical position. While it has been difficult for Tadzhikistan and
Kyrgyzstan to avoid Putin's scheme, it has been somewhat easier for
Uzbekistan and Kazakhstan. The situation for Turkmenistan and Azerbaijan
has been somewhat different because they have alternative transit routes
for their export, and because they rather are competitors to Russia. Armenia
and Georgia have been 'easy to trap' in this respect; while Armenia has
been Russia's closest ally in the post-cold war period and might have less
to loose politically, Georgia has been Russia's most troublesome neighbour
and is therefore the most likely to fall victim to 'purse policies'. A *tour-
de-horizon* will show the stakes.

Recent examples of Russian 'purse policy' in the former Soviet republics

In Central Asia, the 'transit geography' has been a particularly important
Russian instrument. For Kazakhstan the evident counter-strategy has
been to look for alternative outlets for its oil and gas exports, and Russian
irritation has been evident whenever Kazakhstan has tried to diversify
its export routes. In 2002, transit dependency made Kazakhstan sign a
long-term agreement on exports of Kazakh natural gas through Russia,
together with a 15-year agreement on the export of Kazakh oil through
Russia.[37] The Russian irritation over the Kazakh interest in linking into

the Baku–Tibilisi–Ceyhan pipeline (BTC) that skirted Russian territory was obvious, and by early 2006 it seems evident that Kazakhstan will indeed join the BTC.[38] Similar long-term cooperation agreements have been signed with Uzbekistan in April 2004, when Uzbekneftegaz and Russia's Gazprom signed a 15-year production agreement on gas extraction,[39] and in June, when Russia's Lukoil signed a 35-year agreement to develop the Kandym gas field (and where Lukoil would own 90 per cent). Putin felt obliged to reassure the Uzbeks that '(t)his is not Russia investing in Uzbekistan, but Russian business investing'.[40]

Examples of Russian 'purse policy' have been particularly evident in countries with debt problems. Gas production agreements with Tajikistan have been plentiful, and Tajikistan has been heavily dependent on Russian know-how and financing also in developing its hydropower resources. All of this became obvious in 2004 and 2005: in April, Tadzhikistan signed an agreement with Russia's Unified Energy Systems to export electricity to Russia.[41] In June, the UES got involved on 'presidential orders' (according to Chubais himself), in creating a consortium to build the Sangtuda hydroelectric power station together with Iran.[42] In August, a preliminary agreement was reached for Russia to acquire a 51 per cent stake in the Sangtuda station for $100 million, half of which would be paid by writing off some of Tajikistan's debt to Russia. The agreement in its entirety was worth some $500 million.[43] In June 2005, Russian investments into another Tajik power plant, the Roghun power plant, exceeded $500 million.[44]

Kyrgyzstan has been the most sensitive to Putin's 'purse policies' because of its lack of resources to pay off its debts to Russia. Already in 2001, Kyrgyzstan paid off some of its $150 million debt by giving Russia part ownership in 27 of its largest industrial enterprises.[45] In October 2003, agreements were reached on the Russian acquisition of shares in several Soviet-era military plants to further reduce Kyrgyzstan's debt to Russia. Russia bought large shares in some key Kyrgyz industries, and Kyrgyz electricity was to be delivered to Russia.[46] In 2004, Kyrgyzstan and the UES signed a memorandum to finish the construction of Kyrgyzstan's two Kambar-Ata hydroelectric power stations, and later in 2004, the Russian Foreign Minister Sergey Lavrov handed over a list of Kyrgyz enterprises in which Russia would be interested, in exchange for debt relief.[47]

In the Caucasus, Armenia is the most vulnerable and dependent state and also heavily reliant on Russian energy imports. Already in 2002, Armenia finalized an 'assets-for-debts' deal with Russia and agreed to pay its $100 million debt by offering control of the Hrazdan thermal power plant (which produces 30 per cent of the Armenian electricity need) and the Medzamor nuclear power plan (which produces another 40 per cent

of Armenian electricity).[48] Some have described the acquisitions as politically rather than economically motivated.[49] In 2004, Putin and Kocharian
met on several occasions to discuss Armenia's debt. A further Russian
take-over included the Armenian air company Armavia, controlled by
the Russian air company Sibir Airlines.[50] The Russian take-over of the
Armenia Energy Network was finalized in autumn 2005.[51] All of these
examples show that the phenomenon of 'purse policy' is a potential
Russian foreign policy instrument. Of late it has also been developed in
relations with Georgia.

Russia's UES and Gazprom enter Georgia

Georgia is an energy importer, and Russia is the main energy
supplier. Georgia is also highly dependent on Russia both for imports and
for exports. Georgia has been indebted to Russia for energy supplies, as
are many other CIS states. To ensure its energy supply, Georgia has generally been interested in importing gas from several countries, but in July
2003, a 25-year framework cooperation agreement was signed, according to which Gazprom would supply gas, renovate Georgia's pipeline
network, and to transit gas to Armenia in Georgian pipelines.[52] The deal
was severely criticized in Georgia.[53]

Later in 2003, electricity also became a source of domestic conflict when
a subsidiary company of UES acquired a 75 per cent share in the AES-Telasi
electricity distribution company.[54] The UES also received the right to
manage the Khrami-1 and Khrami-2 power stations, as well as a 50 per cent
share of the Transenergy nuclear power plant and all shares in the Mtkvari
power plant. Since then the UES controls the electricity system of Georgia.
Its CEO, Anatoly Chubais, stressed that the acquisition was the result of
purely commercial rather than political interests and that Russia would not
blackmail Georgia by threatening to cut off energy supplies.[55] Although
Shevardnadze seemed to welcome the Russian acquisitions, domestic
opposition was fierce, and the general belief was that Russia would indeed
use Georgian energy dependency to exert political pressure, that it was
going 'to use banks rather than tanks' to seek control of Georgia's strategic
infrastructure.[56] It is, perhaps, more than a coincidence that Chubais was
the father of the idea of a 'liberal empire' in Eurasia.[57]

In May 2004, Russian Prime Minister Mikhail Fradkov promised Russian
participation in joint ventures in the oil, gas, and transport sectors, and
Russian Economic Development and Trade Minister German Gref accompanied Russian businessmen to participate in a Georgian–Russian business forum in Tbilisi, in which the energy sector, highway construction,
agriculture, and the modernization of Soviet-era industry were potential

areas of investment. In Georgia, the debate was intense about whether Putin's new policy was the result of the Russian loss of influence to the United States, or whether it was a change of Russian tactics to regain influence, of 'keeping Tbilisi under its thumb by means of private sector investment into key sectors of the Georgian economy'. The key instrument, as we have seen, has been UES' attempt to take control of the electricity distribution and Gazprom's attempt to monopolize gas deliveries. As one analyst suggested, it does not take much Russian capital to dominate the weak Georgian economy.[58]

In January 2005, a familiar pattern (e.g., from Kyrgyzstan) also appeared in Georgia, when a consortium with Russian interests bought the Chiatura Manganese plant and the Vartsikhe hydroelectric power station for some $130 million. At the same time, Russia's Vneshtorgbank acquired a majority share in the United Bank of Georgia. Part of Georgia's $150 million debt to Russia was restructured, as well, leaving half of the debt to be repaid over 23 years. But this was not all: Georgia's main gas pipeline (from north to south) was sold to Gazprom in exchange for gas supplies. Domestic opposition was strong, and there was even a rift within the Georgian government over the sale.[59] The fact that Georgia was not excluded from the increased gas prices, to take effect in 2006, did not soothe opposition.[60] When the gas pipeline was sabotaged and gas deliveries were halted in January 2006, the general (although incorrect) interpretation in many Georgian opposition circles was that Georgia had got hooked.[61]

All of this points to a familiar pattern, that Russian state-owned or state-controlled energy companies try to get control also of Georgian energy supplies. The difference in comparison to other former Soviet republics is that Russia has had very tense relations with Georgia (over the Chechens in Pankisi Gorge, the Russian military bases left in Georgia, and the Georgian breakaway republics Abkhazia and South Ossetia). Since Russia has failed to subjugate Georgia in the 'traditional' Russian way (by force), it has of late been using the UES and Gazprom to tie Georgia closer to Russia. This might very well turn out to be a much more successful strategy to counter US influence in Georgia.

Russian pipeline politics – Caspian and Black Sea gas and oil pipelines

The larger picture in the Caucasus includes the 'great game' in and around the Caspian Sea where oil and gas production facilities and pipelines constitute an obvious political power base for those in control of the territories where those production facilities and pipelines are located. Russia has been taking an active part in this game. In fact, oil and gas pipelines in the former Soviet space have been seen as the fabric through which the former Soviet Union is still preserved.[62]

In the Caspian and Black Sea regions, the Trans-Caspian gas pipeline (from Turkmenistan's central Karakumi gas fields under the Caspian Sea and via Azerbaijan to Turkey) and the Blue Stream gas pipeline (transporting Russian gas under the Black Sea from southern Russia to Turkey), were meant to solve some transit dependency problems. However important, gas – as a source for heating and electricity – has also been used as a political instrument in Russian policies *vis-à-vis* Belarus, Moldova (and to some extent also Ukraine). But in the Caspian and Caucasus regions oil pipelines have been even more sensitive instruments. By 11 September it had become evident that Russian resistance to new pipelines in the Caucasus region was mainly political. Caspian oil exported to the West and bypassing Russia would give the West greater influence over governments in the region, and at the same time lessen Russian influence.[63]

By far the most controversial oil pipeline construction in the region has been the 1,700 km Baku–Tbilisi–Ceyhan (BTC) oil pipeline crossing the Caucasus from the Azeri oil fields in the Caspian Sea, passing Tbilisi, avoiding 'dangerous' Abkhazia, and crossing the Turkish heartland to the Mediterranean oil export port of Ceyhan. This pipeline has grossly irritated Russia from the very outset, especially since Kazakhstan was interested in joining the project.[64] After eight years of planning, BTC construction finally began in 2003. Security and environmental issues have haunted the project, however.[65] Kazakhstan then joined the BTC pipeline project (planning to transport oil from Kazakhstan by tanker to Baku, where it would be loaded into the BTC pipeline), despite Russian opposition.[66] In Georgia, there were even fears of direct Russian sabotage activities.[67] Environmental problems were also frequent.[68] The BTC was belatedly inaugurated incrementally in summer and fall 2005.

In conclusion, the Caspian Sea, the Caucasus and Black Sea areas are closely interlocked when it comes to oil and gas production and transportation. Russian policies have aimed to tie producers and transporters to Russian pipelines and been opposed to alternative pipeline routes for its neighbouring countries. The persistence of Russian geopolitical thinking has been evident in these policies.

Conclusions: From Geopolitics to geo-economics – the changing nature of Russian imperialism

In conclusion, Russian relations with Georgia have increasingly been governed by 'softer' policies guided by a 'geo-economic' focus, seen as a more effective way of drawing Georgia into a firm Russian embrace than the previous conflict-laden strategies (e.g., on the issue of the Pankisi Gorge and the two remaining Russian military bases in Georgia). Putin has avoided defending the narrower Russian geopolitical interests in Georgia and Abkhazia, and instead tried not to annoy Tbilisi. At the same time Russian big capital has entered Georgia, as part of Putin's more general 'economization' of Russian foreign policy, seen also in his relations to other CIS countries. Putin is acting like a rather modern and benevolent 'imperialist', with non-violent means of re-integrating the former Soviet space. To the victimized weak power, the difference might not be that great, as the Russians demonstrated by the use of economic pressure against Georgia in autumn 2006.[69]

Notes

1　South Caucasus belongs to the middle layer of border territories around Russia – the outer layer is Turkey and Iran, and the inner layer Chechnya, North Ossetia and Dagestan. See Dmitri Trenin, *The End of Eurasia: Russia on the Border between Geopolitics and Globalization* (Washington, DC and Moscow: Carnegie Endowment for International Peace, 2002), pp. 47, 169 and 179–80.

2　Russian–Georgian relations since 1999 have been strongly coloured by (1) the Russian military bases in Georgia; (2) the Georgian conflict regions Abkhazia and South Ossetia; and (3) Chechen warriors hiding out in Northern Georgia (Pankisi Gorge). For the Russian 'sabre-rattling' up to the Georgian 'Rose Revolution', see Bertil Nygren, 'Russia's relations with Georgia under Putin: the Impact of 11 September', in J. Hedenskog, V. Konnander, B. Nygren, I. Oldberg and C. Pursiainen (eds), *Russia as a Great Power. Dimensions of Security under Putin* (London and New York: Routledge, 2005), pp. 156–81.

3　Russia's fundamental foreign policy objectives in the Foreign Policy Concept of June 2000 include 'to form a good-neighbourly belt along the perimeter of Russia's borders, and to promote the elimination of existing and prevent the emergence of potential hotbeds of tension and conflicts in regions adjacent to the Russian Federation'. The Foreign Policy Concept was reproduced in *Diplomaticheskii vestnik*, No. 8, Aug. 2000.

4　South Ossetia is not discussed in this chapter because developments there have been somewhat different and constitute an exception, its status is defined more by the traditionally heavy-handed Russian strategies than by the present Russian 'imperial strategy'. One explanation for this is probably that Putin has not engaged himself personally to the same extent as he has in the Abkhazia conflict.

5　The typical problem in Georgia (as elsewhere in the former Soviet Union) is how many voters there are, who they are, and where they should vote. In the last parliamentary elections in 1999, there were 2.1 million registered voters. After revisions of the voting lists in 2003, these contained 2.9 million names.

The opposition claimed that 600,000 names of deceased remained on the lists, while other voters were excluded. See *RFE/RL Newsline* 9 Oct. 2003. For the general situation at the time, see *RFE/RL Newsline* 14, 16 and 21 Oct. 2003. For all references below to *RFE/RL Newsline*, see <http://www.rferl.org/newsline/default.asp#archive>.

6 *RFE/RL Newsline*, 29 and 31 Oct. 2003.

7 *RFE/RL Newsline*, 3 and 4 Nov. 2003.

8 *RFE/RL Newsline*, 5, 6, 7 and 10 Nov. 2003.

9 See *RFE/RL Caucasus Report*, 12 Nov. 2003; *RFE/RL Newsline*, 12, 13 and 14 Nov. 2003.

10 *RFE/RL Newsline*, 18, 19 and 20 Nov. 2003.

11 Together, the two pro-government factions received a combined total of 123 of the 235 seats.

12 *RFE/RL Newsline*, 21 and 24 Nov. 2003.

13 *RFE/RL Newsline*, 24 and 25 Nov. 2003.

14 See Igor Torbakov, 'Russia turning up pressure on Georgia', *Eurasia Insight*, 1 Dec. 2003, and Igor Torbakov, 'Russian policy makers struggle to respond to political changes in Georgia', *Eurasia Insight*, 8 Jan. 2004. For all references below to *Eurasia Insight*, see <http://www.eurasianet.org/departments/insight/articles/index.shtml>.

15 *RFE/RL Newsline*, 26 and 27 Jan. 2004.

16 For the sequence of events, see Maya Beridze, 'Political tension rise between Georgian government and recalcitrant region of Adjaria', *Eurasia Insight*, 2 March 2004; 'Georgian officials up pressure on Abashidze', *Eurasia Insight*, 17 March 2004; Mevlut Katik, 'Saakashvili, Abashidze back on collision course in Georgia', *Eurasia Insight*, 18 March 2004; Daan van der Schriek, 'As Ajarian leader backpedals, Saakashvili threatens to revive economic blockade', *Eurasia Insight*, 22 March 2004. See also Pavel Felgenhauer, 'Adzharia needs cool heads', *Moscow Times*, 16 March 2004, p. 11; Misha Dzhindzhikashvili, 'Adzharia declares state of emergency', in *Moscow Times*, 16 March 2004, p.4; Simon Ostrovsky, 'Saakashvili strikes bargain in Adzharia', *Moscow Times*, 19 March 2004, p.1; Simon Ostrovsky, 'Adzharian leader revels in defence', *Moscow Times*, 22 March 2004, p.1; Misha Dzhindzhikashvili, 'Tbilisi warns a defiant Adzharia', *Moscow Times*, 23 March 2004, p.4. See also *RFE/RL Caucasus Report*, 19 March 2004. For all references to *RFE/RL Caucasus Report*, see <http://www.rferl.org/reports/caucasus-report/archive2003.asp>.

17 Jaba Devdariani, 'Georgian authorities plan Ajarian end-game', *Eurasia Insight*, 21 April 2004; 'Ajaria declares state of emergency, Georgian leadership urges regional inhabitants to disobey curfew', *Eurasia Insight*, 26 April 2004; Antoine Blua, 'Georgian leaders gives ultimatum to Adjaria', *Eurasia Insight*, 3 May 2004.

18 Tamazi Gendzekhadze, 'Tbilisi offers Abashidze safe passage', *Moscow Times*, 6 May 2004, p. 1.

19 See Sergei Blagov, 'Amid celebration in Batumi, Georgian authorities move to reassert authority in Ajaria', *Eurasia Insight*, 6 May 2004; Anatoly Medetsky, 'Tbilisi takes back Adzharia', *Moscow Times*, 7 May 2004, p. 1.

20 See Irakly Areshidze, 'Did Russia and Georgia make a deal over Ajaria', *Eurasia Insight*, 19 May 2004.

21 *RFE/RL Newsline*, 8, 9, 10 and 23 April 2003.

22 For some of the violent events, see *RFE/RL Newsline*, 1, 7 and 9 Oct. 2003. The haggling over Ardzhinba's medical problems continued; see *RFE/RL Caucasus Report*, 12 Oct. 2001, 31 Jan. 2002, and 3 July 2003.

23 There were more killings of Georgian policemen, a bomb was found on a commuter train, and a Georgian police operation arrested a large Georgian criminal group in southern Abkhazia. See *RFE/RL Newsline*, 6 and 27 Jan. and 4, 5 and 6 Feb. 2004.

24 See *RFE/RL Caucasus Report*, 27 Aug. 2004. In the end, six candidates were registered. *RFE/RL Newsline*, 3 Sep. 2004.

25 See *RFE/RL Caucasus Report*, 30 Sep. 2004; *RFE/RL Newsline*, 4 Oct. 2004; Igor Torbakov, 'Russia mulls recognition of independence for Georgian separatist regions', *Eurasia Insight*, 4 Oct. 2004.

26 For the reporting, see *RFE/RL Newsline*, 5 and 6 Oct. 2004. For the quotes, see *RFE/RL Newsline*, 12 and 13 Oct. 2004. For the events following the announcement of the winner, see also *RFE/RL Newsline*, 14 and 15 Oct. 2004. For an analysis, see 'Outgoing Abkhaz leader says opposition victory is "illegal"', *Moscow Times*, 13 Oct. 2004, p. 2; 'Ex-Abkhaz premier calls vote a fraud', *Moscow Times*, 14 Oct. 2004, p. 2; *RFE/RL Caucasus Report*, 14 Oct. 2004.

27 For the flow of events, see *RFE/RL Newsline*, 29 Oct. and 2, 3 and 4 Nov. 2004. See also John Mackedon, 'Latest developments in Abkhazia hint at Russian intervention', *Eurasia Insight*, 1 Nov. 2004; 'Abkhaz court reverse on vote', *Moscow Times*, 1 Nov. 2004, p. 4; Oliver Bullough, 'Abkhaz rivals turn to Moscow', *in Moscow Times*, 3 Nov. 2004, p. 4; *RFE/RL Caucasus Report*, 5 Nov. 2004.

28 See *RFE/RL Caucasus Report*, 5 Nov. 2004.

29 See *RFE/RL Newsline*, 8 and 15 Nov. 2004; 'Abkhaz president's office is seized', *Moscow Times*, 15 Nov. 2004, p. 3; Sergei Blagov, 'Abkhazia crisis adds to Russia's political headaches in the Caucasus', *Eurasia Insight*, 15 Nov. 2004.

30 *RFE/RL Newsline*, 1 Dec. 2004; *Nezavisimaya Gazeta*, 2 Dec. 2004. See also Theresa Freese, 'Abkhazia: at war with itself', *Eurasia Insight*, 3 Dec. 2004; 'Abkhazia blockade threatened', *Moscow Times*, 2 Dec. 2004, p. 4.

31 See *RFE/RL Newsline*, 6 and 9 Dec. 2004; Sergei Blagov 'Presidential candidates strike deal in Abkhazia', *Eurasia Insight*, 6 Dec. 2004; *RFE/RL Caucasus Report*, 10 Dec. 2004.

32 *RFE/RL Newsline*, 17 and 28 Dec. 2004.

33 See Theresa Freese, 'Gori residents search for reasons behind recent car-bombing', *Eurasia Insight*, 4 Feb. 2005; Jean-Christophe Peuch, 'Georgia: Abkhaz prime minister survives assassination attempt', *Eurasia Insight*, 1 March 2005.

34 Igor Torbakov, 'Russian policymakers air notion of "liberal empire" in Caucasus, Central Asia', *Eurasia Insight*, 27 Oct. 2003.

35 *RFE/RL Newsline*, 27 and 29 Dec. 2005, and 6 Jan. 2006.

36 See Bertil Nygren, 'The Implications for Putin's Policy toward Ukraine and Belarus of NATO and EU Expansions', in Jan Hallenberg and Håkan Karlsson (eds), *Changing Transatlantic Security Relations. Do the US, the EU and Russia Form A New Strategic Triangle?* (New York: Routledge, 2006).

37 See *RFE/RL Newsline*, 6 and 10 June 2002.

122   *Bertil Nygren*

38 *RFE /RL Newsline*, 24, 25, 26 and 27 May, 5 Aug. 13 Oct. and 29 Dec. 2005.
39 The development of the Shakhpakhty field had begun in the seventies, but production was halted in 2002 because of equipment problems. *RFE/RL Newsline*, 15 April 2004.
40 *RFE/RL Newsline*, 17 June 2004.
41 *RFE/RL Newsline*, 20 April 2004. The energy was produced by the Tadzhik Norak hydroelectric power station and transited via Kazakhstan and Uzbekistan.
42 Chubais confessed that he had received 'direct instructions from Putin to get involved in developing the hydropower sector in Tajikistan'. *RFE/RL Newsline*, 10 June 2004.
43 *RFE/RL Newsline*, 27 Aug. 2004. In October, there was another 'energy for debt' discussion on a space surveillance station. Furthermore, Russian Aluminium was to invest $560 million in Tadzhikistan's Roghun hydropower plant and $700 million in aluminium production facilities. *RFE/RL Newsline*, 18 Oct. 2004. In December, the UES signed a protocol with Iran and Tajikistan on the construction of the Sangtuda hydropower plants. *RFE/RL Newsline*, 15 Dec. 2004. The plant would be ready for operaton only in 2009 and with total investments reaching some $500 million. *RFE/RL Newsline*, 18 April 2005. See also *RFE/RL Newsline*, 13 Jan. 2005.
44 *RFE/RL Newsline*, 6 June 2005.
45 See *RFE/RL Newsline*, 9 March and 11 April 2001. For the transfer of shares, see *RFE/RL Newsline*, 12 Sept. 2001. The next year, Kyrgyzstan again proposed paying some $59 million by offering goods and services and a stake in Kyrgyz enterprises. Other deals were also considered. See *RFE/RL Newsline*, 13 March, 12 Sept. and 11 Nov. 2002.
46 *RFE/RL Newsline*, 23 and 24 Oct., 7 Nov. and 23 Dec. 2003.
47 *RFE/RL Newsline*, 23 Aug. 2004. Work on these power plants had been halted in the 1980s because of lack of funding. *RFE/RL Newsline*, 23 Aug. and 13 Oct. 2004.
48 See *RFE/RL Newsline*, 6 Nov. 2002. See also Igor Torbakov, 'Russia seeks to use energy abundance to increase leverage', *Eurasia Insight*, 19 Nov. 2003.
49 See Haroutin Khachatrian, 'Russia moves in Caucasus energy and power sectors could have geopolitical impact', *Eurasia Insight*, 25 Sept. 2003.
50 In February 2004, the defence ministers of the two countries met to review the implementation of earlier agreements on military and military-technological co-operation. *RFE/RL Newsline*, 21 May 2004. In summer 2004, there was a conflict over the five Armenian enterprises ceded to Russia in payment of Armenia's debt. See *RFE/RL Newsline*, 6 Nov. and 5 Dec. 2002, and 15 May 2003.
51 *RFE/RL Newsline*, 11 and 14 July, 30 Aug. and 13 and 26 Sept. 2005.
52 The United States was concerned that the Georgian commitment to buy Russian gas could jeopardize the Azeri Shah Deniz project. *RFE/RL Newsline*, 30 May and 9 June 2003. Shevardnadze was actually approached by the US State Department special envoy for Caspian energy issues Steven Mann who warned that the agreement could damage the BTE gas pipeline project (pipeline from Baku via Tbilisi to Erzerum) and Azerbaijan's Shah Deniz Caspian gas deposit project. *RFE/RL Newsline*, 9 and 10 June 2003.
53 Domestic opposition to the agreement was ascertained. *RFE/RL Newsline*, 28 July 2003.

54 The AES and the Georgian government had been at loggerheads since late 2001. *RFE/RL Newsline*, 1 Aug. 2003. Georgian opposition parties believed the sale to be illegal, since the Georgian government had not been informed in advance. *RFE/RL Newsline*, 4 Aug. 2003.

55 *RFE/RL Newsline*, 7 Aug. 2003.

56 The head of the Georgian Parliament's budget committee, Roman Gotsiridze, quoted in Haroutiun Khachatrian, 'Russian Moves in Caucasus energy and power sectors could have geopolitical impact', *Eurasia Insight*, 25 Sept. 2003.

57 See Igor Torbakov, 'Russia seeks to use energy abundance to increase political leverage', *Eurasia Insight*, 19 Nov. 2003.

58 See Irakly Areshidze, 'Will Russian investment win Georgia's Heart?', *Moscow Times*, 11 May 2004, p. 8; *RFE/RL Newsline*, 26 May and 1 June 2004.

59 *RFE/RL Newsline*, 20 and 26 Jan. and 23 Feb. 2005. This gas pipeline is the only gas import pipeline until the US-sponsored Baku–Tbilisi–Erzurum (BTE or Shah-Deniz) pipeline under construction is finally completed. The late Prime Minister, Zurab Zhvania, openly opposed the sale. Jean-Christophe Peuch, 'President hints at possible Gazprom deal, U.S. unhappy', *RFE/RL Energy*, 25 Feb. 2005.

60 *RFE/RL Newsline*, 30 Nov. and 21 and 22 Dec. 2005.

61 See *RFE/RL Newsline*, 4, 6, 9 Jan. 2006.

62 An article in *Izvestiya* (15 Oct. 2001), 'The Soviet Union Continues to Live with the Help of Pipelines' argued that the oil and gas pipelines built prior to the collapse of the USSR continued to link together the economies of the former Soviet republics. See *RFE/RL Newsline*, 16 Oct. 2001.

63 *RFE/RL Newsline*, 6 Aug. and 31 Oct. 2001.

64 *RFE/RL Newsline*, 26 Feb. and 2 and 8 March 2001.

65 See Michael Lelyveld, 'Georgia/Azerbaijan: Security a concern as pipeline construction set to begin', *Eurasia Insight*, 25 Jan. 2003.

66 *RFE/RL Newsline*, 12 March 2003. Kazakhstan would not need to use the Baku–Ceyhan pipeline until 2008–09, however.

67 In March 2004, Saakashvili warned that foreign political forces could be expected to block the route of the BTC. See *RFE/RL Newsline*, 8 March 2004. In November, Saakashvili accused Georgia's 'enemies' of planning attacks on her energy facilities, after the Baku-Supsa oil pipeline had been attacked as a 'trial run'. Russia dismissed the whole thing as 'absurd and groundless'. *RFE/RL Newsline*, 22 Nov. 2004. The construction was fairly quick once started, although much more expensive than expected. See *RFE/RL Newsline*, 10 Aug. and 3 Dec. 2004.

68 There was widespread environmental opposition. See *RFE/RL Newsline*, 10 Aug. and 20 Oct. 2004.

69 'The Mouse that Roared', *The Economist*, 7 Oct. 2006, and Steven Lee Myers, 'Russia Deports Georgians and Increases Pressures on Businesses and Students', *New York Times*, 7 Oct. 2006, p. A6.

6
Governance and Diplomacy as Attributes of a Great Power: Russia and the Three Enclaves – Kaliningrad, Nagorno-Karabakh and Nakhchivan

Susanne Nies

Is Russia a re-emerging great power? According to Joseph Nye Jr (1989), great power status depends nowadays less on hard power – in the sense of coercive power – than on soft power, to be understood as the ability to attract and persuade. Oldberg demonstrates in his contribution to this volume that President Yeltsin, then his successor Putin, adopted a soft power concept, with Putin shifting from a pure soft power perception in 1999 – technology and high living standards – to a nuclear power perception by 2004 with a new concept of a 'world leader on the energy market' (2005). Oldberg underlines the prime importance of diplomacy, participation in international crisis management and in international organizations as a basis for a great power status. The capacity to assure 'good governance', in the sense of assured democratic control on the state's territory, is definitely the first precondition for a state's ambition to have an impact on the international agenda, as well.

This chapter focuses on the governance and diplomatic aspects of the complex notion of 'great power'. It is devoted to a case study of Russia and its behaviour towards three postsoviet enclaves: Kaliningrad, Nagorno-Karabakh and Nakhchivan. Enclaves are in many cases objects of their international environment and express it and its state at a given time. The three cases are heavily dependent on Russian diplomacy, and permit one to assess its performance, as well as its changes. Kaliningrad, as a part of the territory of the Russian Federation, has been a prime issue between in relations between Russia and the West, especially the EU, since 1991. Kaliningrad has been and continues to be a challenge to both the internal governance and the diplomacy of the Russian Federation.

The two South Caucasian enclaves constitute a test of Russia's international capacities and reliability, especially as the legal heir of the Soviet Union, since the conflict opposes two other successor states of the USSR, Armenia and Azerbaijan, both member states of the CIS.

This chapter is organized as follows: an introduction defines enclaves and governance. The second section is devoted to the case studies: Kaliningrad and Russia's governance on that territory, Kaliningrad as an issue to diplomacy; and on the place of Nagorno-Karabakh and Nakhchivan in Russian diplomacy. The third section elucidates findings.

Introduction: underlying concepts

Enclaves as litmus-tests for governance and diplomacy

Why should we conduct research on Russia's governance of and diplomacy towards three rather small territories? What justifies such an approach? In fact, enclaves are a generally ignored geopolitical phenomenon, and this is all the more surprising since more than one hundred of them figure among today's territorial discontinuities. A number strive towards self-determination and/or independent statehood, as do *de facto* states, rebel movements, and other status quo-contesting actors.[1] Governance is understood here as the key to territorial control. The inherent tension between the need to ensure territorial integrity and local demands for self-determination makes efficient governance of enclaves a difficult task. Enclaves are, after all, isolated geographically. As a result, their affiliation with the metropolitan state may be contested or, alternatively, enclaves may end up as paragons of international cooperation. In the former case, enclaves are places of conflict and war, and in the latter case they become havens of stability similar to microstates. Enclaves are territories cut off from the state of which they legally form a part, bordering on and surrounded by one or more foreign states. These entities not only present a problem in terms of national governance, but a challenge to the existing international system of states. The simple fact that an enclave exists already constitutes a threat to the territorial integrity of the metropolitan state to which the enclave legally belongs. Since international law prescribes no minimal territorial or population size for states, enclaves hold the potential of forming new, independent states.

Enclaves are different places in numerous respects. They share characteristics with islands, *de facto* states, microstates, and other similar entities, but it is the mix of these shared characteristics that ultimately makes them unique. Enclaves may be places of conflict and war, grim and isolated, or, on the contrary, paragons of international cooperation, taking advantage of their geographical location. They might represent store windows, a 'somewhere else', something different from the environment, prosperous, liberal, radiating soft power over the population of a threatened enclaving state, as were West Berlin and Hong Kong. Enclaves are micro-entities with a political history distinct both from that of the heartland to which they belong and the enclaving states surrounding them.

Historically, enclaves have often been subject to sieges by powers seeking to gain control of the enclaved territory, as the cases of Gibraltar and West Berlin demonstrate. In recent times, the threat of sieges has been lessened by the twentieth-century revolutions in transportation and communication technology. In general, siege politics is applied today only by those operating outside of the system and indifferent to international public opinion. Potentially, enclave economies are closed economies, very much like those of islands. In some cases, special economic regimes or zones are established in order to offset the danger of economic suffocation. Due to special economic regimes, tax exemptions and the localization in a heterogeneous economic environment, trade is far from the most important sector of the economy, slightly predominating industrial production.

Enclaves may be subject to rapid demographic change. The population of Königsberg/Kaliningrad changed completely within a decade. Depopulation has been a widespread problem in post-Soviet territory because of the wars of the early 1990s and ongoing economic transition. Tremendous demographic change has accordingly been an important phenomenon in Kaliningrad and Karabakh. The large-scale retreat of Soviet troops, new borders, new citizenship regimes, economic crisis, civil war, and an alarming decrease in both life-expectancy and birth rates has had its effects on all post-Soviet enclaves. An analysis of the political choices and perspectives of enclaves, enclave elite structure, and also the historical narrative in enclaves must take into account influences from immigrant groups from both the enclaving state and exile outside of the enclave.

Enclaves may acquire military and strategic importance, as is the case with Kaliningrad. Their significance can be political, as were West Berlin, Northern Cyprus, or of the enclaves of international organizations. Enclaves may play a role economically, as was true for Hong Kong. Their special situation may be exploited in extreme situations as in war, as is the case with Guantanamo and the argument that US law was not valid there, an opinion later revised after public protest against the treatment of war prisoners there.[2] Enclaves may be of a rather symbolic value, as may become the case in Kaliningrad, which is caught in a dilemma between a necessary liberalization and continued strict control for the sake of Russian public opinion and pressure from the military.

These functions are subject to dynamic changes, initiated by the change of political circumstances – for instance, the decline in the importance of trade routes or the development of relations with a traditional friend or foe. The change in function from military to economic or political significance can be observed quite often. Many enclaves came into being as military bases. They lost this role with the transition from a world of strategic centres to the assertion of complete territorial control by modern nation-states. Now many have gained importance as special economic zones. The unusual economic situation of enclaves has further advanced such developments; Recent changes in military strategy, which may be summed up as a shift from traditional quantitative to a new qualitative experts-based defence, may alter the functions of enclaves in the sense that they could be used both by the military and as free-trade zones. Co-sovereignty could thus be an expression of this trajectory.

Enclaves are more inclined to hard and soft security threats than are other territories: They are often involved in armed conflict, and in most cases exposed to soft security issues such as illegal immigration, cross-border crime, ecological problems and so forth, as the case of Kaliningrad shows.

Governance

If the capacity to 'govern well' is one aspect of a great power status, the notion 'good governance' requires clarification. Good governance is defined as the rule over a territory with low transaction costs. Good governance, as opposed to the notion of bad governance, is to be understood as the pareto-optimum[3] of liberal market economy and central administration, while respecting contemporary normative requirements. The modern usage of the term good governance was developed in the 1970s in the context of the administration of corporate enterprises. It helped express the idea that many administrations had become inefficient and that the trade-off between control and efficiency was worth greater attention.

Today, the criteria for good governance are usually the following:

- *Economic efficiency.* Good governance satisfies the requirement of efficiency, but there necessarily is always a trade-off between equality and efficiency.[4] Ideally, a large portion of a population should benefit from its country's wealth, even if the quantity of distortions due to distributive measures must be minimized. In the first half of the 1990s, state intervention in the social sphere was consciously neglected due to the argument that the population should not be prevented from adapting to new political and economic realities. In the second half of the 1990s, the insight grew that more central management of adjustment processes was needed. Measures such as the GINI coefficient on wealth distribution became important indicators to help achieve a new pareto optimum in the efficiency–equality trade-off.[5]

- *Political efficiency* with respect to public policy, transparency, corruption, democratic participation, and minority rights. On a whole, however, it is very difficult to measure these characteristics, despite such indices as the UNDP Human Development Indicator,[6] the Corruption Perception Index,[7] or the Freedom House Indicator.[8] Since the terrorist attacks of 11 September 2001, security questions have received prominent attention in policy-making. Increased security measures, however, may encroach upon citizens' rights. Thus, a (new) trade-off between security and citizen rights has arisen in the context of good governance.[9]

Russia and Kaliningrad, Nagorno-Karabakh and Nakhchivan

This central section is devoted to a discussion of Kaliningrad, Nagorno-Karabakh and Nakhchivan in Russian domestic and foreign policy. Since the fate of the two South Caucasian enclaves has been tied together in conflict, transforming Nakhchivan in the period 1988–94 into a kind of ransom for Armenia, they will be treated together. Each part of the discussion presents, first, the particularities, historiography, and demography of the enclave, referring, second, to the role of Russia.

The three enclaves have been put on the international agenda with the collapse of the Soviet Union. The conflicts that broke out at that

Table 1: Kaliningrad, Nagorno-Karabakh, Nakhchivan in terms of size and population

	Area (in km²)	*Population*
Kaliningrad	15,100	1,000,000 complete turnover after WWII, ethnic composition like Soviet Union till 1992[10]
Nagorno-Karabakh	4,400	Pre-war population; Currently 130,000,[11] though estimations vary widely. Important ethnic changes since war 1992–94: 1989 76.9% Armenians, 21.5% Azeri; 1999: more than 98% Armenians
Nakhchivan	5,500	3,150,000[12] 96% Azeri, 4% Armenians, no important changes

time suggest that preexisting tension had been frozen during the Soviet period. They differ in terms of size of the territory and the population, as well as the number of enclaving states: Kaliningrad is surrounded by two, Nagorno-Karabakh by one, and Nakhchivan by three states. If the last is not on the international agenda today, it is probably the only one with a high potential for conflict in a near future because of its geopolitical location on the border of Iran.

Kaliningrad in Russian domestic policy and diplomacy

A special status as normalcy

Kaliningrad, the westernmost region of Russia, is located at the lower reaches of the Neman River and comprises a territory of 15,100 square kilometres, representing 0.1 per cent of the total Russian territory. The territory is bordered by 140 km of coast in the west, shares a 200-km border with Lithuania in the north and east and a 210-km border with Poland in the south.[13] The nearest Russian territory is the Pskov oblast, some 600 km away. To access the Russian capital, one must cross three borders and transverse 1,300 km.

Table 2: Distances between Kaliningrad, Russian cities and other capitals

Distances In (km)	Pskov	Moscow	St Petersburg	Stockholm	Copenhagen	Vilnius	Warsaw	Berlin
Kaliningrad	600	1,300	1,000	650	680	340	350	600

Throughout the twentieth century, East Prussia hardly experienced normalcy. Rather, it returned to the turbulent period it passed through at the end of the eighteenth century and the beginning of the nineteenth century.[14] In 1919, East Prussia was cut off from the rest of the German Reich through the provisions of the Versailles Treaty. The region subsequently needed special economic support from Germany, since its economy was too weak to support itself. A German–East Prussian ferry was created by the government in Berlin, in order to maintain a close link between the German mainland and East Prussia, and also in order to support the region's function as an important trading centre. Königsberg, like many places in Central Eastern Europe, was heavily impacted by the events of the Second World War. At the end of the war, it lay in ruins and its German population, which had been at home there since 1255, fled westwards. Formerly German Königsberg and the northern part of East

Prussia were ceded to the Soviet Union by the Potsdam Agreement of 2 August 1945[15] and subsequently integrated into the USSR. The territory was renamed Kaliningrad in 1946,[16] changed affiliation, population, language, and orientation, and became a closed military zone, where the headquarters of the Baltic Fleet were subsequently located. In July 1990, some opening-up occurred. This period of normalcy was brief, however. After the Lithuanian declaration of independence, the territory once again became enclaved. With the collapse of the Soviet Union, Kaliningrad became one of 89 federal subjects of the Russian Federation. The Soviet Union suggested selling Kaliningrad to Germany for a €35 billion during the 2+4 Negotiations – a proposal which had never been evaluated seriously in Germany and was rejected by Poland.

The integration of both enclaving states, Lithuania and Poland, into the EU and NATO[17] has reinforced Kaliningrad's enclavement. Indeed, it seems as though the threefold isolation of Kaliningrad during the twentieth century has become a kind of heritage.

Kaliningrad in Russian domestic and foreign policy

Kaliningrad has been and continues to be a test case for Russian governance as well as its diplomatic skills. The issue was one of demilitarization in the very beginning, of administration and governance in order to offset the specific dilemmas of enclaves (closed economy, etc.) since 1992, an issue of access finally since the integration of Lithuania and Poland into the EU and NATO. Thus, Kaliningrad became an international issue. Energy, ecology and crime remain highly relevant issues Russia and the EU have to address in common, since they share a common interest of avoiding a 'slum in the Baltics' with negative impacts on both of them. The option of remilitarization of Kaliningrad can nevertheless not be excluded at that stage, given a certain revival of cold war rhetoric in East and West. Russia is the more and more dissatisfied with the NATO 19 plus 1 Council, which was established in 2003, and perceives NATO enlargement to parts of the former Soviet Union, as well as the stationing of a new type of anti-ballistic missile system on Polish soil, in Olsztyn very near to the Kaliningrad border,[18] as proof of the continuation of attitudes stemming from the cold war. Kaliningrad continues thus to express the state of East–West relations, depends highly on them, remains volatile and might not continue to liberalize, as should be desirable in the interest of the one million population. Russia's domestic and foreign policy with respect to Kaliningrad has been highly contradictory and risks continuing on that trajectory, at least in the coming years.

Demilitarizing Kaliningrad

At the beginning of the 1990s, nearly everybody in Kaliningrad was directly or indirectly linked to the military. And because of the withdrawal of troops from the former GDR and other Soviet bloc countries, the number increased until 1993. The retiring troops where stationed temporarily in Kaliningrad and then sent off to different parts of Russia. All in all, the reduction of the military presence in Kaliningrad has been spectacular: of the 200,000 soldiers in Kaliningrad in 1990, only 18,000 remained in 2000, and 8,600 in 2006.[19] The movement has nevertheless been contradictory and influenced by the larger international environment. Thus, the Kosovo war and the project of a 'holy Slavic alliance', including Russia, Serbia and Belarus, had an impact on Kaliningrad – demonstrative anti-Western manoeuvres where held in 1999 and 2000, and rumours about a supposed stationing of Russian nuclear weapons, used to compensate conventional weakness and as a threat against the Baltic region and the NATO states, came up at the same time. In 2004, in the context of the polemics over NATO bases in the new member countries (Estonia, Latvia, and Lithuania), the tone changed again in the Russian Administration. 'Theoretically', stated Defence Minister Ivanov, 'a remilitarization of Kaliningrad can not be excluded, if NATO opens up bases in the Baltic states'.[20] The debate over the opening of NATO bases in the Baltic States renewed the discussion in Russia whether it was still important to maintain a significant military presence in Kaliningrad and whether such a presence could be construed as a threat to the West. In reality, and despite all the rhetoric, demilitarization has been constant. If until 2001 Kaliningrad could still be interpreted as a remaining vestige of the East–West conflict, this seemed to be no longer true in 2006 with only the two remaining military facilities of Baltijsk and Primorsk.[21]

A major controversy arose when the Ministry of Defence pursued an isolationist course for the enclave, as opposed to the more liberal approach put forward by other Russian ministries.[22] Today, the victory of the liberal concept is obvious, a move which has been facilitated by the following factors: the emergence of a civil society in Kaliningrad itself, which had hardly existed in the over-militarized formerly closed, zone; the European and international context and Russia's interest in cooperation; and finally the recognition by the Russian government that Kaliningrad would not have the intention of seceding as a 'fourth Baltic republic'. Nevertheless, it is not clear yet whether this victory was temporary, and whether the liberal agenda for Kaliningrad will be sustainable in the medium and long run, in the context of tensions between the two former superpowers and especially the NATO enlargement up to the Russian border.

Administration and governance

The traditional dichotomy between domestic and foreign policy is not applicable to the governance of enclaves. Areas of domestic policy, such as public services – fire departments, police, traffic and transportation, telecommunications, postal service, healthcare, and education, just to name a few – are in the case of enclaves always areas that involve relations with third states: they become a matter of international relations. This unusual linkage between national and foreign policy necessarily makes moot the usual division of competencies between the centre and regions. The choices that a state makes in administrating a territory are usually a consequence of the state's legal traditions and current provisions. The relationship between a state and a subordinate entity, such as an enclave, may be based either on simple conquest or on international treaty, bilateral agreement, or basic constitutional provisions. Administrative structures are subject to everlasting debate in most enclaves. Sometimes they are accommodated, in order to deal with the dysfunctions arising from the trade-off between control and efficiency and to satisfy claims concerning participation and autonomy. Such debates highlight the volatility and chronically provisional character of the status of enclaves.

Kaliningrad is one of 89 federal subjects of the Russian Federation. The enclave has maintained the administrative rulings of 1946, amended in 1955, even after 1991. According to these, the northern part of former East Prussia was segmented into 17 administrative units: 14 administrative rayons, as well as the free cities Kaliningrad, Sovietsk and Cernjachovsk. The amendment of 1955 led only to the abolition of one of the rayons. Four levels of government in Russia currently have a say in Kaliningrad: the federal level, the North-West District (of Russia) level, the territorial level, and the communal level. The Russian government is represented at the federal level as well as the North-West District level, established during the course of federal reform in the summer of 2000. Both the federal and the North-West District levels maintain authorized missions in Kaliningrad: the Consulate[23] and the Plenipotentiary of the Governor in the Kaliningrad Territory. Former commanding Admiral of the Baltic Fleet Vladimir Yegorov governed the oblast' from 2000 until 2005,[24] when the new governor, a well known businessman, 42 year-old Georgi Boos, won the elections. Since the economy and population are concentrated in the city, the mayor and his deputy play an important role as well. The predominant administrative quarrels in Kaliningrad have concerned the questions of military presence, the maintenance of Kaliningrad's special closed status, and the liberal desire to create a 'Hong Kong of the Baltics'. The international context has been highly influential in these quarrels.

Occasional deterioration of Russian–Western relations has reinforced the position of the military in Kaliningrad, In 1995, a worsened relationship led to the abolition of the free trade zone in Kaliningrad, and this was replaced one year later by special economic zone (SEZ) status. Contradictory measures have prevented the enclave from taking off economically, but also the military from reaching its goal, especially considering the tremendous reduction in troop numbers. On 1 July 2006, new federal legislation on special economic zones entered into force: The objective is to establish clear conditions for the functioning of the SEZ in Kaliningrad and to reinforce economic relations between 'small and big Russia'.[25] At the same time, the presence of the secret services in Kaliningrad has been reinforced, and manoeuvres in Baltijsk were held in September 2006.

Access: The visa quarrel

The most controversial issue tied to Kaliningrad's enclavation after NATO and EU enlargement has been the introduction of a visa. Generally, the regulation of visa issues is an indicator of the strength of the relationship between two countries and is therefore a highly sensitive issue. The post-Soviet space was characterized by a low degree of formalized visa procedures, despite the creation of new state borders. Free movement of people was one of the major claims of the popular fronts, considered *the* expression of democracy and liberty.

The so-called Baltic Schengen, an extremely liberal *modus vivendi* established among Poland, Lithuania, and Kaliningrad, as well as a Russian–Lithuanian agreement on the transition of the military and its equipment from the metropolitan state to the enclave, encouraged shuttle trade and good neighbourly relations.[26] The integration of both enclaving states into the EU on 1 May 2004 put an end to the liberal post-Soviet visa regime. Poland and Lithuania may not opt out of the Schengen Agreement, unlike the UK or Denmark in the past.[27] Poland and Lithuania will apply the Schengen rules in full after a transitional period lasting to 2008.[28]

Facts about border crossing

Some nine million border crossings are registered in Kaliningrad every year. An estimated 12,000 people are involved in cross-border shuttle–trading,[29] whereas as many as 45 per cent of Kaliningrad region citizens have not travelled from the region over the past 15 years, while 13 per cent have never been to other regions of Russia. The most active travellers stem from a younger generation aspiring to higher education.[30] Their destinations are mostly the neighbouring regions, not Russia, which is far away and expensive to reach. Thus, a sign announcing 'Moscow, turn to the left' in Kaliningrad's centre must seem a bit surrealistic to its reader. Unlike other metropolitan states, Moscow did not supply substantial subsidies until the issue of visa policy arose in the context of EU enlargement.

After a long silence over Kaliningrad and obvious neglect by Russia, an unprecedented media debate erupted in 2002 concerning visa regulations for Kaliningrad. Russia appointed a special envoy for Kaliningrad, the chair of the Duma committee for External Affairs, Dmitry Rogozin. Until December 2002, Rogozin defended a destructive, maximalist position by calling for 'no visas for trips inside of Russia'.[31] Fantastic proposals of all kinds arose concerning the overall question of how Kaliningrad could be accessed after the enclaving states' integration within the EU: for example, tunnels to Belarus and a corridor through Lithuania. Four hundred and one members of the communist-dominated Duma signed a resolution claiming that the EU was encouraging the further alienation of Kaliningrad and Russia.[32] The position of the EU was initially very dogmatic, as well. EU officials refused to accept any exemptions from the Schengen regime, even if these quite obviously existed already all over the EU, especially in Greece, Spain, Portugal and France.

The EU–Russia summit of 11 November 2002 finally brought an end to the destructive polemics on both sides. On this date, a compromise was reached with the invention of the so-called facilitated transit documents (FTD), which are, in fact, a visa with another name. According to the compromise, Russians travelling to and from Kaliningrad were required to use a FTD to transit through Lithuania beginning on 1 July 2003 and to transit through Poland beginning on 1 October 2003.[33] The transit document is cheap, but has limited validity. The compromise foresaw exemptions for some population groups, especially the population living in regions bordering Lithuania or Poland.[34] Until 31 December 2004, Lithuania accepted Russian national passports. After that, however, Russians were required to produce an international passport, which Russia, however, has had difficulties in producing in sufficient quantities. Even today, some Russians still own only a Soviet passport.

The transit of the military as one particular aspect of access regulations

The movement of Russian troops in and out of Kaliningrad has been a major point of dispute between the EU and Russia. Over the past years, a bilateral Lithuanian–Russian agreement, renewed on an annual basis, enabled Russian military personnel and equipment to pass through Lithuanian territory on the way to Kaliningrad. The EU accession of Lithuania has put an end to this practice for the time being. Even though the number of troops stationed in Kaliningrad was substantially reduced and the opening up of Baltijsk seems to be quite likely, in recent years Russia pressured Lithuania to renew the bilateral agreement. The Russian government finally abandoned its position and is now preparing normal transit documents and passports for the remaining military personnel in Kaliningrad.[35]

Consequences of the introduction of FTD

Despite alarmist scenarios raised by all sides in the debate on introducing a visa regime for Kaliningrad, these scenarios have not played out.[36] Shuttle trade goes on as before. The consequences of the visa regime might even be assessed as extremely positive. In order to offset the potentially negative impact of the visa regime, Russia allocated funds to modernize transit connections, including subventioning flights and creating new and more frequent connections. The EU has extended its commitment to the region by initiating new TACIS projects. During a fact-finding mission in August 2003, the author, who had visited the Kaliningrad territory many times previously, was surprised by the atmosphere of renewal in Kaliningrad, which seemed to her to resemble the atmosphere in the Baltic States right after independence. Russian diplomatic circles, foreign consulates, and the local population were unanimous in their assessment that the situation in Kaliningrad had changed for the better after the introduction of the FTD.[37]

From an enclave of military and strategic significance to a pilot region? An unachieved transition

Kaliningrad as a pilot region between Russia and the EU is a motto that politicians both in Russia and the EU like to employ, and it is sure to determine the debate surrounding Kaliningrad in the coming years. Russian policies towards Kaliningrad have been contradictory since 1991, expressing the desires of conservatives to preserve the military status of Kaliningrad as a war trophy, etc., and those of liberals to open up the territory. After fifteen years, the general move seemed to be clear towards a liberal scenario, symbolized by the unprecedented demilitarization, and by the recent change of the governor from a military man to a successful economist. The Russian vice minister for foreign affairs, Vladimir Titov, reaffirmed during a meeting in Kaliningrad at the beginning of March 2006 that Russia would make the transformation of Kaliningrad into a kind of Hong Kong on the Baltic Sea a priority, translated by efficient cooperation with neighbouring states.[38] Is this move sustainable? In the light of conflicts between Russia and former Soviet Republics – for example the energy crisis with Ukraine in January 2006 or the confrontation with Georgia in October 2006 over their relationship with NATO and especially the United States – that reveal Russian sensitivity to the EU's and NATO's move eastwards, a reversal of Russian policy concerning Kaliningrad cannot yet be excluded.

Nagorno-Karabakh and Nakhchivan[39] in Russian diplomacy

The fact that Armenia and Azerbaijan are integrated only weakly into the international system, with a rather weak Commonwealth of Independent States (CIS) as their first reference, and that they are part of a region rampant with armed conflict has had an impact on the outcome of conflicts over Nakhchivan and Nagorno-Karabakh in the Caucasus.

Much as in its dealing with Kaliningrad, the policy of Moscow towards Karabakh went through several phases. Initially, in the context of rising tension surrounding perestroika and glasnost in the mid-1980s, Karabakh was one expression of a generalized phenomenon of rising nationalism and the quest for independence, a new identity, and change of an outdated Soviet situation. The next phase occurred with the peaceful dissolution of the Soviet Union and the setting up of 15 successor states. The Karabakh conflict became international, with Nakhchivan involved as a kind of ransom. Russia was to develop a new strategy towards 'the near abroad' – a strategy that was in the beginning contradictory. The third phase saw Russia as a member of the Minsk group (OSCE) in charge of brokering a solution to the conflict, once a ceasefire was imposed through the pressure of the international community via the UN. Russia assumed the role of an 'honest arbitrator', distancing itself from its initial ally Armenia in favour of a neutral and internationally credible position. Russia is viewed as a reliable and predictable partner in this process. With the recent negotiations over the future status of Kosovo, Russia initiated a new diplomatic approach by tying together the question of recognizing Kosovo as an independent state and similar recognition of Abkhazia, Southern Ossetia, Transdniestria and Karabakh. This linkage is not new. The special status of Karabakh had been modelled upon that of Abkhazia in 1923. By tying these issues together Russia's goal is to prevent Kosovar independence and thereby to show solidarity with its traditional Serbian ally.

Nagorno-Karabakh

The autonomous territory of Nagorno-Karabakh is located toward the eastern end of the South Caucasus. It extends over a territory of 4,400 sq. km and is inhabited by approximately 200,000 persons, mostly of Armenian origin (80 per cent of the population). The special status of the territory dates back to 1921, when Stalin transferred Azerbaijani territory to Armenia and Armenian territory to Azerbaijan according to the principle *divide et impera*. The current status of the enclave is not grounded in law, and, although Nagorno-Karabakh declared its statehood, this status has not been recognized by the international community.

History and historiography

As is typical in places that are home to two or more ancient populations and subject to repeated invasion, state building is connected to competing accounts of national history in Nagorno-Karabakh. Nagorno-Karabakh has been contested by Azeris and Armenians for centuries. The two groups use different names to designate the same places. Armenians boast of the region's early conversion to Christianity in the third century, which they say proves that the Armenians are legitimate heirs to the enclave. The Azeris see the region as part of the ancient Caucasian Albanian kingdom dating back to 400 BC[40] and claim that it has been populated by indigenous Caucasian and Turkic people ever since. In the fourth century, these people, already known as Azerbaijanis, adopted Christianity as a state religion. Azeri history tells us that Arabs invaded the kingdom, conquered it in the eighth century and converted it to Islam by force. The exiled Azeri nobility tried in vain to re-establish the kingdom in the ninth and tenth centuries. Despite evident differences, there are some points of agreement between the two versions of history. Both historiographies claim that the ninth and tenth centuries AD was a period of flourishing culture and wealth, a Christian period when a number of monasteries – called Khachkars by the Armenians – were erected all over the region.

For Azeris and Armenians, the Middle Ages were a period of violent religious war and invasion by the Arabs, Turks, and Mongols. The divide between the two cultures appears afterwards, with the conversion of Azeris to Islam and the repartition of the region due to the settlement of Christian Armenians and Islamic Azerbaijanis on two sides of a divide. This divide was reinforced when the entire Caucasus region was exposed to a violent war between the Iranian Khanate and the Russian Empire. According to the Azeris, Prince Panah Ali-khan Javanshir valiantly defended Karabakh against the Iranian Khanate in 1747 with the support of the Russians. In the eyes of the Armenians, this event was actually an act of conquest.

Regardless, the region was divided into four provinces afterwards: Elizabetpol, Yerevan, Baku and Tbilisi. Azeris and Armenians were united in their struggle against Tsarist oppression, culminating in a violent uprising beginning in 1905. The 1917 Bolshevik Revolution led to the independence of Armenia and Azerbaijan, both of which claimed sovereignty over Nagorno-Karabakh. Both parties to the conflict soon were entangled in a violent war, after which the territory was integrated into Azerbaijan in 1921. Nevertheless, a group of Russian, Armenian and Azerbaijani Bolsheviks decided to grant Karabakh an autonomous status from 1923 onwards, following the Abkhazia model in Georgia. Thus, the conflict was suspended during the Soviet period. Nagorno-Karabakh gained its capital in the beginning of the 1920s at the site of a former village called Xankandi and renamed after Armenian communist leader Stepan Shaumyan-Stepanakert. While Azeris prefer to refer to the city by its former name, Armenians kept to the Soviet name, perhaps also as a signal of closeness to Moscow. Stepanakert is populated by less than 50,000 inhabitants today, slightly less than in Soviet times.

Economy

Nagorno-Karabakh once depended heavily on Azerbaijan, as did Armenia.[41] Until 1989, 87 per cent of Armenian goods were transported through the neighbouring country and resources were supplied from the latter. Today, isolation and subsistence economy, as well as shuttle trading instead of production, characterizes the economy of both Armenia and of Karabakh. In economic terms, support from Russia and the diaspora proved to be the only means to improve the conditions of the poorest post-Soviet republic. Nagorno-Karabakh[42] is a still a subsistence economy dependent on aid from outside, especially from the metropolitan state.

The Armenian dram is used as a currency in Nagorno-Karabakh as a sign of the close connection between *de facto* state and the metropolitan state. According to Armenian data, the wealthy Armenian diaspora has overcome wartime damage, estimated at more than $2 billion thanks to donations and investments.[43] However, the high rate of unemployment and emigration, both of which are an expression of the unsettled political future, prevented the territory from attaining normalcy. Armenia, itself poor in resources and severely damaged by the earthquake of 1988, which caused more than 25,000 injuries, has suffered tremendously from the post-Soviet transition and political conflict. Completely isolated in 1990–91 because of its policies in Karabakh, it suffered from economic blockade from Moscow, Turkey, and Georgia. Baku stopped providing energy and oil in November 1991, at a time when Armenia received 2 per cent of its energy from the latter and 16 per cent from the Russian Federation. Its only nuclear power plant was damaged in the 1988 earthquake, but it was later repaired, in order to reduce the negative consequences of the embargo.[44] The cold winter of 1996 turned out to be a nightmare for 3.5 million Armenian citizens who were without adequate heating. Imports from Iran became increasingly important during the war and Iran saw the war as a convenient opportunity to increase trade with the Caucasus region. Iranian trucks are a common feature in the region. After the war, in 1994, substantial aid came from Moscow, while the blockade by Turkey and Azerbaijan have continued to the present. The embargos were especially dramatic, since the Soviet economy had been based upon close regional ties. In 1993, Turkey decided to suspend humanitarian aid to Armenia, leaving only one bridge from Iran for humanitarian aid to enter Armenia.

Nakhchivan

Nakhchivan is an Azeri enclave in the Southern Caucasus, separated from its metropolitan state by Armenia to the northwest. It borders the Araz river and Iran on the southwest. After a land exchange with Iran in 1932, Turkey obtained a common border with the enclave some ten kilometres in length along the Araz River at Sederek. This strategic change proved to be decisive only some sixty years later, when the enclavation of the territory could be indirectly offset by access to the enclave through Turkey. The territory covers 50,500 sq km and is inhabited by 3,150,000 citizens, the vast majority of whom are of Azeri extraction. The enclave is rich in minerals, with deposits of marble, lime, gypsum, and oil, which was discovered some years ago. Mineral springs are located in several cities such as Badamli, Sirab, Nagajir, and Kiziljir. These cities were health resorts in Soviet times.

Legal status

Nakhchivan is an autonomous republic of Azerbaijan. The constitution of November 1995 makes Azerbaijan a secular, democratic, and unitary republic with a legislature of 125 deputies, and a strong president and administration. Deputies from Nakhchivan are represented in the parliament, the Milli Melis. The region has been since Soviet times the place of origin of prominent Azeri leaders, such as the family of the presidents Aliev.

History and historiography

Nakhchivan was first mentioned by Ptolemy in his *Geography*, written in the middle of the first century AD. The territory's name changed as a result of numerous invasions and occupations throughout history.[45]

Nakhchivan's history allegedly began with its founding by the Biblical Noah in 1500 BC. The region contains some of the most important archaeological sites of the South Caucasus and has been subject to conquest since Alexander the Great's rule in the fourth century BC. It was ruled by the Arabs in the seventh century, invaded by the Seljuks in the ninth, and by the Mongols in the twelfth century. The cities of the region were important Persian trading centres in medieval times. Julfa, located on the silk-road, was inhabited by Armenians until 1604, when the Persian Shah displaced the entire population of craftsmen and their families to his new capital of Esfahan.[46] The first railway connections were established in 1906, creating the Armenia–Nakhchivan–Julfa line, which is cut off from rail traffic today. Nakhchivan, capital of an independent Khanate in the eighteenth century, became part of the Russian Empire in 1828 as a result of the Russian–Persian war of 1804–13. In 1920, the region was established as an independent Soviet republic. One year later, its leaders favoured integration with Azerbaijan in the larger context of the Transcaucasian SFSR, uniting Azerbaijan, Armenia, and Georgia. Boundaries where rearranged in 1924. Nakhchivan became an independent Autonomous Soviet Socialist Republic, Armenia, Georgia and Azerbaijan reappeared, and the province of Zangezour was affiliated with Armenia, thus isolating Nakhchivan from the rest of Azerbaijan. The autonomous Soviet republic declared independence even before Lithuania, in January 1990. This independence was not accepted, and the enclave reintegrated with Azerbaijan to become independent together with Baku in September 1991.

Economy

Unlike Nagorno-Karabakh, Nakhchivan did not experience a devastating war, although the post-Soviet economic transition has presented significant challenges to the local economy. Very much as in other post-Soviet peripheries far from the new capitals, the enclave has transited to a kind of subsistence economy. It does not benefit directly from the metropolitan state's wealth in natural resources and it relies heavily on regional transit trade and a share of the related black market, as well as on agriculture. Agricultural production consists mostly of cotton and tobacco. There is also a mining and food industry. A large silkworm breeding enterprise is run in Ordubad. Azeri geologists discovered oil fields in 1960, continuing their exploration since 1998 with an Azeri–US joint venture.[47]

Access

No special visa is required for the enclave any longer, but only a general visa for Azerbaijan. The issue of access is a relatively small handicap to the expansion of the enclave's economy, because Turkey and Iran maintain friendly relations with the metropolitan state and share the latter's hostility towards Armenia. As a result, Nakhchivan participates in cross-region trade with Iran, Turkey, Azerbaijan and even Moscow. Flight connections link the enclave with Baku four times a day. The strategically important Sederek bridge was reopened to Iran, as was the Umud Körpüsü 'bridge of hope' across the Azer river, on 28 May 1992, thus creating a direct land link between Turkey and Azerbaijan. The border was closed during Soviet times, and the bridge was built only in 1992. Although the Iranian and Turkish land crossings require bribes, time and bureaucratic procedures, they do not prevent the enclave from serving as a centre of trade.

Nagorno-Karabakh and Nakhchivan in Russian foreign policy

From conflict to war and the linkage of Karabakh and Nakhchivan (1988–92)

In 1988 a petition with over 80,000 signatures was sent to the Communist Party in Moscow asking for the restitution of the enclave to Armenia. The General Secretary refused any revision of the status of Nagorno-Karabakh, so that on 13 February 1988 the soviet of the autonomous territory of Nagorno-Karabakh officially requested integration into Armenia. Violent incidents between Azeris and Armenians were the consequence of this vote. Ethnic conflict broke out and was manifested in the brutal anti-Armenian massacre at Sum Gait, which inevitably conjured up among Armenians the memory of the 1915 genocide. The declaration of independence of the Republic of Karabakh in early 1992 resulted in a full-scale war between Armenia and Azerbaijan, whose relations were already poisoned by decades of conflict over Karabakh, especially the confrontations of the immediate past. Baku claimed that its borders were inviolable, a claim supported by the Soviet Union. Soviet troops arrived in Baku in January 1990, in order to re-establish peace and order after 1,500 victims had already been killed in armed conflict. The Soviet presence was greeted with resistance and by embargos of Nakhchivan by the Armenians and of Nagorno-Karabakh by the Azeris. The Azeri blockade was far more effective, since Georgia assisted Azerbaijan in suffocating the economies of Armenia and Nagorno-Karabakh. Little reconstruction of the enclave occurred and no humanitarian aid could access the region. Faced with such a severe embargo, the Armenian parliament declared the unification of the country with Karabakh. Armenian villages were attacked by Azeris in the districts of Khanlar and Chaumianovsk, leading to the outbreak of full-scale war on 13 and 14 January 1991. Popular fronts from the Baltic States, far from the strongest factions in the USSR, took the initiative to mediate between the two sides. This initiative did not prevent the intervention of mercenaries and arms dealers in the conflict, supplying arms from Russia and Lebanon. A state of emergency was declared and 30,000 Soviet troops were sent to Baku in order to restore order. The Soviet Ministry of Defence justified the intervention by stating, first, that there was a clear danger that Soviet power in the region could be undermined, second that it feared the secession of Azerbaijan, and third that it was necessary to fight Islamism in the region. 'Black January', as it came to be known later, claimed 500 lives. Since the Armenians felt that they could not rely on Soviet support and were afraid that Turkey too would side with the Soviet Union, Armenia tried to find common ground with Ankara – an unsuccessful attempt, it turned out. In November 1991, the Azerbaijani parliament suspended the autonomy of Nagorno-Karabakh and integrated it fully into Azerbaijan.

Internationalization of the conflict after the dissolution of the Soviet Union

The conflict obtained an international dimension when both Armenia and Azerbaijan gained *de facto* independence from the Soviet Union in September 1991. An estimated 35,000 people died and nearly one million people became refugees, driven onto Azerbaijani territory. In May 1992, the Karabakh defence forces conquered some strategic places including Shushi, a city in Karabakh overlooking Stepanakert, and Lachine, a strip of land connecting Karabakh with Armenia. The conquest of Lachine, an almost special territory since the 1920s and the capital of the short-lived Kurdish Autonomous Province (often named as 'Red Kurdistan' (1923–29)) altered the geopolitics of the enclave entirely. The Azeri economic blockade on Karabakh was thereby broken. War continued until 1994, causing both Armenians and Azerbaijanis to flee the region. The violent confrontations, deportations, sieges, pogroms, and partisan war were in many ways reminiscent of the civil wars of 1905 and 1917–18. Armenia constructed a modern road along the Lachine corridor, financed by the Armenian diaspora, which had been called upon by Robert Kocharian, the former president of the enclave and later president of Armenia, replacing Ter Petrosjan in 1998. The Armenian-occupied territories of approximately 8,000 sq km have been repopulated since 1994 with Armenian refugees from Azerbaijan proper.

In order to offset Azeri pressure, Armenia put pressure on Nakhchivan, 'its Azeri enclave', in early 1992. The 1921 Soviet–Turkish Treaty of Kars allowed Turkey to intervene if Nakhchivan was ever threatened by a 'third force', with this third force being Armenia, of course. This clause was invoked for the first time in 1992 at the behest of Haidar Alyev, then President of Azerbaijan. The Turkish threat against Armenia equalled a NATO threat against Russia, and thus Armenia decided against invading the enclave. As a consequence, the Azeri enclave Nakhchivan has experienced a shift from the Soviet empire to the Turkish cultural sphere. Much as the Lachine corridor to Nagorno-Karabakh, the opening of the bridge of hopes from Turkey to Nakhchivan in May 1992 relativized the effects of enclavation. The international constellation – that is, Turkey's backing of Azerbaijan and the former's affiliation with NATO – make any change of the current situation impossible. As is the case for Nagorno-Karabakh, there exists a *de facto* pacification without normalization. The opening up of borders with Armenia and the creation of a liberal trade zone are unlikely in the near future.

The current situation in Karabakh has not changed since 1994. The front lines between the armies of Azerbaijan and Mountain Karabakh remain with their network of wire fences and minefields across one kilometre of no-man's land. Regular exchanges of sniper fire are as much part of the border's 'normalcy' as a large quantity of men and material committed to holding the line.[48] A report of the European Parliament considered poverty and corruption and a democratic deficit as the most important problems of the region.[49] Closed borders, interrupted railway lines, roads, pipelines, a distorted economy in the region as a consequence, an ongoing mental war between Armenia and Azerbaijan make clear the absence of normalcy.

Mediation in the frozen conflict

The ceasefire of May 1994 put an end to war, and international negotiations were led under the auspices of the OSCE, with eleven countries forming the so-called Minsk Group, with a French, US and Russian co-presidency. Since 1997, the Group has proposed a number of solutions, such as demilitarization (June 1997), autonomy (December 1997), and co-sovereignty (November 1998). But all were thwarted by the veto of at least one party. The aim of the Minsk Group is to propose an acceptable solution to all conflicting parties. No solution is in sight yet to the most serious problems, which include the following. First, the government of non-recognized Karabakh does not participate in the negotiations and does not necessarily feel bound by results brokered by Armenia.[50] There is a clear risk of the emergence of two Armenian states, a theory defended already today by the Karabakhi president Kotcharian. Karabakh becomes thus more alienated from Armenia and the rest of the world – a common fate of *de facto* states, which are barely part of diplomacy and official negotiations and, thus, left out, as well, in reconstruction programmes, etc. In the case of Karabakh, a clear shift in attitudes towards independence as the only option is visible today.

The second problem concerns the attitudes in Armenia and Azerbaijan, with nationalist propaganda from one against the other and each serving as a scapegoat for the other helping to displace domestic problems from the political agenda. In this context it was revealing that both presidents Aliev and Kocharian insisted, during the fruitless negotiations of the Minsk Group in Rambouillet in February 2006, that negotiations have to be continued, that the Minsk process was very important to them, that a peaceful solution to the conflict had to be found. If ever the negotiations were suspended, nationalists would gain more influence in their respective countries, they maintained.[51] The current discussions focus on a progressive retreat of Armenian forces and their substitution by an international peacekeeping force, as well as a referendum on the future status of Karabakh. Armenia declared its readiness to disengage from most of the buffer zones, if international guarantees for Karabakh's security are provided. The strategically important Lachine corridor would not be returned. Negotiations are today about the context of a solution, not the solution itself. Getting used to one or more decades of peace, even without an official settlement or a peace treaty might be a first step towards a solution later, as much as the non-regulation bears in itself the risk of renewed violence.

Russia behaves today as a neutral arbitrator in the conflict and does not favour officially Armenia or Azerbaijan, which is different from the initial years of the conflict, when the Soviet Union still existed. At that time Moscow favoured Aserbaijan. Armenia, angry about Gorbachev's preference, refused then to ratify, on 19 March 1991, the new Federation Treaty. Erevan finally ratified it in December 1991, claiming that the Republic of Karabakh should also become a member of the CIS – a claim which Moscow rejected. President Yeltsin maintained continuity with Gorbachev's position in supporting Baku and rejecting the claims of Erevan. Only in 1994, for the sake of strategic and economic interests, Russia changed its position on the dispute. Although Armenia is dependent on Russian raw materials and food, Russia imports computer technology, especially for the military. In addition, the common adversary Turkey ties the Russian–Armenian alliance. Thus, both states signed, on 19 October 1994, an agreement on military bases in Gumri (formerly Leninakan) as well as on a Russian border force in Armenia.

Unitl 1994, the West considered the conflict internal – no South Caucasian policy deserving that name existed at that time. Putin shifted towards a diplomacy of neutrality between Baku and Erevan and thus abandonned the politics of support for Armenia. The payoff was the recognition of Russia as a honest arbiter, a reliable partner in an international conflict in the former Soviet Union. In that sense the recent linkage between the cases of Karabakh and Kosovo does not express a Russian desire for Karabakh independence, but rather the refusal to accept that of Kosovo. Although Russia has intense relations with Transdniestria, Abkhazia and South Ossetia, it never engaged similarly with Karabakh. The exchanges that occur are relatively important, however, at the everyday level, in the sense that students from Karabakh attend Russian universities, future diplomats study at MGIMO, and that the elite of the non-recognized Stepanakert is comprised of members of the former Soviet elite. It is astonishing to meet in Stepanakert not narrow-minded nationalists, but representatives of a vanished empire with the knowledge of global diplomatic issues associated with such an empire.

It presently seems unlikely that there will be any substantial changes in Nagorno-Karabakh's status quo in the near future. Public opinion in Karabakh itself seems to agree. A survey in 2005 among the Karabakh population concerning the perspectives in the short, medium and long term revealed that the majority does not expect an opening up of the border in less than 25 years.[52] The international community, represented by the OSCE Minsk Group, as well as the EU, has no tool to remedy the situation, so that declarations of principles have replaced real politics. Nevertheless, the end of one of the most violent wars of the end of the twentieth century is in itself an important success, as most observers admit. The main aim of the Minsk Group could thus be to bridge to a future where a more internationally integrated Azerbaijan and Armenia could be able to agree on a solution. In a near future the frozen conflict has to be prevented from heating up again – a partial disengagement of Armenia from the buffer zone backed up with international guarantees could be negotiated, and both countries should get used to peaceful coexistence, even with for the time being closed borders. To date, Russian diplomacy does not offset any constructive solution, but participates in common with France and the United States in the Minsk process.

Russia, a re-emerging great power? Insights from the case studies: Russian governance and diplomacy towards three post-Soviet enclaves

Concerning the future evolution of Kaliningrad, Karabakh and Nakhchivan general considerations concerning enclaves are valid for them as well.

Enclaves are often weak and volatile, with an uncommonly fast evolution and a culture difficult to assess within the parameters commonly used to assess the culture of other territorial entities. In any case, enclaves are territorial and political discontinuities calling for special regulations. And this is precisely what often creates a dilemma for international security. Enclaves have resisted complete integration into the administrative structures of the metropolitan states to which they belong, and this accounts for their particular nature. As for Kaliningrad, the most important question is whether the ambition of creating a 'Hong Kong on the Baltic' will become reality. Kaliningrad has been subject to a conflict between the military and liberals over the future destiny of the enclave. Rumours have been used in this quarrel to back arguments. It is clear today that the liberal position has won out, with a containment of the military in Baltijsk and an important reduction of military spending and troops in Kaliningrad. Following the changes of the past 15 years, it is more likely that Kaliningrad will follow the West Berlin trajectory, being a highly subventioned place instead of a productive economic place. The proximity of St Petersburg as a predominant Russian trading centre, but also the absence of a liberal elite, of any tradition in a liberal sense, could be serious obstacles to an economic take off of the region. A remilitarization of Kaliningrad is unlikely, but legally not impossible.

As for Karabakh the solution of the conflict is not in sight for the short term. The integration of Armenia and Azerbaijan into the international community – with the EU neighbourhood policy and NATO playing a role – could be part of a solution modelled upon the containment of the Greek–Turkish conflict. Priority should be given to the permanence of peace after the conflict and to integration, including the population of Nagorno-Karabakh (but not Karabakh as a state). Therefore, European neighbourhood policy should include the enclaves as well – on the model of Turkish northern Republic of Cyprus – stating clearly that cooperation does not mean political recognition.

The potential for conflict involving Nakhchivan should not be underestimated – the location of the enclave, its separation inside of Armenia and the proximity to a potential conflict in Iran are serious arguments to include this neglected place, as well, in an international strategy.

Is Russia a re-emerging great power? Great power status depends heavily on soft power, the capacity to initiate diplomatic processes, to contribute with new proposals – in that sense Russia is surely not a great power. As for Russian governance and diplomacy towards Kaliningrad on the one hand, and Nagorno-Karabakh and Nakhchivan on the other hand, Russian governance and diplomacy provided the following insights.

First, diplomacy proved to be reliable This trend has been often been overlooked because of domestic-oriented rhetoric. In Karabakh, Russia, as the heir of the Soviet Union, is integrated fully in the framework set up by the international community, thus participating as a 'honest arbitrator' and neutral partner in the Minsk process. This 'playing in conformity with the rules of the game' has to be considered as an important transition in post-Soviet diplomacy, since Russia could have opted for engagement with one or the other. But the goal of being a 'neutral broker' in post-Soviet territories, to be a reliable partner in international relations and diplomacy, prevented the country from opting for this approach. An important diplomatic initiative, on the other hand, has not been presented by Moscow either – whether because of an absence of ideas, impact, or interest is not clear. As a matter of fact, the Russian presence in the Southern Caucasus is not comparable to that of Soviet Union in 1991. A challenge to the continuation of today's reliable participation of Russia in the Minsk process could stem from any revived post-cold war antagonism between Washington and Moscow in the Southern Caucasus.

In one sense, questionning the role of Russia as a great power parallels similar questions concerning the West. The EU is also not a great power now, because of contradictory policies and the absence of substantial foreign and security tools. But is not the lack of new ideas in both Russia and the EU about dealing with their common neighbourhood a major factor in determining that neither is rally a great power at the present time?

Notes

1 Cf. for an extensive discussion on enclaves, see Susanne Nies, *Sand in the Works: Enclaves Challenging Metropolitan States. The Cases of Cabinda, Ceuta, Melilla, Gibraltar, Kaliningrad, Mountain Karabakh and Nakhchivan* (Paris: HDR, Sciences Po, 2004, published at GRIN, Germany, 2005), available at <http://www.hausarbeiten.de/faecher/hausarbeit/po5/25725.html>.

2 On 13 March 2003, the US Supreme Court confirmed the non-validity of US law in Guantanamo. On 28 June 2004, this decision was reversed and Guantanamo since has been considered as a space subject to at least some of the legal procedures in force elsewhere in the United States.

3 For the definition of the pareto-optimum and pareto-efficiency, see David Begg, Stanley Fischer and Rudiger Dornbusch, *Economics*, 4th edn, (New York: McGraw-Hill, 1994), p. 257. An allocation is pareto-efficient for a given set of consumer tastes, resources, and technology, if it is impossible to move to another allocation which would make some people better off and nobody worse off., Ute Arentzen, *Gabler Volkswirtschaftslexikon* (Wiesbaden: 1997), p. 849.

4   For a discussion on the subject of the equality–efficiency trade-off, see Arthur M. Okun, *Equality and Efficiency, The Big Trade Off* (Washington, DC: Brookings Institution, 1975).

5   GINI index: See Arentzen, as note 3 above, p. 855. The GINI index indicates, represented in most cases with the Lorenz-curve, the correlation between households and share of the GDP of a country. Perfect equality corresponds to a GINI index of O, complete inequality to 1: one person or households detains the entire GDP.

6   For a definition of the Human Development Index (HDI), see <http://www.undp.org>.

7   For a definition of the Corruption Perception Indicator see <http://www.globalcorruptionreport.org>.

8   Freedom House Indicator, see <http://www.freedomhouse.org>.

9   The civil control of governments, including the disappearing military factor, has led to the change in the face in modern governance, as was mentioned already. An increased preoccupation with security may reverse this change, even if military and police have been subject to substantial changes, a high degree of professionalization, quality instead of quantity, etc.

10   Until 1989, Kaliningrad, followed by Moscow and St Petersburg, had the highest percentage of inhabitants born outside of the region in all of the Soviet Union. Considering that the share of the locally born population is on the rise, rumours about 'undue foreign infiltration and influence' may quieten down in the future.

11   Current population data are available at <http://www.travel-images.com/az-karabakh.html>.

12   Sources: Nakhchivan <http://www.fortunecity.com/campus/purdue/47/naxcivan.html>.

13   Katharina Amani, *Regionalentwicklung im Westen Russlands. Das Beispiel der Oblast' Kaliningrad* (Greifswald: Ernst Moritz Arndt Universität, 1998), p. 6.

14   Eastern Prussia had already been subject to enclavation in 1772, after the first partition of Poland, and became during the Napoleonic Wars, from 1808–13/15, capital of the besieged Prussia.

15   Volle Cornides, *The Potsdam Agreement, Um den Frieden mit Deutschland,* Oberursel 1948, Amtsblatt des Alliierten Kontrollrats in Deutschland, Ergänzungsblatt Nr.1, S.13 ff., DGAP (ed.) *Dokumente zur Berlin-Frage 1944–62* (Munich: Oldenburg Verlag, 1962), Ch. V, p. 21–8; § VI DGAP 1962: 26.

16   Nearly total destruction of Königsberg occurred in August 1944, at the time of the German–Soviet confrontations. Unconditional surrender of the territory occurred on 9 April 1945. After the war, the destruction continued with war films using the German facades and destroying them in reality, and the Breshnev modernization at the end of the 1960s. See Sergej Henke, *Der russische Traum* (Hamburg: Kovacs, 2003); Leonid Smirnyagin, *The Kaliningrad Issue: the Sensation that Need not have Been,* Briefing Papers Carnegie Endowment Moscow, Vol. 4, Issue 05 (Moscow: 2002), insists on the banal character of the renamed places: Pionerskii, Pravdinsk, Slavsk, Svetlogorsk, as well as Kaliningrad. These names reflect the military use and neglect of the territory.

17   Poland joined NATO in 1999, Lithuania in March 2004; both countries entered the EU in March 2004.

18   *Le Figaro*, 5 Oct. 2006.

19   Statement by Fleet Admiral Valujev, *Rossijskie Vesti*, 16.5.2002: 8, at <http://
     www.securities.co.uk>. According to this statement the military presence in
     Kaliningrad was to be reduced to 8,600 troops by 2002.
20   Laure Mandeville, Interview with Russian Defence Minister Sergei Ivanov,
     Le Figaro, 21 March 2004.
21   Bill Gertz, 'Russia To Slash Ground Forces, Rely on Nukes', *Washington Times*,
     17 Oct. 1997, p. A1; see also *Washington Post*, 6 June 2000, p. A14. The CIA
     supposedly found tactical nuclear weapons in Kaliningrad.
22   Sander Huisman, A *New European Policy for Kaliningrad*, Occasional Paper 33,
     (Paris: ISS, March 2002 at <http://www.iss-eu.org/ocassion/occ33html>, p. 10.
23   As is the case with the consulate of Armenia in Nagorno Karabakh, this post
     is referred to in daily speech as 'the embassy'.
24   The deputy is Michail Cikel. See *Kto est' kto v Kaliningrade* (Kaliningrad: 2001).
25   Kaliningrad is waiting for strategic investors, – see <http:www.rost.com>.
     Legislation adopted by the Duma 23 Dec. 2005, signed by the president on
     17 Jan. 2006.
26   Polish and Lithuanian citizens on one side and Kaliningrad citizens on the other,
     buy vouchers at negligable prices of about one euro, in order to enter the neigh-
     bouring country. They might stay for a maximum of 30 days without a visa. In
     the beginning, during 2003–04, the interior Russian passport sufficed to transit.
27   The agreement of 14 June 1985 among Germany, France, Belgium, Luxemburg
     and the Netherlands concerning the progressive abolition of border controls
     between their countries, entered in force in 1990. In 1995, Spain, Portugal,
     Italy, Greece, Austria, Finland and Sweden joined in, as well as association
     treaties with Norway and Iceland, in 1995. The Amsterdam Treaty integrated
     the Schengen Agreement into the *Acquis Communautaire*, with a remaining
     special status – opting out – for the UK, Ireland and Denmark. This option
     does not exist any further for those joining in after 1999, when the Amsterdam
     Treaty came into force.
28   The integration into the Schengen space is proceeded via a gradualist strat-
     egy: if the candidate country applies, it is integrated some two years later. In
     the case of the fifth enlargement countries, the setback of integration is due
     to the delays in operability of the Schengen-Information-System II, SIS II.
     See <http://europa.eu.int/scadplus/leg/de/cig/g4000s.htm>.
29   Heinz Timmermann, 'Kaliningrad – eine Pilotregion für die Gestaltung der
     Partnerschaft EU-Russland?', *Osteuropa*, 9 (2001), p. 1042. According to
     Lyndelle Fairlie, the residents of Kalingrad leave their region 14 times as
     often as other Russian citizens. Lyndelle D. Fairlie, 'Kaliningrad. A Russian
     Exclave in Search of New Roles', in Paul Gansler *et al.* (eds), *Border Regions in
     Functional Transition* (Berlin: 1996), pp. 213–37.
30   IOM (International Organization for Migration), Vilnius Office, *Migration and
     Transit as seen by Kaliningrad population. Representative public opinion survey of
     the Kaliningrad population*, official publication of the International Organization
     for Migration (Vilnius: IOM, 2005), p. 27
31   Cited in Michail Vinogradov, 'The Duma protects Kaliningrad', *Izvestia*, 20 June
     2002, p. 2.
32   'Not one centimetre of Russian territory ... ', *Rusika Izvestia*, 20 June 2002.
33   See <www.strana.ru>; Susan Glasser, 'Russia, EU Agree on Travel to and
     From Kaliningrad', *Washington Post*, 12 Nov. 2002.

34 The transit document exists in two different forms: first, for multiple entry, to be issued by the Lithuanian and Polish consulates, and second, for single entry, to be bought with the train ticket or after verification of identity at the border. Polish and Lithuanian authorities may refuse this document; data will be registered by the border authorities.

35 *Königsberger Express.*

36 See, e.g., 'Inaccessible Kaliningrad', *Courrier International*, 21 July 2003.

37 For a detailed presentation, see IOM, *Kaliningrad Transit: Secure Borders, Free Transit* (Vilnius: IOM, 2005).

38 Itar-Tass, 6 March 2006.

39 For literature on Nagorno-Karabakh, see Levon Chobarjian (ed.), *The Making of Mountain-Karabagh: From Secession to Republic* (Basingstoke: Palgrave Macmillan, 2001); Per Gahrton, *Report on the South Caucasus. European Parliament, European Parliament* documents, 2004; Thomas De Waal, *The Black Garden: Armenia and Azerbaijan through Peace and War* (London: New York University Press, 2003); Svante E. Cornell, *Autonomy and Conflict: Extraterritoriality and Separatism in the South Caucasus – Cases in Georgia* (Uppsala: Uppsala University, Department of Peace and Conflict research, 2002); David D. Laitin and Ronald Grigor Suny, 'Thinking Way out of Karabakh', *Middle East Policy*, 7/1 (Oct. 1999), pp. 145–76; Dov Lynch, *Endgames*, unpublished manuscript (2004); Dov Lynch, *Russian Peacekeeping Strategies towards the CIS: The Cases of Moldova, Georgia and Tajikistan* (London: RIIA and Macmillan, 2000); Dov Lynch, *Managing Separatist States: A Eurasian Case Study*, Occasional Paper No. 32 (Paris: WEU Institute for Strategic Studies, 2001); Dov Lynch, 'Separatist States and Post-Soviet Conflicts', *International Affairs*, 78/4 (Oct. 2002), pp. 831–48; Charles King, 'The Ethnic War: Understanding Eurasia's Unrecognized States', *World Politics*, 53, (July 2001), pp. 525–52; Larry Minear and Neil McSeearlane, *Humanitarian Action and Politics, The case of Nagorno Karabakh* (Providence, RI: Brown University, Thomas J.Watson Jr Institute for Insternational Studies, Occasional Paper No. 25, 1997); Tim Potier, *Conflict in Nagorno Karabakh, Abkhazia, and South Ossetia: A Legal Appraisal* (Dodrecht: University Press, 2000); Barnett R. Rubin, *Post-Soviet Political Order: Conflict and State-Building* (London: Routledge, 1998); Graham Smith, and VivienLaw, *Nation-Building in the Post-Soviet Borderlands: The Politics of National Identity* (Cambridge: Cambridge University Press, 1998).

40 This kingdom is not related to current Albania.

41 For the dependency of Nagorno-Karabakh on Azerbaijan in Soviet times, see Dov Lynch, *Endgames*, unpublished manuscript (2004), p. 23.

42 The economy of Nagorno-Karabakh is dominated by the tobacco industry, wine and the cultivation of silkworms.

43 'Troisième Rencontre à Genève des Hommes d' affaires arméniens d' Europe', 7 May 2002, at <http://www.armenianforum.org>.

44 Henrik Bischof, *Der Karabakh Konflikt: Moskaus Hand in Transkaukasien* (Bonn: Friedrich-Ebert-Stiftung, 1995), p. 8, and at <http://www.fes.de/fulltext/aussenpolitik/00035.html>.

45 The name is of Greek origin, meaning 'the land of sweet water'.

46 The Julfa quarter in Nakhchivan suffered from severe destruction in the 1990s. On 16 February 2006, the European Parliament condemned the serious

destruction of this ancient Armenian cultural place, around the seventeenth-century Vank cathedral.

47 Source: <http://www.fortunecity.com/campus/purdue/47/naxcivan.html>.
48 The army of Moutain Karabakh consists of 20,000 men, trained in Ivanovka, near Stepanakkert. See <http://www.travel-images.com/az-karabakh.html>.
49 Gahrton 26 Feb. 2004, South Caucasus report to the EU parliament.
50 Fact-finding mission of the author to Karabakh, April–May 2005, report Susanne Nies (unpublished manuscript containing interviews, etc.).
51 Courrier International 799/2006, *Situation figée au Haut-Karabakh.*
52 Susanne Nies, fact-finding mission, Karabakh, May 2005.

7
Russia and China in the New Central Asia: The Security Agenda

John Berryman

The implosion of the Soviet Union in late 1991 triggered the steepest decline not associated with military defeat of any major power in modern history. Nonetheless, Russia remains the largest polity in the world, its territory comprising 30 per cent of the vast space of Eurasia, with land and sea borders totalling almost 62,000 kilometres. The Russian Federation (RF) has retained most of its old northern and northwestern borders, together with the border with North Korea and a 4,300-km border with China. However, in Europe, Russia's borders were returned to those of the seventeenth century, while its southern borders in the Caucasus and Central Asia were rolled back by almost 1,500-km to where they had been in the 1800s. South of the undefended 7,000-km border between Russia and Kazakhstan, the longest international land border in the world, the five new Central Asian successor states form a huge but fragile buffer zone. Containing around 50 million inhabitants, including 30 million Muslims and six million ethnic Russians, these secular post-Soviet regimes separate Russia's own Muslim regions, containing some 13 per cent of the RF population, from the Muslim south of Iran, Afghanistan and Pakistan. Locked between the EU to the west and China to the east, and between the Artic north and an unstable Muslim south, Russia has the potential to become either the regional hegemon or the 'sick man' of Eurasia.[1]

This chapter examines Russian security policy and the new Central Asia, focusing on the challenge posed by China's reemerging role in the region. The first section seeks to explain the less than successful efforts in the Yeltsin years to deal with the security challenges posed by the new Central Asia. The second section traces China's long-standing concerns for the security of its northwestern province bordering the region, focusing on the development of the Shanghai Cooperation Organization (SCO). The third section reviews Putin's efforts to re-engage with the Central Asian states and the fourth section examines Russia's reassertion of its position in Central Asia. The chapter concludes by examining the prospects for Russia and China in the region.

Russia and the new Central Asia

During the Soviet period, to prevent any sort of 'domino theory' effect, pan-Islamic connections between the inhabitants of the five Central Asian republics, other Muslim regions within the Soviet Union, and the peoples of surrounding Islamic states, were firmly suppressed. Following the collapse of the Soviet Union, the question posed was whether Russia could maintain stability within the post-Soviet space without adopting a neo-imperial policy. The liberal institutionalist view was that Russia should learn to coexist with the newly independent states as equal partners and accept the possibility that Central Asia would become a part of a 'larger Middle East'. Realists, however, argued that the containment of Islam and the stabilization of relations between states of the former Soviet Union (FSU) was conceivable only with great power protection. In this view ideological conflicts had been replaced by geopolitical struggles for spheres of influence. If Russia did not offer some form of direction, the Central Asian buffer zone could eventually comprise an unstable bloc of hostile states. It was argued that 'unless the Russian Federation is leader in its own region of the world, still less can it expect to become a power of truly global stature'.[2] Indeed, the Moscow-based Armenian scholar and Presidential Council member, Andranik Migranyan, suggested that the entire post-Soviet geopolitical space should be explicitly declared a vital sphere within which Russia's interests could be neither denied nor ignored. Migranyan urged that Moscow should, in an echo of the US Monroe Doctrine, seek international recognition of Russia as the regional hegemon.[3] However, the Monroe Doctrine of 1823 was the proclamation of an aspiring hegemon. Russia, by contrast, confronts the difficult task of imperial retrenchment with the possibility of losing its position as the regional hegemon. The centrist formulation of the Russian Council on Defence and Foreign Policy that Russia should pursue an 'enlightened post-imperial integrationist course', eschewing any consideration of coercive re-integration of the post-Soviet states, consequently secured wide support within the policy-making elite.[4]

Although a framework for post-imperial integration was established in the form of the Commonwealth of Independent States (CIS), Russia's initial focus on integration into Western economic and political structures encouraged an indifference towards the CIS, exacerbated by a proprietorial view of the Central Asian states. Scores of multilateral agreements were signed within the CIS, but thanks to the huge asymmetries in size and power between the RF and the other member states, the general tendency for locally dominant states to use regional multilateral organizations to achieve their objectives, and for small states to use them to constrain larger ones, was quickly evident.[5] Lacking the necessary mechanisms whereby they might be given some real influence on policy, the post-Soviet states saw many of the agreements as instruments of Moscow's neo-imperial strategy. Looking to develop new economic ties with the international community, the post-Soviet states were fearful that close cooperation with Russia would run the risk of recreating the centre–periphery relations of the Soviet period. Most of the agreements were therefore never implemented.[6] Proposals for a CIS Economic Union, Free Trade Zones, Customs Union, Eurasian Economic Community and Single Economic Space, likewise failed to create an integrated economic union. In sum, after a decade of independence Central Asia remained a weak subcomplex within a larger CIS complex in which the residual dominance of the regional hegemon was eroding.[7] The shortcomings of the CIS integration process were such that critics such as Konstantin Zatulin, Director of the Russian Academy of Sciences Institute for the Studies of the CIS, and Andranik Migranyan, concluded that the CIS was a 'fiction'.[8] Aleksei Arbatov, Russia's leading liberal security analyst, likewise dismissed the CIS as 'an absurd hybrid of NATO, the European Union and the UN, and it is not effective in any of its incarnations'.[9]

Within the sphere of military-security policy coordination, the 1992 CIS Tashkent Collective Security Treaty (CST), a subregional agreement signed initially by Russia, Kazakhstan, Kyrgyzstan, Tajikistan, Uzbekistan and Armenia, gained three additional members in late 1993, when Georgia, Azerbaijan and Belarus joined. Although nominally a collective security agreement, the reality was that as the dominant power, Russia, was bound to provide military protection, including in theory a nuclear umbrella, to these nine weak states in Europe, the Caucasus and Central Asia. The Central Asian states looked to Moscow to provide a security guarantee against China and, after 1996, the Taliban regime in Afghanistan. Since Russia was wary of taking on security commitments, with the exception of the 1995 agreement to establish a CIS Joint Air Defence System, most of the collective decisions and documents of the CST were never implemented. By the time Azerbaijan, Georgia and Uzbekistan withdrew from the CST in 1999, with Uzbekistan joining the newly established anti-CIS subregional grouping of Georgia, Ukraine, Azerbaijan and Moldova (GUAM), the CST was effectively moribund.[10] In view of the shortcomings of the multilateral arrangements reached within the CIS and CST, Moscow resorted to bilateral agreements to maintain its strong residual links with the Central Asian states. Following the breakup of the Soviet Union, the majority of the states of the FSU remained heavily indebted to Russia, which had provided the republics with a massive annual subsidy of close to 67 billion roubles.[11] Control of the Soviet-era oil and gas pipelines linking these states to Russia provided Moscow with additional leverage.[12] Nonetheless, after signing bilateral Treaties of Friendship, Cooperation and Mutual Assistance with Moscow, alongside discounted energy prices, Central Asian states have received weapons, technical equipment and Russian military training assistance at discounted rates.[13]

With respect to Russia's military position along its southern flank, following the nationalization or disbanding of 11 divisions in the former Transcaucasian republics and 11 divisions in the former Central Asian republics, 22,000 Russian border troops and military units remained in the South Caucasus and 40,000 Russian troops remained in Central Asia. In April 1994, Yeltsin directed the Russian Foreign and Defence Ministries to negotiate agreements with CIS states and Latvia to establish almost thirty Russian bases. In the event, thanks to the shortfall in resources, hopes of establishing a Russian forward security zone in the CIS region were abandoned as Russian troops were steadily withdrawn from their deployments along the external borders of the CIS. By 1999, Russian troops and border guards had departed from all Central Asian states with the exception of Tajikistan, where 11,500 Russian-officered border guards were deployed along the 1,344-km Tajik–Afghan border, backed up by the presence of Russia's long-established 8,200-strong 201st Motor Rifle Division (MRD).[14] Under the terms of the 1999 Russo–Tajik agreement, the forces of the 201st MRD have been reduced to 5,500 contract troops and in October 2004 a permanent base for the division was established at Dushanbe. In September 2005, Russian responsibility for the border troops was transferred to the Tajik authorities.[15] Russian military personnel also remain in Tajikistan at the space surveillance radar station at Nurek and in Kazakhstan at the Baikonur space launch centre, the Sary-Shagan anti-missile testing range, and the ballistic missile early warning system (BMEWS) *Dnepr* and *Dnestr* space surveillance radars at Balkash.[16]

Russia's enforced strategic drawdown was accompanied by the vigorous engagement of NATO PfP programmes in the region, and in 1999 the Pentagon transferred responsibility for the Central Asian states to the key military zone of US Central Command.[17] These moves were seen in Moscow as evidence of Washington's determination to seize the opportunity offered by Russia's weakness to 'consolidate and perpetuate the prevailing geopolitical pluralism' in the post-Soviet states and roll-back Russian influence in the Caucasus and Central Asia, thereby enhancing US global strategic dominance.[18] Fears that Central Asia might also become contested territory between Russia and China only added to Moscow's concerns.[19]

Andrew Hurrell has observed that a declining hegemon invariably seeks 'the creation of common institutions to pursue its interests, to share burdens, to solve common problems and to generate international support and legitimacy for its policies'.[20] The development of a new multilateral framework for interstate cooperation in the region – the 'Shanghai Five' – was largely a Chinese initiative. However, it offered Moscow the opportunity to establish a measure of shared responsibility with Beijing for the maintenance of the stability and security of Central Asia.[21] It was an opportunity Russia seized, in a calculated gamble embarking on a radically new course by allowing and even encouraging Chinese involvement in the region.[22]

China and the new Central Asia: From the 'Group of Five' to the SCO

Although acquired by the Qing dynasty in 1757, Chinese Turkestan was not incorporated as a province in the Chinese empire until 1884. The 17 million people of the Xinjiang Uighur Autonomous Region (XUAR) includes around eight million Uighurs, a Muslim people of Turkic ethnicity with links to almost 180,000 Uighurs who live in Kazakhstan and 50,000 in Kyrgyzstan, together with more than one million Kazakhs and 200,000 Kyrgyz. Notwithstanding the development of its oil and gas reserves, the use of repressive measures, and the mass transfer of Han Chinese to Xinjiang since the 1950s, the authorities in Beijing remain deeply concerned to prevent the development of 'separatist' and 'splittist' forces in the XUAR. Apart from the challenge they pose to the stability of the province, such movements might additionally encourage Mongols in China's Inner Mongolia AR to seek unity with the newly independent Mongolia.[23]

During the fifty years of Tsarist colonization and seventy years of Soviet rule of Central Asia, repeated efforts were made to encroach on China's vulnerable northwestern flank. During 1927–42, Xinjiang was a virtual protectorate of the Soviet Union, while 1944–49 saw the establishment of the short-lived Soviet-sponsored Republic of East Turkestan.[24] During the Sino–Soviet dispute, apart from massively increasing its military forces along its Central Asian borders with China and stationing first-echelon forces within the Mongolian People's Republic in striking distance of Beijing, the Soviet Union fuelled separatist sentiments in Xinjiang by giving special status to ethnic Uighurs in Soviet Central Asia. According to retired military intelligence officer, Vladimir Suvurov, Moscow even helped to set up the United Revolutionary Front of East Turkestan in Almaty in 1975.[25] In response, China deployed 12 People's Liberation Army (PLA) MRDs and associated forces totalling 200,000 troops in the Lanzhou Military District (MD) bordering Central Asia and revived claims to sections of Kazakh, Kyrgyz, and Tajik territory. Despite the normalization of Sino–Soviet relations in the 1980s, China's control over the XUAR was not relaxed.[26] With the implosion of the Soviet Union and the emergence of potentially unstable Central Asian neighbours, China's primary regional security concern was the stability of its northwestern province. Strategic cooperation to maintain stability in the region and curtail the intrusion of extra-regional powers suited Beijing as much as Moscow.[27] In contrast to its relations with the newly independent neighbour of Mongolia, where Beijing made clear its determination to block Russian aspirations to treat it as within its sphere of influence, China recognised the pre-eminence of Russia in Central Asia. This 'Holy Alliance' to freeze the geopolitical status quo in Central Asia, driven by a congruence of regional security concerns in Beijing and Moscow, represented something closer to 'suspended competition' than active cooperation.[28]

Apart from its concern to check the development of separatism in the XUAR, Beijing was quick to see the contribution Central Asia's energy resources might make to China's energy security policy. Since 1993, China has been a net importer of oil, and thanks in part to China's voracious demand over the past decade world oil prices have risen 1,000 per cent from $6.90 to $69 a barrel. In 2004, China edged out Japan to become the world's second largest importer of oil and by 2020 it is estimated that China will be reliant on international suppliers for 60 per cent of its oil and 30 per cent of its natural gas, most delivered by oil tankers and liquid natural gas tankers. Since China currently lacks a 'blue-water' navy, these vessels are vulnerable to interdiction on the high seas. China is therefore looking to the development of secure pipelines from nearby states, ranging from Russia and the Central Asian states to Iran, to contribute to a more reliable and diversified range of suppliers. In 1997, China secured agreements to develop two oilfields in Kazakhstan and build a 3,200-km pipeline to Xinjiang to connect with the Tarim Basin pipeline and on to Shanghai. Part of the pipeline was opened in December 2005. Although at this stage Central Asia provides only 10 per cent of China's total oil imports, it is clear that the development of energy links between the Central Asian states and China will only add to the international challenge to Russia's current dominance of the regional oil supply systems.[29]

Following the broad resolution of the Sino–Russian border disputes by the agreements of 1991 and 1994, in 1996 and 1997 China, Russia, Kazakhstan, Kyrgyzstan and Tajikistan signed agreements on military confidence-building measures (CBMs) on their respective borders and mutual force reductions in the border areas which will remain in effect until 2020, with the possibility of their prolongation for another five years. These historic agreements were the most comprehensive arms-control accords in Asia since 1945 and were the first multilateral security agreements to be signed by Beijing. For Moscow these agreements reduced the possibility of complications with China on what had been the outer border of the Soviet Union and permitted Russia to re-deploy military forces to counterbalance NATO's proposed eastward expansion. For Beijing, stability on China's western borders permitted a redeployment of border troops to the Fujian coast facing Taiwan and the South China Sea.[30]

To monitor the agreements, it was agreed that annual summit meetings of the 'Group of Five' would be held. Thanks to the growing challenge of radical Islam and terrorism, the focus of the consultations quickly extended beyond CBMs to include these issues. Following the bombings in central Tashkent in February 1999, the incursion of fighters of the Islamic Movement of Uzbekistan (IMU) into southern Kyrgyzstan in August 1999 triggered Uzbek participation in anti-terrorist operations. To secure wider support for the transnational struggle with the IMU, in July 2000 Uzbekistan attended as an observer the 'Group of Five' summit in Dushanbe, the capital of Tajikistan, at which it was agreed that a joint Regional Anti-Terrorist Centre (RATC) for information exchange and analytical work should be established in Bishkek. At the Shanghai summit in June 2001, despite Russian misgivings, Uzbekistan was admitted as the sixth member of the group, which was retitled the Shanghai Cooperation Organisation (SCO). The Shanghai Convention on Combating Terrorism, Separatism and Extremism was approved. Although the SCO stated that it was not aimed at any third parties, US plans for missile defence were condemned. Both Russia and China saw the advantages to be derived from the development of an Asian cooperative security system which excluded the United States and provided them with a platform from which to express their rhetorical preference for a multipolar world.[31]

As the title of the organization suggests, it is above all Beijing that has promoted the SCO. As something of an 'outside power' lacking any sort of sponsored multilateral framework for consultation in the region, such as that provided for Moscow by the CIS and CST, China has been anxious to foster a regional institution which would provide it with an entry point into the affairs of Central Asia and reinforce its bilateral relations with the Central Asian states. In the global context, China's membership of the SCO has underlined Beijing's preparedness to participate in multilateral forums to further regional and global cooperation. As the largest regional security system in the world, embracing one quarter of the land surface of the planet, the SCO provides an example of a multilateral approach to security in Asia in contrast to Washington's unilateral or bilateral alliance approach.[32]

Putin's reengagement with Central Asia

As Director of the Federal Security Service from July 1998 and Secretary of the Russian Security Council from March 1999, Putin's meteoric rise to power coincided with the intensification of activity by Islamist insurgents. Following his appointment as Prime Minister and designated successor to Yeltsin in August 1999, Putin signalled that terrorism and regional stability within the CIS would be priorities for Russia's foreign and security policy. In contrast to the somewhat condescending patrician tone that Yeltsin had adopted in his meetings with Central Asian leaders, Putin assumed a brisk and straightforward approach. Following a visit to Tajikistan in November 1999, his visits to Tashkent in December 1999 and May 2000 opened a new phase of limited accord in Uzbekistan's fluctuating relationship with Russia. Thanks to Putin's visits, over thirty bilateral agreements were reached for Russia to supply Uzbekistan with substantial quantities of military equipment and communication systems, while Tashkent now agreed to participate in the CIS air defence system.[33]

Alongside the strengthening of these bilateral links, Putin sought to reinvigorate the collective security potential of the CIS. The mounting of *Southern Shield of the Commonwealth 99* in October–November 1999, a CIS anti-terrorist exercise involving Russia, Kyrgyzstan, Tajikistan and Uzbekistan, was followed in March 2000 by a full counter-terrorist exercise in Tajikistan, *Southern Shield of the Commonwealth 2000*, which included troops from Kazakhstan along with participants from Armenia and Belarus. Thirteen thousand troops took part in what was probably the largest such exercise ever held in Central Asia. In April, a CIS summit agreed to establish a RATC in Moscow with an office in Bishkek, headed by a Russian general, Boris Mylnikov, former deputy head of the anti-terrorist department of the Federal Security Service and from 1975 to 1991 a KGB operative.

The subsequent proposal for a RATC put forward by the Shanghai Forum at its Dushanbe summit a month later, exposed the emerging rivalry between the SCO and the CIS as regional security organisations.[34]

In May 2001, an important CST summit in Yerevan, the capital of Armenia, agreed to Russian proposals that three groups of Collective Rapid Deployment Forces (CRDFs) should be established: a western group (Russia and Belarus); a 1,500-strong Caucasus group (Russia and Armenia); and a Central Asian group. The latter would comprise one specially designated battalion each supplied by Kazakhstan, Kyrgyzstan and Tajikistan as well as elements of Russia's 201st MRD deployed in Tajikistan. It would total some 3,000 troops and a joint military command would be established in Moscow with a coordinating staff, headed by a Russian commander, Major-General Sergei Chernomordin, located in Bishkek. Apart from their potential contribution to anti-terrorist operations, the establishment of these CRDF groups brought closer Moscow's ambition to establish full regional groups of forces within the Tashkent Treaty space. The creation of the merged Volga-Urals MD in September 2001 provided a better focused rear headquarters at Ekaterinburg for operations by Russian forces in Central Asia.[35]

Given their common efforts to contain the spread of Islamic extremism, after the terrorist attacks of 11 September 2001 in the United States it was not difficult for Russia, China and the Central Asian states to support the US 'Global War on Terror' (GWOT). On 14 September, the prime ministers of the SCO issued a statement condemning the attacks. Some of the Central Asian states indicated their land and air space would be available for use by US and coalition forces in the anti-Taliban *Operation Enduring Freedom* in Afghanistan. Apart from high-quality intelligence, Russia made available to the anti-Taliban forces at least fifty T-55 tanks and thirty armoured personnel carriers. The subsequent direct 'intrusion' of US forces into Central Asia established the region as a higher profile element in both US–Russian and US–Chinese relations, thereby shattering any prospect of a settled Russo–Chinese condominium over inner Asia and freeing up the ability of the states of the region to seek the bilateral support of a variety of patrons. The opening provided by the GWOT enabled Putin to secure a strategic partnership with the United States, thereby supplanting China in the role of America's strategic partner in the region and downgrading the strategic partnership only recently forged between Russia and China. The softening of Putin's opposition to Washington's plans for missile defence (MD), undertaken with only minimal consultation with Beijing, and Putin's restrained response to the abrupt December 2001 US announcement of its intended unilateral withdrawal from the Anti-Ballistic Missile Treaty, followed by the swift negotiation of the Russo–American Strategic Offensive Reductions Treaty in Moscow in May 2002, only added to China's concerns. These misgivings over Russia's apparent compliance with US priorities were not alleviated by the reassurances offered by Russian Defence Minister Sergei Ivanov in a special visit to Beijing.[36] Lacking the substantial nuclear forces of the RF, Beijing feared that a US pre-emptive first-use nuclear strategy, linked to a workable MD system, might neutralize China's vulnerable minimum deterrence force and remove constraints on US policy in the event of a confrontation with China over Taiwan.[37] Moreover, long-standing Chinese fears of strategic encirclement by the United States seemed to be confirmed with the establishment of new American bases within striking distance of China's western frontiers, complementing the existing US forward bases off China's eastern borders in Japan and South Korea. Little interest was shown by Washington in compensating Beijing for this 'intrusion' into China's backyard. The US Department of State's reluctant classification of the East Turkestan Islamic Movement operating in Xinjiang as a terrorist organization in August 2002 represented only a token return for China's lukewarm support for the US war on terror.[38] However, neither China nor Russia sought to block the deployment of US forces into Central Asia. For both powers the benefits of the US GWOT, together with their reluctance to jeopardize their respective trade and financial links with the West, dictated that they avoid any costly confrontation with Washington.

With some member states hosting US forces, for the moment the SCO was sidelined. Tashkent's disinterest in the SCO as a regional security provider was apparent when it declined to send representatives to SCO meetings and little was achieved at the SCO summit in St Petersburg in May 2002.[39] At the May 2003 SCO summit in Moscow, the SCO charter adopted was not made public and a modest annual budget of only $4 million was agreed. The Chinese ambassador to Moscow, Zhang Deguang, a fluent Russian speaker, was identified as the first SCO Secretary-General and China agreed to meet the cost of his office in Beijing (not Shanghai) over the first three years. At the June 2004 SCO summit in Tashkent, in recognition of Uzbekistan's wish for an antiterrorist centre on its territory, the SCO RATC was established in Tashkent rather than Bishkek with a staff of thirty.[40] Undeterred by the slow institutional development of the SCO, in October 2002 China conducted military exercises across its 858-km Tienshan mountain-range border with Kyrgyzstan, the PLA's first military exercise with a foreign country. In a very limited operation China contributed only 100 soldiers, 10 vehicles and several helicopters, while Kyrgyzstan committed only 60 border guards and five armoured vehicles.[41]

In August 2003, the first SCO military exercise, *Coalition 2003*, was held in Kazakhstan, Kyrgyzstan and western China, more than 1,000 troops from five member states taking part. Uzbekistan, which had participated in the GUUAM command-staff exercises the previous month, claimed its troops were not adequately prepared for the exercise and held separate exercises along its borders with Tajikistan. Chinese military activity in Kazakhstan and Kyrgyzstan was accompanied by an increase in China's military aid to these two Central Asian states, totalling respectively $3 million and $1.2 million.[42] In 2006, all six SCO member states participated in large-scale anti-terrorist exercises.[43]

Russia's strategic reassertion in Central Asia

The deployment of US and coalition forces in Central Asia, coupled with mounting Chinese military-security activity in the region, has triggered a reinvigoration of Moscow's preferred regional security system, the CST, and a reassertion of Russia's strategic position in Central Asia.

In May 2002, the CST's Collective Security Council agreed that the CST should be upgraded into a regional security organization, renamed as the Collective Security Treaty Organisation (CSTO). In October, its charter, modelled ostensibly on NATO, was approved and the former director of Russia's Federal Border Service, Colonel-General Nikolai Bordyuzha, was appointed Secretary-General of the CSTO. Although the CSTO has been recognized by the OSCE and the SCO and granted observer status in the General Assembly of the UN, efforts by Moscow to develop institutional contacts between NATO and the CSTO were rebuffed. Bordyuzha's proposal in December 2005 to establish a Eurasian Advisory Council that could include representatives from the CSTO, SCO, NATO, the EU and the Eurasian Economic Community has likewise been ignored.[44] Despite the upgrading of the CSTO along NATO lines, establishment of NATO-style collective security structures and groups of integrated forces, as envisaged in the Yeltsin years by the Secretary of the Council of CIS Defence Ministers, Leonid Ivashov, and by the CIS Staff on Coordination of Military Cooperation, has yet to be secured.[45]

The decision of the CSTO's Collective Security Council in December 2002 to establish a CRDF base in Kyrgyzstan signalled Moscow's determination to bolster its military position in the region. In return for a rescheduling of part of its $133 million debt to Russia, Kyrgyzstan agreed that a largely Russian-funded and Russian-equipped CRDF aviation unit should be established on its territory to provide close-air support for anti-terrorist operations. The former Soviet flight-training base at Kant,

20 km east of Bishkek, was selected. It is suggested that Moscow moved to establish the base at Kant after learning that the United States was looking to acquire the base in addition to its facility at Ganci, Manas International Airport, close to Bishkek.[46] Following the formal inauguration of the CSTO at its summit in Dushanbe in April 2003, in October Putin formally opened the Kant airbase.

Having earlier insisted upon the closure on cost grounds of the last Soviet overseas bases in Vietnam and Cuba in 2002, Russia has established at Kant its first post-Soviet outpost abroad. Located only 35 km from the US-led coalition airbase at Ganci, it highlights Russia's preparedness to challenge, albeit implicitly rather openly, the US presence in Central Asia. Its location only some 300 km from China's border also constitutes a challenge to China. According to high level sources in Bishkek, extensive consultations between Moscow and Beijing preceded the opening of the base. The Russian presence at the base initially comprised around 300 personnel and sixteen Russian aircraft plus ten Kyrgyz aircraft.[47] Given the modest size of the deployment, the establishment of the airbase was seen to be primarily political in character, symbolizing Russia's resolve not to be marginalized by the United States and China in one of its key spheres of influence. In December 2003, it was agreed that two battalions rather than one would each be assigned to the CRDF by Russia, Kazakhstan and Kyrgyzstan, and three would be provided by Tajikistan.[48] In January 2004, a CSTO Joint Staff was established and in August the first large CSTO CRDF exercise was mounted. Involving 2,000 of the 4,500 troops available, *Rubezh 2004* drew upon units provided by Russia, Kazakhstan, Kyrgyzstan and Tajikistan.[49]

With the upgrading of the CSTO and the activation of its CRDF, the potential for parallelism or rivalry between the CSTO and the SCO and Russo–Chinese rivalry within the SCO has grown. However, in response to the 'colour' revolutions, Russo–Chinese collaboration has, for the moment, been strengthened. In the wake of what was perceived in Moscow to be the Western-inspired and manipulated 'Rose Revolution' in Georgia in November 2003 and 'Orange Revolution' in Ukraine in December 2004, following a questionable parliamentary election peaceful mass demonstrations ousted President Askar Akayev of Kyrgyzstan in the 'Tulip Revolution' of March 2005. His ignominious flight to Moscow was followed by only a reshuffle of the political elite rather than its turnover and in July elections legitimized the presidency of Kurmanbeck Bakiyev who had assumed control in March. By contrast, the bloody crackdown on political unrest in the eastern town of Andijon in Uzbekistan in May 2005 attested to the determination of President Karimov to hold on to power.

The widespread Western criticism of Karimov's action exposed policy differences in Washington over the wisdom of US support for the regime in exchange for the use of Uzbekistan's Karshi Khanabad (K2) airbase. In sharp contrast, Moscow and Beijing provided staunch support for Karimov. Russian Foreign Minister, Sergei Lavrov, alluded to 'Taliban-like provocation', while a Chinese Foreign Ministry spokesman expressed approval of Karimov's crackdown on 'the three forces of separatism, terrorism and extremism'.[50]

At the SCO summit in Astana, Kazakhstan, on 5 July 2005, all six member states called upon the Western coalition states involved in the military operations in Afghanistan to set a timetable for the withdrawal of their troops and bases from the territories of SCO member states. Outraged by criticisms of his regime and calls for an international investigation of the Andijon events, on 29 July President Karimov announced that the lease of K2 would be terminated and that Washington would be expected to have withdrawn all US forces from the base by the end of the year. (On 21 November the last US plane left K2). Tashkent's break with Washington was accompanied by the forging of closer relations between Uzbekistan and Russia and China. Karimov's red carpet visit to Beijing in May, in which a $600 million joint venture energy deal was signed, was followed by his visit to Moscow in June, during which a secret memorandum on military cooperation was signed. The first ever joint Russian–Chinese military exercises at Vladivostok and on the Shandong Peninsula in August, and the first-ever joint Russian–Uzbek counter-terrorist exercises in Uzbekistan in September, were followed by another visit to Moscow by President Karimov on 14 November, during which a mutual security pact was signed and which will facilitate the deployment of Russian forces on Uzbek territory. In December, an agreement was reached for joint Russo–Uzbek production of 40 IL-76 transport aircraft for sale to China, thereby helping to liquidate Uzbekistan's $500 million debt to Russia.[51]

By contrast, seeking to maintain good relations with Washington as well as Moscow, Kyrgyz President Bakiyev reaffirmed the status of the US base at Ganci during a hasty July 2005 visit to Bishkek by US Defense Secretary Donald Rumsfeld. Bakiyev subsequently informed Washington that the annual rent for the use of the Ganci airbase would rise a hundredfold from $2.7 million to $207 million. The Krygyz authorities argued the new sum was in line with international practice and Washington eventually agreed to pay an annual rent of between $150–200 million.[52]

In contrast to the increased charges demanded for the use of Ganci by US and coalition forces, Russia's use of the CSTO Kant airbase remained rent-free, and there were even rumours that the CRDF presence in

Kyrgyzstan would be increased, possibly in the form of a second base at Osh in the volatile and densely populated Ferghana valley.[53] However, on a visit to the Kant base in February 2006, Russian Air Force Commander Vladimir Mikhailov announced that, although the air component would be increased by some 150 per cent, boosting personnel from 300 to 750, no new Russian bases for Central Asia were under consideration, leaving Kant and the 201st MRD in Tajikistan as the only standing bases in the region. Mikhailov hinted that a 'stand-by' base might be established by Russia in the western strategic salient of Belarus, probably located near Russia's new BMEWS *Volga* radar at Baranovichi. Established to replace the recently constructed Soviet radar station in Skrunda in Latvia, which closed in August 1998, the Baranovichi station commenced experimental operations in December 1999. Mikhailov made clear that these initiatives to buttress Russia's position in zones of special interest were a response to what was perceived to be a renewed strategic encirclement of Russia by the United States and NATO. During the cold war, the Soviet Union had sought to push its front lines away from its own borders onto the territories of its socialist allies. A more assertive Russia was now establishing its own forward bases on the territories of its CSTO allies.[54] This reinvigoration of Russia's strategic position in Central Asia forms part of Putin's broader project to 'restore what was lost with the fall of the Soviet Union' ... on a new, modern basis' and re-establish Russia as a Eurasian great power.[55] Notwithstanding understandable reservations in Moscow as to the durability of its new relationship with the erratic Karimov, in January 2006 Uzbekistan was admitted to the Eurasian Economic Community and in June readmitted to the CSTO – an organization Uzbekistan had left seven years earlier after seven years of membership.[56]

Conclusion

How have the 'colour' revolutions affected the position of the major players in the New Great Game in Central Asia? For the moment, the US position in Central Asia has been weakened by its withdrawal from Uzbekistan and the perceptions of the other autocratic local leaderships that they should not look to Washington for support against 'colour' revolutions. Moscow and Beijing have, to date, cooperated closely in opposing all manifestations of popular protest in Central Asia. However, prospects for a stable Russo–Chinese condominium in Central Asia are uncertain. It seems that Beijing accepts Moscow's role as the primary power broker and security manager of Central Asia – a region which is not yet a high priority for China. Apart from the preservation of internal order and stability to facilitate the continuation of China's 'peaceful rise', the strategic priorities for the authorities in Beijing currently lie in East Asia, notably Taiwan and the South China Sea. Russian–Chinese bilateral trade, especially energy supplies, has seen a sixfold increase from $5.7 billion *per annum* to $30 billion *per annum*, which may well double to $60 billion by 2010. China is therefore anxious not to jeopardize its valuable strategic partnership with Moscow. Beijing refrained from responding to the bruising rebuff it sustained when, after nine years of talks, in the summer of 2003 Putin abruptly shelved the Angarsk–Daquing oil pipeline project in favour of consideration of a possible Japanese-financed oil pipeline to the Russian port of Perevoznaya on the Pacific coast.[57] Determined to avoid an over-dependence on China as a market for Russian oil and gas and to keep open the possibility of supplying the wider Asia-Pacific market, a replacement agreement to conduct a feasibility study for a possible spur pipeline from Russia to China was not reached until Putin's visit to Beijing in March 2006.[58] Although Beijing may, for the present, be holding back from any challenge to Russia in Central Asia, it seems likely that over time China's rapidly developing trade and energy links with the region will erode historic Central Asian suspicions and open the way for the development of more intense Sino–Russian strategic rivalry in Central Asia. Within five years of the collapse of the Soviet Union, China's trade with post-Soviet Central Asia doubled to $872 million. By 2000, it had risen to almost $2 billion and by 2004 China's trade with Kazakhstan and Krgyzstan was second only to that of Russia.[59]

While recognizing the importance of its strategic partnership with China, Russia maintains a close watch over China's activities in Central Asia. Whatever the truth of unconfirmed reports that Chinese designs on the recently vacated K2 base triggered a movement of Russian military personnel to the vicinity of the base, it is clear that Moscow has not abandoned its efforts to maintain Russia's position as the regional security manager in Central Asia.[60] Russia moved quickly to fill the geopolitical vacuum left in Uzbekistan by the withdrawal of US forces, while its efforts to develop the CSTO as a Russian-led tightly integrated military-focused regional security system stand in sharp contrast to the SCO's Chinese-led broad, loose and economically focused cooperative security framework. The attendance of Pakistan, India, Mongolia and Iran as observers at recent SCO summits has accentuated this contrast.[61] The wide membership and shallow commitment offered by the SCO may condemn it to remain little more than another ineffectual 'talking shop', comparable to the ASEAN Regional Forum.[62] Parallelism rather than outright rivalry therefore best characterizes current relations between the CSTO and the

SCO. In the longer term it is recognized that, since China's economy has doubled in size while Russia's has shrunk by almost half, with the consequence that the Chinese economy is now four times the size of the Russian economy, this continued shift in power relations will lead to a further reworking of Russo–Chinese relations which will profoundly impact on their relations in Central Asia.[63] As two astute Russian analysts have observed, it may be that: 'From a long-term or even medium-term perspective, the Shanghai process leads to the gradual 'friendly' replacement of Russian influence in Central Asia with that of China.'[64]

The development of Russo–Chinese relations in the region will of course be crucially affected by US and NATO policy. For the moment, both Russia and China still welcome US suppression of terrorism and promotion of stability in the region. Recognising that the two regions have become arenas of geopolitical competition, the NATO Istanbul summit in 2004 identified the Caucasus and Central Asia as strategically important regions requiring 'special focus' by the alliance.[65] However, the development of US security relations with Azerbaijan, including possible bases at Nasosnaya near Baku or Ganca in western Azerbaijan, and US and NATO support for Georgiain its confrontation with Russia, may bring about a refocusing of US and NATO strategy in Eurasia away from Central Asia to the hydrocarbon resources of the Caspian and the northern flank of Iran to curb possible WMD proliferation.[66] A diminished US role in Central Asia may therefore open the way to more unrestrained Russo–Chinese competition in the region. The outcome of the New Great Game in Central Asia remains uncertain.

Notes

1 Zbigniew Brzezinski, *The Grand Chessboard: American Primacy and its Geostrategic Imperatives* (New York: Basic Books, 1997), ch. 4; David Kerr, 'Chinese Relations with the Russian Far East', in Michael J. Bradshaw (ed.), *The Russian Far East and Pacific Asia: Unfulfilled Potential* (Richmond: Curzon, 2001), pp. 182–3.

2 See Roland Dannreuther, 'Russia, Central Asia and the Persian Gulf', *Survival*, 35/4 (1993–94), pp. 92–112; Irina Zviagelskaia, *The Russian Policy Debate on Central Asia* (London: Royal Institute of International Affairs, 1995); David Kerr, 'The New Eurasianism: The Rise of Geopolitics in Russia's Foreign Policy', *Europe-Asia Studies*, 47/6 (1995), p. 982; Andrei P. Tsygankov, 'From International Institutionalism to Revolutionary Expansionism: The Foreign Policy Discourse of Contemporary Russia', *Mershon International Studies Review* 41 (1997), pp. 247–68; and Boris Rumer, 'The Search for Stability in Central

Asia', in Boris Rumer (ed.) *Central Asia: A Gathering Storm?* (Armonk, NY: Sharpe, 2002), pp. 49–51.

3   Robert H. Donaldson and Joseph L. Nogee, *The Foreign Policy of Russia: Changing System, Enduring Interests* (Armonk, NY: Sharpe, 2005), pp. 126–7, 208, 383.

4   Neil Malcolm, 'Foreign Policy Making', in Neil Malcolm, Alex Pravda, Roy Allison and Margot Light (eds), *Internal Factors in Russian Foreign Policy* (Oxford: Oxford University Press for Royal Institute of International Affairs, 1996), pp. 137–8.

5   See S. Neil MacFarlane, 'On the Frontlines in the Near Abroad: the CIS and the OSCE in Georgia's Civil Wars', *Third World Quarterly*, 18/3 (1997), pp. 509–25; Sean Kay, 'Geopolitical constraints and institutional innovation: the dynamics of multilateralism in Eurasia', in James Sperling, Sean Kay and Victor S. Papacosma (eds), *Limiting Institutions: The Challenge of Eurasian Security Governance* (Manchester: Manchester University Press, 2003) p. 125.

6   See Philip Roeder, 'From Hierarchy to Hegemony: The Post-Soviet Security Complex', in David A. Lake and Patrick M Morgan (eds), *Regional Orders: Building Security in a New World* (Pennsylvania: Pennsylvania State University Press, 1997); and Martha Brill Olcott, Anders Aslund and Sherman Garnett, *Getting it Wrong: Regional Cooperation and the Commonwealth of Independent States* (Washington, DC: Carnegie Endowment for International Peace, 1999).

7   See Andrei Kortunov, 'Russia, the "Near Abroad" and the West', in Gail Lapidus (ed.), *The New Russia: Troubled Transformation* (Boulder, CO: Westview Press, 1995); Medhi Mozaffari, '"CIS" Southern Belt: Regional Cooperation and Integration', in Mehdi Mozaffari (ed.), *Security Policies in the Commonwealth of Independent States* (Basingstoke: Macmillan, 1997), pp. 148–9; Bruno Coppieters, Alexei Zverev and Dmitri Trenin (eds), *Commonwealth and Independence in Post-Soviet Eurasia* (London: Frank Cass, 1998); Barry Buzan and Ole Wæver, *Regions and Powers: The Structure of International Security* (Cambridge: Cambridge University Press, 2003), pp. 423, 428–9.

8   Konstantin Zatulin and Andranik Migranyan, 'SNG posle Kishineva: nachalo kontsa istorii' (The CIS after Kishinev: the beginning of the end of history) *Sodruzhestvo NG* (supplement to *Nezavisimaya* Gazeta) no. 1. 2 December 1997.

9   Greg Austin and Alexey Muraviev, *The Armed Forces of Russia in Asia* (London: I.B. Tauris, 2000), p. 80.

10 Andrei Zagorski, 'CIS regional security policy structures', in Roy Allison and Christoph Bluth (eds), *Security Dilemmas in Russia and Eurasia* (London: Royal Institute of International Affairs, 1998) p. 287; and Rumer, as note 2 above, pp. 38–41.

11 Jonathan Steele, 'Fear and folly in Moscow', *The Guardian*, 21 Feb. 1992; and Andrei Kortunov and Andrei Shoumikhin, 'Russia and Central Asia: Evolution of Mutual Perceptions, Policies and Interdependence', in Yonjin Zhang and Rouben Azizian (eds), *Ethnic Challenges beyond Borders: Chinese and Russian Perspectives of the Central Asian Conundrum* (Basingstoke: Macmillan, 1998), p. 28.

12 Rumer, as note 2 above, p. 51.

13 Roy Allison, 'Strategic Reassertion in Russia's Central Asia Policy', *International Affairs*, 80/2 (2004), pp. 290–91.

14 See Jed C. Snyder, 'Russian Security Interests in the Southern Periphery', *Jane's Intelligence Review*, 6/12 (1994), pp. 548–51; Raymond Garthoff, 'Russian Military Doctrine and Deployments', in Bruce Parrott (ed.), *State*

Building and Military Power in Russia and the New States of Eurasia (Armonk, NY: New York: Sharpe, 1995); Michael Jasinski, *Russian Military Capabilities in Central Asia* (Centre for Nonproliferation Studies, Monterey Institute of International Studies, September 2001), at <www.cns.miis.edu/research/wtc01/rusmil.htm>; Jonson, 'The Security Dimension of Russia's Policy in South Central Asia', in Gabriel Gorodetsky (ed.), *Russia Between East and West: Russian Foreign Policy on the Threshold of the Twenty-First Century* (London: Frank Cass, 2003), p. 138.

15 Mikhail Gavryushin, 'Should They Stay or Should They Go?: The Future of Russian Border Guards in Tajikistan', *Russian Military Review*, 7 (2004), pp. 25–6; International Institute for Strategic Studies, *The Military Balance 2006* (London: Routledge, 2006), p. 218.

16 Pavel Podvig (ed.), *Russian Strategic Nuclear Forces* (Cambridge, MA: MIT Press, 2001), pp. 422–7.

17 Dana Priest, *The Mission: Waging War and Keeping Peace with America's Military* (New York: W.W. Norton, 2003), Ch. 5.

18 Brzezinski, as note 1 above, p. 51; Sergei Mikoyan, 'Russia, the US and Regional Conflict in Eurasia', *Survival*, 40/3 (1998), pp. 112–26.

19 Vladimir Shlapentokh, 'Russia, China and the Far East: Old Geopolitics or a New Peaceful Cooperation?', *Communist and post-Communist Studies*, 28/3 (1995), p. 313.

20 Andrew Hurrell, 'Regionalism in Theoretical Perspective', in Louise Fawcett and Andrew Hurrell (eds), *Regionalism in World Politics: Regional Organisations and International Order* (Oxford: Oxford University Press, 1995), pp. 52–3.

21 William C. Wohlforth, 'Russia', in Richard J. Ellings and Aaron L. Friedberg with Michael Wills (eds), *Strategic Asia 2002–03: Strategic Aftershocks* (Seattle, WA: National Bureau of Asian Research, 2002), p. 205.

22 Nikolai Sokov, 'The Not-So-Great-Game in Central Asia', PONARS memo No. 403 (December 2005), at <www.csis.org/ruseura/ponars/index.htm>.

23 David Bachman, 'Making Xinjiang Safe for the Han? Contradictions and Ironies of Chinese Governance in China's Northwest', in Morris Rossabi (ed.), *Governing China's Multiethnic Frontiers* (Seattle: University of Washington Press, 2004).

24 Martha Brill Olcott, 'Russo-Chinese Relations and Central Asia', in Sherman W. Garnett (ed.), *Rapprochement or Rivalry? Russo-Chinese Relations in a Changing Asia* (Washington, DC: Carnegie Endowment for International Peace, 2000), pp. 375–83.

25 Elizabeth Wishnick, *Strategic Consequence of the Iraq War: US Security Interest in Central Asia Reassessed* (Carlisle, PA: Strategic Studies Institute, US Army War College, May 2003), p. 27, at <www.carlisle.army.mil/ssi>.

26 Jennifer Anderson, *The Limits of Sino-Russian Partnership* (Oxford: Oxford University Press for International Institute for Strategic Studies, Adelphi Paper 315, 1997), pp. 47–8; Roy Allison, 'Central Asian military reform. National, regional and international influences', in Sally N. Cummings, (ed.), *Oil, Transition and Security in Central Asia* (London: RoutledgeCurzon, 2003), p. 223; E. Wayne Merry, 'Moscow's Retreat and Beijing's Rise as a Regional Great Power', *Problems of Post-Communism*, 50/3 (2003), pp. 17–31.

27 Guangeheng Xing, 'China and Central Asia', in Roy Allison and Lena Jonson (eds), *Central Asian Security: The New International Context* (London: Royal Institute of International Affairs, 2001), p. 166.

28 Anderson, as note 26 above, pp. 49–51, 57–8.

29   Philip Andrews-Speed, Xuanli Liao and Roland Dannreuther, *The Strategic Implications of China's Energy Needs* (Oxford: Oxford University Press for International Institute for Strategic Studies, Adelphi Paper 346, 2002); Robert G. Sutter, *China's Rise in Asia: Promises and Perils* (Lanham, MD: Rowman and Littlefield, 2005), pp. 250, 259; Charles E. Ziegler, 'Energy in the Caspian Basin and Central Asia', in Roger E. Kanet (ed.), *The New Security Environment: The Impact on Russia, Central and Eastern Europe* (Aldershot: Ashgate, 2005), pp. 203–7; Daojiong Zha, 'Chinese Energy Security: Domestic and International Issues, *Survival*, 48/1 (2006), pp. 179–90.

30   Lowell Dittmer, 'The Emerging Northeast Asian Regional Order', in Samuel S. Kim (ed.), *The International Relations of Northeast Asia* (Lanham, MD: Rowman & Littlefield, 2004), pp. 337–8.

31   'Russia has Misgivings about Shanghai Cooperation Organisation', *Eurasia Insight*, 20 June 2001; Bates Gill and Matthew Oresman, *China's New Journey to the West: China's Emergence in Central Asia and Implications for US Interests* (Washington, DC: Centre for Strategic and International Studies, 2003), pp. 7–8.

32   Jeanne L. Wilson, *Strategic Partners: Russian-Chinese Relations in the Post-Soviet Era* (Armonk, NY: Sharpe 2004), pp. 53–4, 59; Michael D. Swaine, 'China: Exploiting a Strategic Opening', in Ashley J. Tellis and Michael Wills (eds), *Strategic Asia 2004–05: Confronting Terrorism in the Pursuit of Power* (Seattle, WA: National Bureau of Asian Research, 2004), p. 72.

33   Allison, as note 26 above, p. 221.

34   Roy Allison, 'Structures and Frameworks for Security Policy Cooperation in Central Asia', in Allison and Jonson (eds), *Central Asian Security*, as note 27 above, pp. 228–9.

35   Haroutin Khachatarian, 'Creation of Rapid Deployment Force Marks Potential Watershed in Collective Security Treaty Development', *Eurasia Insight*, 30 May 2001; International Institute for Strategic Studies, *The Military Balance 2001/2002* (Oxford: Oxford University Press, 2001), p. 108; Roger N. McDermott, *Kazakhstan's Armed Forces: Reform or Decay?* (Camberley: Conflict Studies Research Centre, Royal Military Academy 2002), p. 11.

36   Rex Li, 'A rising power with global aspirations: China', in Mary Buckley and Rick Fawn (eds), *Global Responses to Terrorism: 9/11, Afghanistan and Beyond* (London: Routledge, 2006), p. 215.

37   International Institute for Strategic Studies, 'China's response to missile defences: confronting a strategic *fait accompli*', *Strategic Comments*, 8/1 (2002).

38   Martha Brill Olcott, *Central Asia's Second Chance* (Washington, DC: Carnegie Endowment for International Peace, 2005), p. 197.

39   June Teufel Dreyer, 'Encroaching on the Middle Kingdom? China's View of its Place in the World', in Christopher Marsh and June Teufel Dreyer (eds), *US–China Relations in the Twenty-First Century: Policies, Prospects and Difficulties* (Lanham, MD: Lexington Books, 2003), p. 97.

40   Gill and Oresman, as note 31 above, pp. 8–10, 20; Annette Bohr, 'Regionalism in Central Asia: new geopolitics, old regional order', *International Affairs*, 80/3 (2004), p. 490; International Institute for Strategic Studies, 'The Shanghai Cooperation Organisation', *Strategic Comments*, 12/7 (2006).

41   Henry Plater-Zyberk, *Kyrgyzstan: Focusing on Security* (Camberley: Conflict Studies Research Centre, Royal Military Academy, K41, 2003), p. 9; Tamara

Makarenko, 'Foreign bases complicate terror assessments in Central Asia', *Jane's Intelligence Review*, 15/6 (2003), p. 34.

42 Wishnick, as note 25 above, p. 29; International Institute for Strategic Studies, *The Military Balance 2003/2004*, (Oxford: Oxford University Press, 2003), p. 128; Bohr, as note 40 above p. 499.

43 Institute for Strategic Studies, as note 40 above.

44 Olcott, as note 38 above, p. 187; International Institute for Strategic Studies, as note 15 above p. 148; Richard Weitz, 'Averting a New Great Game in Central Asia', *Washington Quarterly*, 29/3 (2006), p. 164.

45 Alexander A. Konovalov, 'The changing role of military factors', in Vladimir Baranovsky (ed.), *Russia and Europe: The Emerging Security Agenda* (Oxford: Oxford University Press for the Stockholm International Peace Research Institute, 1997), pp. 214–18; Roy Allison, 'Regionalism and Security in Central Asia', *International Affairs*, 80/3 (2004), pp. 470–72.

46 Igor Torbakov, 'Moscow Aims to Restore its Influence in Central Asia', *Eurasia Insight*, 5 Dec. 2002.

47 Russia provided five SU-25 *Frogfoot* (NATO designation) ground-attack aircraft; five SU-27 *Flanker* long-range strike aircraft; and six IL-76 *Candid* military transports. Kyrgyzstan supplied two elderly Mi-8 *Hip* helicopters; one IL-18 *Coot* air reconnaissance aircraft; four L-39 *Albatros* trainer aircraft; plus three An-26 *Curl* military transport aircraft.

48 William D. O'Malley and Roger N. McDermott, *Kyrgyzstan's Security Tightrope: Balancing its Relations with Moscow and Washington* (Fort Leavenworth, K: Foreign Military Studies Office, 2003), pp. 6, 10–12 at <http://fmso.leaven. army.mil/fmsopubs/ISSUES/Kyrgyzstan/Kyrgyzstan.htm>; John Berryman, 'Putin's International Security Priorities', in Roger E. Kanet (ed.), *The New Security Environment: The Impact on Russia, Central and Eastern Europe* (Aldershot: Ashgate, 2005), pp. 41–43; Lena Jonson, *Vladimir Putin and Central Asia* (London: I. B. Tauris, 2005), pp. 96–7; Alexander Golts, 'Playing with Fire in Central Asia', *Moscow Times*, 27 Sept. 2005, at <www.themoscowtimes. com/stories/2005/09/27/006_print.html>.

49 Erica Marat, 'CSTO's Anti-Terrorist Exercises "*Rubezh-2004*" Score High Rating Among Member States', *Central Asia-Caucasus Analyst*, 25 Aug. 2004, at <www.cacianalyst.org/view_article>; International Institute for Strategic Studies, *The Military Balance 2004/2005* (Oxford: Oxford University Press, 2004), p. 143; Jonson, *Vladimir Putin and Central Asia*, as note 48 above, p. 188.

50 Stephen Blank, 'New Turns in Chinese Policy Towards Central Asia', *Central Asia-Caucasus Analyst*, 15 June 2005, at <www.cacianalyst.org/view_article>.

51 Golts, as note 48 above; Igor Torbakov, 'Uzbekistan Emerges as Russia's New "Strategic Bridgehead"', in Central Asia', *Eurasia Insight*, 14 Dec. 2005; Stephen Blank, 'Russia Looks to Build a New Security System in Central Asia', *Eurasia Insight*, 4 Jan. 2006.

52 Olga Dzyubenko, 'Kyrgyzstan wants US to pay more for military base', *Reuters*, 15 Feb. 2006, at *Johnson's Russia List*, No. 43.

53 Igor Torbakov, 'Kyrgyz, Russian Officials Mull Military Base Possibility in Southern Kyrgyzstan', *Eurasia Insight*, 2 June 2005; International Institute for Strategic Studies, *The Military Balance 2005/2006* (London: Routledge, 2005), p. 223.

54 Podvig, as note 16 above, p. 425; Aleksandr Babakin and Viktor Myasnikov, 'The Creation of an "Anti-Warsaw Bloc": the generals have set their sights on yet another military base', *Nezavisimaya Gazeta*, 1 March 2006, at *Johnson's Russia List*, No. 52; *The Military Balance 2006*, as note 15 above, p. 149.

55 Ilan Berman, 'The New Battleground: Central Asia and the Caucasus', *Washington Quarterly*, 28/1 (2004–05), p. 66.

56 'Uzbekistan Rejoins a Security Bloc', *Moscow Times*, 26 June 2006, at <www.themoscowtimes.com/stories/2006/06/26/018-print.html>.

57 Lyle Goldstein, and Vitaly Kozyrev, 'China, Japan and the Scramble for Siberia', *Survival*, 48/1 (2006), pp. 163–78.

58 Valeria Korchagina, 'China Offers $400 million for Oil Pipeline', *Moscow Times*, 23 March 2006, at <www.themoscowtimes.com/stories/2006/03/23/001_print.html>.

59 Guangcheng Xing, 'China's Foreign Policy Toward Kazakhstan', in Robert Legvold (ed.), *Thinking Strategically: The Major Powers, Kazakhstan and the Central Asian Nexus* (Cambridge: MA: MIT Press, 2003), pp. 120–21; Sutter, as note 29 above, p. 259.

60 Sokov, as note 22 above, p. 227.

61 David Wall, 'Shanghai Cooperation Organisation: Five Candles, Three Evils', *The World Today*, 62/6 (2006), pp. 20–21.

62 Dittmer, as note 30 above, pp. 343–5.

63 Dmitri Trenin, *The End of Eurasia: Russia on the Border between Geopolitics and Globalization* (Washington, DC: Carnegie Endowment for International Peace, 2002), p. 195; Stephen Blank, 'China in Central Asia: The Hegemon in Waiting?', in Ariel Cohen (ed.), *Eurasia in Balance: The US and the Regional Power Shift* (Aldershot: Ashgate, 2005).

64 Dmitri Trenin and Alexei V. Malashenko, with Anatol Lieven, *Russia's Restless Frontier: The Chechnya Factor in Post-Soviet Russia* (Washington, DC: Carnegie Endowment for International Peace, 2004), p. 206.

65 Mevlut Katik, 'NATO Embraces Central Asia and the Caucasus at Istanbul Summit', *Eurasia Insight*, 30 June 2004; Berman, as note 55 above, pp. 59–69.

66 International Institute for Strategic Studies, 'Uzbekistan casts out America', *Strategic Comments*, 11/6 (2005).

8
The US Challenge to Russian Influence in Central Asia and the Caucasus[1]

Roger E. Kanet and Larisa Homarac

Over the past decade and a half, since the implosion of the former Soviet Union, the United States has emerged as an active player in Central Asia and the Caucasus, competing for influence throughout the region with both the Russian Federation and China. The rationale most often provided by US governmental sources for the expansion of US interest and involvement in the area comprises two central, but interrelated, elements. The first is a series of arguments associated with the importance of supporting political stability throughout the region and doing everything possible to strengthen democratic forces. This is based on the assumption that, in the long term, democratic governance will contribute to stability, as well as to the improvement of the overall quality of life for the peoples of the region and ultimately to a more peaceful international environment. A second set of arguments, presented most forcefully since the terror attacks on New York and Washington on 11 September 2001, relates directly to the 'war on terror' proclaimed by President George W. Bush and to the goal of rooting out the influence of the Taliban and al-Qaeda in Afghanistan. Former Soviet basing facilities in Central Asia have been used – with the initial agreement of the Russian government – to contribute to carrying out the attack against terrorist forces.

Yet, these two sets of publicly announced objectives in building new relationships with the countries of Central Asia and the Caucasus are not the sole determinants of US policy. In fact, before the Supreme Court's selection of the current Bush Administration as winner of the presidential election in autumn 2000 and the 9/11 terrorist attacks on the United States the Clinton Administration had already established and expanded security relations with the post-Soviet states within the context of NATO's Partnership for Peace Program. In testimony to Congress on 17 March 1999, then NIS Ambassador Stephan Sestanovich summed up the Clinton administration's policy toward Central Asia as pursuing four interrelated goals: (1) democratization; (2) market-oriented reform; (3) greater integration with western political and military institutions; and (4) responsible security policies on nonproliferation, anti-terrorism, and drug trafficking. Sestanovich noted that securing the sovereignty, independence and territorial integrity of Central Asian states was the cornerstone of US policy.[2] More specifically the United States strove for goals that can be defined as desirable rather than essential. United States' policy in the region emphasized: 'denuclearization assistance to Kazakhstan, low-level military to military aid, both bilateral and multi-lateral, through NATO's Partnership for Peace Program), and various forms of democratization and economic assistance throughout the region'.[3]

In addition to the stated purpose of facilitating the democratic transi-tion in civilian–military relations, the objectives concerned US access to the vast energy resources of the region and, a related factor, the attempt to ensure that Moscow would not be in a position to reassert its control over the region as it reemerged as a great power in world affairs, as other analysts have already demonstrated.[4] Both of these objectives have con-tinued to influence US policy in the Bush Administration and probably will remain central factors in US policy in the future – depending upon the way in which the current power struggle in the region eventually plays out. However, concerns about energy and about Russia's role in the region were not the only important issues from a US perspective. Even before the terrorist attacks of September 2001 other, more specific, objectives dealt with such matters as state failure, armed conflict, major political and eco-nomic unrest in the CASC region that might contribute to criminalization and drug trafficking, as well as potentially leading to sectarian civil wars of the sort that had emerged in Afghanistan after the Soviet withdrawal. If this part of the world were to become a safe haven for drug trafficking and terrorism, it would be impossible to develop the economic infrastruc-ture and, therefore, make use of the region's energy resources. While ter-rorist attacks pose a different kind of threat from those that come from another state – that is, they do not endanger directly US sovereignty – they still can damage greatly US national values and way of life.[5]

The 9/11 terrorist attacks in the United States represented the turning point in US involvement in the Central Asian and Southern Caucasus (CASC) states. For the first time the United States acquired temporary basing facilities in the region in response to a changing security envir-onment, as Uzbekistan, Kyrgyzstan, and Tajikistan became frontline states in operation Enduring Freedom.[6] Although other goals, such as democratization and transformation of the economy, still remained important, anti-terrorism became the core of US policy in the region. In testimony to a newly created Senate Foreign Relations Sub-Committee on Central Asia and the Caucasus in December 2001, Assistant Secretary of State Elizabeth Jones[7] emphasized three sets of long-term interests that the United States would continue to pursue in the region: (1) preventing the spread of terrorism; (2) assisting the Central Asian states with economic and political reform and the establishment of the rule of law, and (3) ensuring the security and transparent development of Caspian energy resources.

Although the United States has not promised security guarantees to the countries of the region, it did sign agreements with Uzbekistan before the deterioration of relations in 2005 that implied that any threat to Uzbekistan would elicit US concern. In addition, significant financial assistance was given to Uzbekistan which received 'an extra $25 million in foreign military financing, $18 million in nonproliferation, anti-terrorism, de-mining and related programs and $40.5 million in Freedom Support Act funds'.[8] Although Russia has extended its support to the United States in their joint fight against terror and facilitated the initial expansion of US military involvement in Central Asia, the Russians are still very concerned about long-term US involvement in its 'backyard'.[9]

In order to understand Russia's attitudes and its decision-making concerning Central Asia and South Caucasus it is vital to understand the Russian relationship to the CIS states in an historical context. As Oliker and Szayna note, Russian rule over the region of Turkistan and Transcaspia dates back to the nineteenth century, with the inner Asian region initially divided into spheres of influence by China and Russia. After the middle of the century, Moscow asserted and then maintained:

> control during both Tsarist and Soviet periods, and CASC states were important sources of resources for the successive empires. Over time, to many in Russia, such imperial possessions became a component of Russia's self-definition, and proof of its importance as a state and as a great power ... Moreover, many ethnic Russians lived in these regions during Soviet times and, despite emigration following the collapse of the Soviet Union, many remain, particularly in Kazakhstan.[10]

Therefore, it is not surprising that even after fifteen years of CIS independence, Russians have a difficult time accepting this fact. Russia's economy depends to a substantial degree on the economic and political stability of the CIS states and also on its relationship with individual states. The Soviet-designed and built network of oil and gas pipelines has enabled

Russia to create an oil monopoly and ensure the dependence of the Central Asian and South Caucasus states on Russia.[11] For this reason Russia has pursued policies aimed at weakening the CASC states and keeping them more dependent on Russia, which includes continuous opposition to any export routes or the construction of new pipelines that avoid Russian territory. Although Russia is not the 'empire' that it once was, the Putin administration has emphasized the fact that Central Asia and the Caucasus are among their vital interests and that they will do everything to maximize their geopolitical position and build upon historical and cultural connections in that region. This is an integral part of a policy committed to reestablishing Russia as a major global power, beginning in what in the 1990s was referred to as the 'near abroad', and expanding Russia's political and security impact, as well as its economic influence, beyond the territories of the former USSR.

In a long year-end interview published in *Nezavisimaia gazeta* on 26 December 2000 president Putin stated: 'relations with CIS countries – not with the CIS organization, but with CIS member countries – have certainly been and will be priority Number One for us'.[12] Although the CIS states and the Russian Federation signed numerous mutual security and economic agreements throughout the 1990s, they did not have a significant impact, since the agreements were never really implemented. Many CIS states still depend heavily on Russia for their security and see it in their own interests to maintain a good relationship. Nevertheless, as Ilan Berman has noted, 'Moscow's reemergence in the post-Soviet space has also been driven by the revival of an old idea: Russia as empire.[13] The revival of Russia as an empire has been much more feasible under the Putin administration, which has significantly weakened the legislative and executive restraints that had limited presidential power.[14] As a result, policy and decision making in the Kremlin have become increasingly unilateral and authoritarian, creating very limited political outlets for dissent or change. This permits Putin to take virtually any approach to foreign and security policy that he and his key advisors determine is most appropriate. As Richard Staar has pointed out:

> key appointments to government posts and periodic institutional purges have enabled Putin to create a vibrant subculture of former KGB officers within the Kremlin bureaucracy. These so-called *silovski* today occupy upward of 60 percent of the key decision-making positions within the Russian government and constitute an important bloc of political support for official presidential policies. Together, these dynamics have given Putin a sweeping mandate to pursue his neo-imperial aspirations.[15]

The Putin government, despite its brutal and oppressive military policy towards Chechnya, has not been able to suppress the Chechen separatist movement. In fact, that movement has contributed to an expansion of Islamic extremism not only in Russia, but also in Central Asia and in the Chinese province of Xinjiang.[16] Considering Russia's large Muslim population in the North Caucasus and the strengthening of radical Islamic political movements such as IMU and Hizb ut-Tahrir, Russia's leaders fear the spread of Islamic radicalism throughout Russia. This new fear of Islamic extremism in Central Asia and the Caucasus was an important driving force for the new Military Doctrine developed at the outset of Putin's presidency and approved by presidential decree on 21 April 2000. The doctrine begins with the following assessment of the political military situation facing Russia: (1) the threat of a large-scale war, including nuclear war, has declined; (2) regional power centres, ethnic and regional extremism, and separatism have been strengthened; (3) local wars and armed conflict have spread; and (4) there has been a proliferation of nuclear and other weapons of mass destruction.[17]

Following from this assessment the main threats to Russian military security were identified as: (1) territorial claims; (2) the refusal by others to recognize Russian interests; (3) armed conflict close to the borders of the Commonwealth of Independent States (CIS); (4) the expansion of foreign blocs and alliances (NATO); (5) the stationing of troops close to CIS borders; and (6) international terrorism.

It is clear from this list of challenges to Russian security interests that the establishment of permanent US military bases in Central Asia and the further expansion of NATO into Russia's own 'backyard' would be perceived in Moscow as threats. The Russian leadership has made clear that, when the war in Afghanistan is over, US troops in Central Asia are expected to withdraw. Russia has persistently attempted to tie CIS states, including those in the Caucasus, to its own policy preferences and has tried to resist the advance of US influence throughout the region by punishing those states economically and militarily that chose to align with the United States or to go their own way. The relationship between Russia and Georgia, for example, was already strained in the 1990s, when Russia assisted Abkhaz separatists against the Georgian government during the 1992 war. Moreover, the Russians accused Georgian President Shevardnadze of permitting Chechen rebels to hide on Georgian territory in the Pankisi Gorge. When claims that the American-owned gas company AES Corporation was selling gas to Georgia at a cheaper price than Russia were revealed, Russia responded by cutting its oil and gas supplies once again to Georgia as a warning that it did not accept US interference. Russia's ability to pressure Georgia through the visa regime and energy supply cutbacks remained strong, and Russian analysts continued to 'chide Tbilisi for wanting it both ways, that is to join NATO by 2005 and still enjoy the advantages of free movement in, and energy from, Russia'[18] In autumn 2006, Russia responded to Georgian complaints and actions targeted at Moscow by declaring full scale economic war on Georgia[19]

Tajikistan and Armenia have been Russia's closest allies and have welcomed Russian troops. Colonel General Sherali Khayrulloev, for example, has noted that Tajikistan considers Russia its main partner for military cooperation:

> The Tajik armed forces were set up thanks to Russia's assistance, military-technical cooperation between our countries is at a very high level today ... Soviet standards are no worse ... we have a similar structure of the armed forces, similar armaments and military hardware. And what is most important, the Russian military educational system is not inferior to any other[20]

Other former republics of the USSR have been less eager than Tajikistan and Armenia to cooperate with Russia. Kyrgyzstan has accepted limited military and political assistance, whereas Kazakhstan has minimized its dependence on Russia by merely maintaining its military and political relationship through the Shanghai Cooperation Organisation.[21] On the contrary, Turkmenistan has remained isolationist, Georgia continues to demand that Russian troops leave its territory, and Azerbaijan and Uzbekistan have refused to accept Russian military assistance. Kazakhstan, Kyrgyzstan, Georgia, Uzbekistan and Azerbaijan turned instead towards the United States and Turkey for political and military support. Certainly Russia will not give up its interests in the CASC region, as its recent security activities throughout the region attest; however, the question still remains whether Russia, as a relatively weak actor on the global stage and a country itself in a profound political and economic transition, is capable of providing stability and control in case of a conflict.

> For Russia to achieve post-imperial stability it would first have to become post-imperial. A state based on the national principle, much like Britain, France, Spain and Austria after their empires crumbled. Russia's central problem, which poses a constant threat to the sovereignty of numerous neighbors, is its inability or unwillingness to forge a distinct national and clearly delimit its territorial reach. In order to become a nation-state, the ruling elite would need to divest itself of any pretensions to

pan-Slavism, Eurasianism, or other messianic, state expanding, and 'great power' ambitions couched as 'national interests' Only such a drastic reorientation would provide Moscow with opportunities for confidence building and cooperation with countries such as Ukraine and Georgia or Poland and Romania.[22]

The United States and Russia share an interest in fighting global terrorism, and the potential exists for a partnership in terms of energy resources. Former Russian Prime Minister. Evgenii Primakov, for example, has accused the United States of ignoring Russian interests and of treating Russia as just another 'post-industrialist' nation by 'diverting all its attention to China'.[23] The US–Russian relationship will determine policy development in Central Asia and Caucasus. The primary concern will be whether the United States and Russia decide to cooperate or compete in the area. Presently, there is evidence that the two countries, after a period of leaning more towards cooperation, are becoming more confrontational.[24] Robert Legvold, a long-time observer of Russian politics, points out three ways to think about US involvement in Central Asia:

> The first would continue past practices, treating these states as fragmented and, while not to be dismissed, of a lower-order priority ... The United States does not have a compelling reasons to become deeply engaged in the region. The second perspective views Eurasia as key to international peace and stability, and Central Asia as critical to the course of developments in Eurasia. The third perspective too regards the post-Soviet space as crucial for the stability of the international order and Central Asia as key to what happens in the post-Soviet space ... however, the second view starts from a preoccupation with control over this space, the third worries more about the loss of control within this space.[25]

It does not matter which perspective one considers most suitable strategically for developing a sound Central Asian policy. One fact remains essential; namely, Russian interests cannot be ignored. Whether the United States will maximize its goals in CASC by assuming a larger role than currently and encouraging a higher level of independence of CASC states from Russia or simply limit its involvement to maintaining a few bases in the region and not doing more than at the present will greatly depend on the nature of the US–Russian relationship. The fate of Central Asia and the Caucasus depends directly on whether US–Russian cooperation will grow and, thus, direct their involvement towards reconstructing the

CASC region where more stable and democratic institutions can thrive and benefit both. If rivalry becomes the dominant focus of decision-making, Central Asia will be a huge burden on the relationship.

Not only are Russia and the United States key players in the CASC region, but China and Iran have increasingly assumed a more important role. The major players have two strategic options. First, as a 'regional concert' they could 'seek to induce a pattern of self-restraint, in the process attempting to rally all to the notion that their mutual interests should take precedence over the individual interests of the major powers'.[26] Another option would be to focus on sources of the instability within the region and to develop a 'stability plan' that resembles the stability pact in the Balkans. Scholars such as James Goldgeier argue that, although there is significant cooperation between Russia and the United States today in the struggle against international terrorism, underlying rivalries will remain, certainly unless and until Russia is truly integrated into Europe. '[O]nly if Russia stays on the democratic path and integrates more fully into Europe will a true partnership between the two countries become a sustained possibility'.[27]

Many saw the G-8 summit in St Petersburg in July 2006 as a test of how fully Russia has integrated in the European-type market economy. 'This summit is a huge test for Russia', the UK's Douglas Alexander said. The UK position echoes EU energy commissioner Andris Piebalgs' view that EU energy security can only come about via the Europeanization of Russia in political and economic terms.[28] Certainly, mutual interests such as the struggle against terrorism, international energy policies and stabilization in the CASC are foundation stones upon which a partnership between the United States and Russia can be built. However, this time it is up to Washington not Moscow to match their rhetoric with actions and to determine how far they intend such a joint venture to go.

Nationalism and unilateralism in US policy

Before continuing our assessment of US policy in Central Asia and the Caucasus and the possibilities for Russian–US cooperation in the region, it is important to place that policy within the overall context of more general US foreign and security policy. As several authors have pointed out, US policy has become increasingly assertive, unilateral and nationalist in orientation since the end of the cold war.[29] Even during the administration of Bill Clinton, who regularly touted the importance of international institutions and collaborative relations with allies, the United States tended to pursue a basically unilateralist approach to foreign and security policy. In fact, the multilateral rhetoric of the Administration tended to hide the reality of growing nationalist and unilateralist views among substantial portions of the political elite, including especially elected members of the House of Representatives and the Senate.

Under George W. Bush, all pretence of a commitment to the use of international law and institutions as a central component of US foreign policy was abandoned. Although, periodically, lip service has been paid to diplomatic and other non-coercive instruments in the search for security, in particular since the invasion of Iraq, the focus of US behaviour has been on the use of military instruments and geopolitical concerns. US interests, as defined in Washington, take precedence over all other matters in influencing US policy. The debates associated with the run-up to the US invasion of Iraq in 2003 are most illustrative of the unilateralist approach to foreign policy.

As we look more specifically at US policy toward the Russian Federation within the general orientation that we have laid out, we note that, regardless of the rhetorical flourishes about shared interests, an important component of US policy ever since the collapse of the USSR has been the containment of Russian influence and the concomitant expansion of a US presence in the peripheral areas of the former Soviet Union. Throughout the 1990s, for example, Washington periodically criticized Moscow for its attempts – often quite blatant attempts – to reestablish control over portions of what was then generally referred to as the 'near abroad'.(30) Although the major thrust of Russian initiatives at that time, and thus of US criticism, generally related to the CIS countries of Europe, concerns were also voiced about Russian efforts to reintegrate Central Asia into a Moscow-centred political system. By the late 1990s, Russian foreign policy under Foreign Minister, later Prime Minister, Evgenii Primakov was explicitly oriented toward establishing such a system, in part to counter what Moscow viewed as US attempts to isolate it and preclude its reemergence as a major regional and even world power.(31)

Although US–Russian relations reached their post-1991 nadir early in the Bush Administration with both countries expelling diplomats, 9/11 resulted in a dramatic shift in policy in both Moscow and Washington. President Putin opted to support Washington in the 'war on terror', including facilitating US access to military basing facilities in Central Asia, as part of a 'bandwagoning' approach to supporting US policy initiatives. While Russia in the late 1990s had attempted to deal with US global dominance by pursuing a Eurasian approach of allying with like-minded states opposed to that dominance, Putin obviously decided that, for the time being at least, joining in support of the United States would provide greater benefits to Moscow. The result was a substantial improvement in the tone of US–Russian relations. However, this did not mean that the United States abandoned its objectives in relations with other CIS countries, in particular in Central Asia. For example, Washington continued to push for options for oil and gas pipelines that would skirt Russia and, therefore, reduce the potential of Russia's gaining further leverage over either Central Asian exporters or the Western purchasers of energy.[32]

US policy in Central Asia

In fact, there is one area in which Russian and US policy interests overlap significantly in Central Asia – namely, in ensuring that the region does not contribute to global terrorism. For Russia the single most important source of security concerns relates to Chechnya and the stimulus that Russian efforts forcibly to reimpose central control have given to the emergence of Islamic fundamentalism in Russia. Attacks in Moscow itself, but more importantly the growing challenge to Russian control of the Russian Caucasus, indicate the relevance of that concern. Directly related to this issue is Moscow's fear of the expanding influence of political Islam across the predominantly Muslim states in Central Asia. This concern has been the centerpiece of Russian policy toward these states and has dictated Russian military and security support for the regimes in power, as John Berryman has documented in his chapter in this volume. As we already noted, the Russian concern is paralleled by American fears that an unstable Central Asia could provide Al-Qaeda and other terrorist organizations the type of environment that Afghanistan once provided. But, as others have shown, even in the general area of the struggle against terrorism Russian and US perceptions and objectives differ appreciably. President Putin has attempted to obtain support for a policy in Chechnya and elsewhere that is far more repressive than one that Washington, and the West more generally, is willing to accept.[33]

It is here that Russian objectives appear to come directly in to conflict with a least two of the stated objectives of the United States. The first, which has become one of the core rhetorical goals of US foreign policy under George W. Bush, relates to the commitment to supporting the establishment of democratic political systems – even if this involves regime change. Until the end of cold war this objective in US policy was tempered by the realities of US global influence and the competition with the USSR. However, as others have demonstrated, an important element of US policy throughout much of its history has been based on the view of the superiority of the US political system and the conviction that the extension of democratic governance would contribute to global peace and security and to the overall interests of the United States.[34] Throughout most of the latter half of the twentieth century, the United States was not in a position to push these objectives forcefully, in large part because of the global security competition with the USSR. However, with the collapse of the Soviet Union, the growing military capacity of the United States, and the terrorist attack of September 2001, external – as well as internal – limitations on US policy initiatives dissolved. In Afghanistan and again in Iraq, the United States has demonstrated its ability and willingness to use its immense military might in order to replace regimes that it finds inimical to its interests – although it has not found a way to establish and consolidate the kind of regime that it prefers and its actions may well prove to be counterproductive in the overall struggle against global terrorist groups.

The central issue here is that US policy objectives call for the establishment of certain types of political regimes, even in Russia and other portions of the former Soviet Union.[35] For Washington, democratic regimes committed to free market economies, as defined by the United States, are viewed as essential for the long-term security interests of the United States and the world. If this means regime change, then the United States – at least a substantial portion of its current political elite – is willing to pursue that objective. As we shall see below, it is precisely on this issue that the United States has come into conflict with at least one of its nominal partners in Central Asia in the fight against terror.

The second area in which Russian and US interests are destined to come into conflict – in Central Asia, as well as elsewhere – concerns the US effort to maintain its global, and regional, dominant position in relationship to the Russian Federation. This is an objective regularly and loudly denied in Washington, although one that ever since the collapse of the former USSR has been widely criticized in Moscow. Evidence of this aspect of US policy can be seen most clearly in the various efforts since the mid-1990s to strengthen the ability of CIS member states to resist Russian domination and, specifically in the case of the Central Asian and Caspian Basis states to reduce Russia's ability to exert influence over the burgeoning oil and gas production of the region by locating pipelines so that they skirt Russian territory.[36]

Prior to 9/11, US security interests and involvement in Central Asia were quite limited, although the US military was already considering its possible role in the region.[37] Immediately after the collapse of the Soviet Union the primary US concern was to eliminate the remnants of nuclear weaponry left behind in Kazakhstan. Moreover, through NATO's Partnership for Peace Program the United States initiated efforts to integrate the new countries of the region into Western political and security organization.[38] Almost immediately, however, as the potential of the region for the production of natural gas and oil became evident, Western companies, including those based in the United States, and the US government began to exhibit a growing interest in the region.[39]

As we have already noted, by summer 2001, shortly before the terrorist attacks in the United States, US relations with Russia had deteriorated significantly – to the point that both sides expelled diplomats and engaged in mutual recrimination against one another. One of the charges of the Russian side related explicitly to the perceived effort of the United States to contain Russian influence within the member countries of the CIS and to extend US involvement throughout the region. In fact, by the late 1990s, the United States had already committed itself to military engagement in Central Asia with the Silk Road Strategy Act that provided security assistance with the stated objective of providing regional stability and support for democratization.[40]

Besides supporting the development of democratization and free market economies, the United States has actively pursued policies that would weaken Russia's influence in Central Asia by attempting to strengthen CIS states' sovereignty and independence. Elizabeth Sherwood-Randall, US Deputy Assistant Secretary of Defense for Russia, Ukraine, and Eurasia during 1994–96, stated that a coherent US Caucasus policy began to emerge in 1994, earlier than had previously been suspected. The Pentagon's main concern was the role of regional armed forces, including Russia's efforts at subverting the new states and intervening militarily in their territories.[41] In response, the United States strengthened its bilateral ties with Turkey and reinforced the development of independent security policy in the new states of Central Asia and the Caucasus. Russia, as well as the political elites of Central Asia, was well aware of the geopolitical interests that also undergirded this policy. Central Asia and the Caucasus have become an important area of direct US–Russian tensions today not just because of economic and political issues, but because the area includes ethnic fractures, separatism and Islamic radicalism that are crucial for future stability, not only of the CIS states but also for future security of the United States' European allies.

NATO Secretary General Javier Solana stated that Europe cannot be fully secure, if the Caucasus remains outside the European security zone.[42] He restated this position later as EU High Representative for Common Foreign and Security Policy during a meeting of foreign ministers of the three Caucasian countries hosted by the EU.[43] Uzbekistan has been a special concern for the international community, since the government of Islam

Karimov staged a crackdown on demonstrators in the eastern city of Andijon on 13 May 2005. Many analysts see the tension in Uzbekistan as a source of further instability in the rest of the region. Yury Federov, a former aide to President Putin, states:

> Internal developments in Uzbekistan are really worrisome; the ruling regime keeps itself in power through repression, and many people in Uzbekistan believe that repression in the final end cannot save the current regime from the crash, which may lead, in turn, to a general destabilization of the situation in the country and in the neighboring region ..., in the event of any trouble, the densely populated Ferghana Valley, which runs through Uzbekistan, Kyrgyzstan, and Tajikistan, could be the 'epicenter' of instability.[44]

If regional conflict were to spread, Russia's handling of the issue would be most important since Russia's still has significant military and economic, as well as ideological and cultural, influence in this region. It also is important to point out that Russian print and television media have a major impact on the local interpretation of events in Central Asia. Various analysts maintain that Western influence is waning and that that of Russia over its former satellite of Uzbekistan is increasing.[45] Thus, Washington and the EU states should use forums such as the G-8 Summit in St Petersburg to attempt to persuade Moscow to pressure the Uzbeks towards moderation.

The G-8 Summit in St Petersburg was expected to be pivotal in terms of Russian policy toward Central Asia and the Caucasus, as well as how the US–Russian relationship will develop in the light of the increasingly harsh criticism of the Kremlin's authoritarian behaviour in Russia and towards CIS states.[46] President Putin has been strongly denounced by Western governments for using Russia's superior political and economic position to support pro-Russian undemocratic regimes in Central Asia and the Caucasus. However, these issues were hardly touched upon at the Summit, given the importance of the Iranian nuclear issue and other crisis situations.

The incompatibilities of US policy in Central Asia

As we noted at the outset of this discussion, US policy in Central Asia cuts across a number of objectives – from supporting the war on terror and encouraging the emergence of democratic regimes in the region to containing, even limiting, Russian influence and ensuring access for the

United States and the West to the energy resources of the area. As has become increasingly evident, these objectives are in many respects incompatible. First, the extensive military support and politico-military cooperation of the United States with countries such as Uzbekistan and Tajikistan in return for US access to military facilities used to support the war in Afghanistan have not contributed to democratization of what are inherently authoritarian regimes. In fact, US pressures on these regimes to open up their political processes and criticism of local responses to democratically oriented political protests have greatly strained relations between the two sides. From the perspective of dominant local political elites, the threat to stability, defined in terms of maintenance of the status quo, cannot be dealt with as Washington expects. More importantly the way in which Washington perceives the democratization process might further destabilize the region and inflame conflicts throughout the region. Stephen Blank has argued that 'The US attempt to induce democratization from above – through reliable clients – and from outside by its own efforts may itself be a factor that generates the ethnic tensions and economic polarization that fuel such conflict'.[47]

President Bush has called President Lukashenko of Belarus 'Europe's last dictator'. The truth is that the democratization process has also been very slow in Central Asia and the Caucasus. In fact, CASC states have slipped further from democracy into rather semi-authoritarian regimes.[48] Kazakhstan's President Nursultan Nazarbayev, who has sent critics to jail or into exile, has been the president since 1989. He recently 'won' re-election to another seven-year term. Turkmenistan's dictator, Saparmurat Niyazov, likes to be called 'Turkmenbashi' or leader of all Turkmens. He came to power in 1985, and his parliament named him president-for-life in 1999. In Azerbaijan, a 2003 presidential election looked more like dynastic succession, when the late Heydar Aliyev was succeeded by his son, Ilham.[49] Robert Legvold points out:

> the United States, instead of treating democracy-building as an abstract, mechanical process and economic reform as a checklist of universally prescribed steps, should focus more on how Central Asian governments can calibrate economic and political policies advancing the process, but in ways preserving peace. This is not for a moment an invitation to look the other way when governments abuse human rights ... or when they corrupt democratic forms for their own ends.[50]

The May 2005 riots and the government crackdown in Uzbekistan raised most clearly the question of the compatibility of US support for authoritarian regimes, supposedly in the name of the global war on terror, and the latters' rhetorical commitment to supporting human rights and democratization. On the other side, it raised in the minds of authoritarian leaderships in Central Asia the question of the potential costs of a long-term relationship with the United States.[51] The military and economic support that the United States has provided are simply not sufficient, in the view of the current authoritarian leadership, to warrant what is viewed as unwanted US advice and interference in local affairs.[52]

This entire set of issues feeds directly into another aspect of US policy – the effort to contain the reemergence of Russian influence in the region and to prevent Russia from benefiting significantly, either politically or economically, from the vast energy resources of the region. As Douglas Blum noted almost a decade ago:

> It is difficult to escape the conclusion that America's Caspian policy is predicted on the illusion of a 'unipolar moment' where Washington alone can orchestrate, and indefinitely maintain a congenial alignment of international forces. The implication is that it is possible to fashion relations in the Caspian region so as to constrain Russian decision-making with relatively little Russian resistance.[53]

Ever since President Putin facilitated the United States gaining formal access to Central Asian bases after 9/11, the Russians have made most clear that they view the US presence as temporary and tied directly to the war in Afghanistan against the Taliban and al-Qaeda. That statement has been repeated over and over by high-level Russian officials and was reinforced by the collective position taken by the Shanghai Cooperation Organization at its 5 July 2005 meeting, which calls for the host governments to establish the conditions for the withdrawal of US troops.[54] From the perspective of Moscow, developments in the CIS in the recent past have been quite disconcerting. Georgia under President Mikhail Saakashvili has shifted its policy orientation toward the West and has, with the public support given by President Bush, called upon Moscow to withdraw its remaining troops from Georgian territory.[55] The current Ukraine government, which came to power only after massive demonstrations against fraudulent elections resulted in a new election, has moved even more energetically than Georgia to strengthen its ties with the West – although its internal political problems have weakened its ability to act effectively. In both of these cases the result has been a lessening of Russia's role and influence in former Soviet space. Moscow is not about to accept a similar situation in Central Asia.

What we now observe in Central Asia is a coincidence of the interests of several of the indigenous states, along with those of Russia and China, all of which are concerned for not necessarily the same reasons about the long-term implications of a continued US presence. The insecurity of local political elites about stability and their own tenure in office provides Moscow – and Beijing, another important member of the Shanghai Cooperation Organization that shares Russia's concerns about the US presence – the opportunity to strengthen their ties with the countries of the region. For Beijing Central Asian gas and oil represent a partial solution, at least, to their long-term need for energy to fuel their economic growth.[56]

It is difficult to imagine that the United States will long succeed in Central Asia in pursuing the policies that it has initiated. Moreover, there is a danger that US policy towards Central Asia may prove counter-productive: 'to defend the peace against terrorism, the United States has ended up cooperating with the very tyrants responsible for the repression that increases support for home-grown anti-government and trans-national movements'[57] The US concentration on combating terrorism without addressing many other potential sources of instability in the region, such as conflicts over water resources, border disputes, refugee issues, drug trafficking and human rights abuses, could backfire, thus endangering US troops and undermining US credibility. It is essential that the United States acknowledge the lack of cooperation between individual CIS states and recognizes potential problems and frictions between neighbouring states which could spill over and create unrest in the whole region. Legvold ascribes this distrust among the individual states to the long-time Soviet suppression and political isolation of the CASC region as part of Russian policy in the 'near abroad': 'The remnants of the Soviet Union hold the post-Soviet space together, but like a thicket of briar trapping small animals, in ways that leave the weaker states wary of their neighbors, particularly Russia, and the Russians weary of their neighbors and ungenerous toward them'[58]

As the Central Asian states are picking up the pieces from the ruins of the former Soviet Union and trying to modernize their economic and political systems, new orders, new stakes and new political patterns are being established. Although CIS states are sovereign, they are still weak states. After the disintegration of the former USSR most of them lost their social safety net, and not only have their economies worsened, but also the educational and health systems in the CASC are at abysmal levels. 'Besides this basic measure of economic dislocation, evidence of its human cost accumulated, the kind that implies the risk of social and political unrest.'[59]

As the young Central Asian states attempt to define themselves as nations, new ties are being built with the states of Eurasia's rim – including China, of course, but also India, Pakistan and Iran. Considering the growing power of China and its need for energy to fuel its economic growth, as well as the increasingly important role of Iran as an actor in the Middle East, the stakes for the United States in Central Asia are much higher than commonly recognized. Bearing in mind the ethnic diversity of the region makes it even more difficult for the United States to achieve its agenda in the CASC by focusing on one issue – that is, combating terrorism.

The region is far too important for Russia and China, and the local political elites are increasingly aware that some of their core interests will be much better served by re-establishing a closer relationship with Moscow,[60] balanced now by strengthening economic ties with China. Despite its overall superior strength on the global stage, the United States simply does not have the ability locally to exert the economic or political or effective military clout needed to outbid Moscow and Beijing. Probably more important still is the fact that the security interests of the elites of the region are not likely to be served, in their view, by a tightening of the relationship with Washington. Local leaders see Moscow and Beijing as their main future trading partners and, considering the policies that the United States has so far pursued (e.g., ignoring repressive domestic government policies such as in Uzbekistan), are increasingly distrustful of Washington's *modus operandi* in Central Asia. Uzbekistan so far has benefited the most from the US military and economic assistance and neighbouring countries, Kazakhstan, Kyrgyzstan and Tajikistan, fear the emergence of Uzbekistan as a possible hegemon in the region. 'Although Uzbekistan's neighbors, often dramatically exaggerate Uzbekistan's capacities', Martha Brill Olcott notes, 'it remains true that weak but militarized societies unquestionably make bad neighbors and civil unrest in Uzbekistan might prove far more destabilizing in the long run to Kazakhstan, Kyrgyzstan, and Tajikistan than any deliberate policy that Tashkent might pursue'.[61] In case of a conflict Kyrgyzstan, Kazakhstan, and Tajikistan are more likely to trust Russia as a reliable partner than the United States and, therefore, they have continued to remain active members, for example, of collective security agreements that include Russia.

While the US strategic position is still strong, it is difficult to predict whether its current role in the region will remain, especially when one takes into account the difficult challenges that the United States continues to face in Afghanistan and Iraq. Directly relevant to this issue is Legvold's assessment that 'The failure of the peace process in the Middle East, as well as the growth of anti-Americanism in the Muslim parts of the world as a result of the US response to terrorism, make the United States more dependent on partnership with Russia and other countries in regions where the United States now has expanding interest, such as Central Asia'.[62]

The tragedy of 11 September did not just bring dramatic change in American foreign policy, but it also opened an opportunity for building new ties and forms of cooperation. It is important that post-Soviet space does not become isolated as a result of the competition between the major powers. Historically, Central Asia has been the bridge between Asia and Europe, and it is in the major powers' interests to help to reconstruct the still fragile and weak countries in Central Asia and the Caucasus into stable and peaceful societies. This daunting task will be only possible by strengthening US–European–Russian ties, not by a continuation of efforts to maintain spheres of influence.

Notes

1 An earlier, but similar, version of this chapter was published as 'O Desafio dos Estados Unidos à Influencia Russa na Ásia Central e no Cáucaso', [The U.S. Challenge to Russian Influence in Central Asia and the Caucasus], *Relações Internacionais* (Lisbon), no 12 (December 2006), pp. 29–48, with the agreement that it would appear here in English.
2 Cited in Frank T. Tsongas, 'Central Asia Official Outlines US Policy', *RFE/RL Newsline,* 14 March 1999, at <http://www.rferl.org/>.
3 Olga Oliker and Thomas Szayna (eds), *Faultlines of Conflict in Central Asia and the South Caucasus: Implications for the U.S. Army* (Santa Monica, CA: RAND Corporation, 2003), pp. 220–21.
4 For discussions of US policy, see Oliker and Szayna, ibid.; Celeste A. Wallander, 'U.S. Policy toward Russia and Eurasia in the 1990s', in Brian Loveman (ed.), *Strategy for Empire: U.S. Regional Security Policy in the Post-Cold War Era* (Lanham, MD: SR Books, 2004), pp. 155–72; Rajan Menon, ' "Greater Central Asia", Russia and the West: Challenges and Opportunities for Cooperation', in Alexander J. Moyl, Blair A. Ruble and Lilia Shevtsova (eds), *Russia's Engagement with the West: Transformation and Integration in the Twenty-First Century* (Armonk, NY: M.E. Sharpe, 2005), pp. 209–22; and Lena Jonson and Saadat Olimova, 'The USA and Central Asia: Responses to U.S. Engagement in Tajikistan', unpublished paper prepared for presentation at the World International Studies Committee First Global International Studies Conference, Istanbul, 24–27 Aug. 2005. See, also, the perceptive analysis of Russian policy in the region by John Berryman in the Chapter 7 of this volume.
5 Oliker and Szayna, as note 2 above, p. 223.
6 Elizabeth Wishnick, *Growing U.S. Security Interests in Central Asia*, Strategic Studies Institute of the U.S. Army War College, unpublished manuscript, Oct. 2002, at <https://www.strategicstudiesinstitute.army.mil/pubs/display.cfm?pubID=110>, p. 1.

7   Elizabeth Jones, 'U.S.-Central Asian Cooperatin', Testimony to the Sub-committee on Central Asia and the Caucasus, Foreign Relations Committee, US Senate, 13 Dec. 2001, p. 9.

8   Wishnick, as note 6 above, p. 7.

9   On Russia's initial support for US military presence in Central Asia after 9/11, see Lena Jonson, 'Understanding Russia's Foreign Policy Change: The Cases of Central Asia and Iraq', in Jakob Hedenskog *et al.* (eds), *Russia as a Great Power: Dimensions of Security Under Putin*, (London and New York: Routledge, 2005), pp. 182–200.

10 Oliker and Szayna, as note 2 above, p. 191.

11 Igor Torbakov speaks of Russia's efforts to establish a 'liberal empire' through-out former Soviet space by assuring control over energy extraction and distri-bution. Igor Torbakov, 'Russian policymakers air notion of 'liberal empire' in Caucasus, Central Asia', *Eurasia Insight*, 27 Oct. 2003.

12 Cited in J.L. Black, *Vladimir Putin and the New World Order: Looking East, Looking West?* (Lanham, MD: Rowman & Littlefield, 2004), p. 289.

13 Ilan Berman, 'The New Battleground: Central Asia and the Caucasus', *Washington Quarterly*, 28/1 (2004–05).

14 John Berryman, in his chapter in this volume, discusses in detail recent security collaboration between Russia and the countries of Central Asia.

15 Richard F. Staar, 'Decision Making in Russia', *Mediterranean Quarterly*, 13/2 (2002), pp. 9–26.

16 For an excellent assessment of Russian policy in Chcchnya and its relation-ship to Islamic fundamentalism across Euraisa, see Matthew Evangelista, *The Chechen Wars: Will Russia Go the Way of the Soviet Union?* (Washington, DC: Brookings Institution Press, 2002). On the expansion of the Islamist chal-lenge to Russin rule, see John B. Dunlop and Rajan Menon, 'Chaos in the North Caucasus and Russia's Future', *Survival*, 48/2, (2006), pp. 97–114.

17 *The Military Doctrine of the Russian Federation*. Signed by President Vladimir Putin, 21 April 2000. Available in English at <http://www.freerepublic.com/forum/a394aa0466bfe.htm>.

18 Black, as note 12 above, p. 239; see, also, Molly Corso, 'Georgian-Russian Relations Continue to Deteriorate', *Power and Interest News Report*, 7 Dec. 2005, at <http://www.pinr.com>.

19 Steven Lee Myers, 'Russia Deports Georgians and Increases Pressures on Businesses and Students', *New York Times*, 7 Oct. 2006 at <http://www.nytimes.com/2006/10/07/world/europe/07moscow.html>; "The Mouse that Roared", *The Economist*, 7 Oct. 2006, p. 62.

20 'Tajik Defense Minister says Cooperation with Russia a Priority', Interfax, 29 March 2006. *RFE'RL Newsline*, 10/5a, 30 March, at <http://www.rferl.org/>.

21 Oliker and Szayna, as note 2 above.

22 'Think tanks says Russia needs clear Central Asian strategy', 'Interfax' 3 March 2006. *RFE/RL Newsline*, 10/40, at <http://www.rferl.org/>.

23 Yevgeny Primakov, 'Russia and the U.S. in Need of Trust and Cooperation', *Johnsons's Russia List*, 30 March 2006, at <http://www.cdi.org/russia/johnson/>.

24 Vice-President Richard Cheney's criticisms of Russia at meetings in Lithuania in early May 2006 and the ensuing Russian–US exchange of verbal attacks is evidence of this shift. John O'Neill, 'Cheney Criticizes Russia on Human Rights',

New York Times, 4 May 2006, at <http://www.nytimes.com/2006/05/04/ world/europe/04cnd-cheney.html?ex=1304395200&en=6f0569a075de8218&ei= 5088&partner=rssnyt&emc=rss>.

25 Robert Legvold, 'U.S. Policy Toward Kazakhstan' in Robert Legvold (ed.), *Thinking Strategically: The Major Powers, Kazakhstan, and the Central Asian Nexus* (Cambridge, MA: MIT Press, 2003), p. 100.

26 Ibid., p. 105

27 James M. Goldgeier, 'Prospects for U.S.-Russian Cooperation', in Andrew C. Kuchins (ed.), *Russia after the Fall* (Washington, DC: Carnegie Endowment for International Peace, 2002), p. 291.

28 Cited in Andrew Rettman, 'Russia's G8 Summit will Flop, Former Putin Aide Predicts', *EUobserver*, 31 March 2006, at <http://euobserver.com/>.

29 Andrew J. Bacevich, *American Empire: The Realities and Consequences of U.S. Diplomacy* (Cambridge, MA: Harvard University Press, 2002); Andrew J. Bacevich, *The New American Militarism: How Americans are Seduced by War* (New York: Oxford University Press, 2005); Chalmers Johnson, *The Sorrows of Empire: Militarism, Secrecy and the End of the Republic* (New York: Metropolitan Books, 2004); Roger E. Kanet, 'The Bush Revolution in U.S. Security Policy', in Roger E. Kanet (ed.), *The New Security Environment: The Impact on Russia, Central and Eastern Europe* (Aldershot: Ashgate, 2005), pp. 11–29; and Anatol Lieven, *America Right or Wrong: An Anatomy of American Nationalism* (Oxford: Oxford University Press, 2004).

30 Alexander V. Kozhemiakin and Roger E. Kanet, 'Russia as a Regional Peacekeeper', in Roger E. Kanet (ed.), *Resolving Regional Conflicts* (Champaign, IL: University of Illinois Press, 1998), pp. 225–39; and Gabriela Marin Thornton and Roger E. Kanet, 'The Russian Federation and the Commonwealth of Independent States', in Roger E. Kanet (ed.), *The New Security Environment: The Impact on Russia, Central and Eastern Europe* (Aldershot: Ashgate, 2005), pp. 165–82.

31 Roger E. Kanet, 'Zwischen Konsens und Konfrontation: Rußland und die Vereinigten Staaten', *Osteuropa*, 51/4–5 (2001), pp. 509–21.

32 The first of these, the Baku–Ceyhan oil pipeline, was opened in May 2005. It begins in Azerbaijan and brings oil from the Caspian area via Georgia to the Mediterranean coast of Turkey. At the same time, however, a gas pipeline from Russia to Turkey under the Black Sea has also begun operating. See Aida Sultanova, 'Pipelines to Speed Flow of Caspian Oil to West', AP Report, *Miami Herald*, 25 May 2005, p. 18A; Erin E. Arvedlund, 'Pipeline Done, Oil from Azerbaijan Begins Flowing to Turkey', *New York Times*, 26 May 2005, p. C6; 'Oil Over Troubled Waters', *The Economist*, 28 May 2005, p. 54; and Charles E. Ziegler, 'Energy in the Caspian Basin and Central Asia', in Roger E. Kanet (ed.), *The New Security Environment: The Impact on Russia, Central and Eastern Europe* (Aldershot: Ashgate, 2005) pp. 210–18.

33 Andrew S. Weiss, 'Russia: The Accidental Alliance', in Daniel Benjamin (ed.), *America and the World in the Age of Terror: A New Landscape in International Relations* (Washington, DC: CSIS Press, 2005), pp. 125–72; and Evangelista, as note 16 above.

34 See Bacevich, The New American Militarism as note 29 above; John Lewis Gaddis, *Surprise, Security, and the American Experience* (Cambridge, MA: Harvard University Press, 2004); Lieven, as note 29 above and Christopher Layne,

The Peace of Illusions: American Grand Strategy from 1940 to the Present (Ithaca, NY: Cornell University Press, 2006).

35   For example, while taking part in a conference of Black Sea and Baltic leaders concerning democracy in early May 2006, US Vice-President Dick Cheney roundly condemned the Russian government for its human rights abuses and for attempting to coerce its neighbouring states. He called upon President Putin and the Russians to return a policy committed to establishing a liberal democracy in Russia. See O'Neill, as note 24 above.

36   Robert Ebel and Rajan Menon (eds.), *Energy and Conflict in Central Asia and the Caucasus* (Lanham, MD and New York: Rowman & Littlefield, 2000); and Ziegler, as note 32 above.

37   Richard Sokolsky and Tanya Charlick-Paley, *NATO and Caspian Security: A Mission Too Far?* (Santa Monica, CA: RAND Corporation, 1999).

38   Wishnick, as note 6 above.

39   Ottar Skagan, *Caspian Gas* (London: Royal Institute of International Affairs, 1997); Ebel and Menon, as note 36 above.

40   Wishnick, as note 6 above.

41   See Black, as note 12 above.

42   Cited in Blank, see note 47 below.

43   Ahto Lobjakas, 'EU: South Caucasus Countries Discuss "Frozen Conflicts", Closer Ties', *Radio Free Europe/Radio Liberty,* 13 Dec. 2005, at <http://www.rferl.org/featuresarticle/2005/12/f77a9a29-7360-4a75-9e4a-20f41e42badb.html>.

44   Cited in Rettman, as note 28 above; see, also, Martha Brill Olcott, *Central Asia's Second Chance* (Washington, DC: Carnegie Endowment for International Peace, 2005).

45   Ibid., pp. 200–05.

46   O'Neill, as note 24 above.

47   Stephen J. Blank, 'U.S. Military Engagement with Transcaucasia and Central Asia', unpublished manuscript (June 2000). Available online at the website of the Strategic Studies Institute of the US Army War College, p. 9.

48   Marina Ottaway provides a perceptive study of the rise of semi-authoritarian regimes, including the case of Azerbaijan. Marina Ottaway, *Democracy Challenged: The Rise of Semi-Authoritarianism* (Washington, DC: Carnegie Endowment for International Peace, 2003).

49   For an excellent recent assessment of political developments in the countries of Central Asia see Olcott, as note 44 above.

50   Legvold, as note 58 below, p. 78.

51   Rouben Azizian, *Central Asia and the United States 2004–2005: Moving beyond Counter-Terrorism?* (Honolulu: Asia-Pacific Center for Security Studies, 2005).

52   For a perceptive background assessment, see Institute for War and Peace Reporting, 'Will US Policy Backfire in Central Asia?', *Reporting Central Asia,* 273 30 March 2004, at <http://www.iwpr.net/indes.pl?arhive/rca/rac_100403_273_1_eng.txt>.

53   Douglas Blum, *Sustainable Development and the New Oil Boom: Comparative and Competitive Outcomes in the Caspian Sea Program on New Approaches to Russian Security,* Working Papers Series No. 4 (Cambridge, MA: Davis Center for Russian Studies, Harvard University, 1997), p. 21.

54   Both Moscow and Beijing, the most important members of the organisation, have become increasing concerned that the United States views its presence

in Central as the beginning of a long-term policy that has important geopoliti-cal implications that extended far beyond the current war on terror. See Oliver Lee, 'Geopolitics in Central Asia Today', ZAMAN Online, Istanbul, 7 July 2005, at <http://www.zaman.com?bl=20050707&hn=21424> (accessed 20 July 2005); Vladimir Socor, 'U.S. Military Presence at Risk in Central Asia', *Eurasia Daily Monitor*, 2/132, 8 July 2005, at <http://www.jamestown.org/ edm/>, Daniel Kimmage, 'Central Asia: CSO-Shoring up the Post-Soviet Status Quo', *RFE/RL Central Asia Report*, 5/26, 14 July 2005.

55 Elisabeth Bumiller, 'Bush Encourages Georgia with a Warning to Russia' *New York Times*, 11 May 2005, p. A3.

56 See Ziegler, as note 32 above; and Kimmage, as note 54 above.

57 Wishnick, as note 6 above.

58 Robert Legvold, 'Great Power Stakes in Central Asia', in Robert Legvold (ed.) *Thinking Strategically: The Major Powers, Kazakhstan, and the Central Asian Nexus* (Cambridge, MA: MIT Press, 2003), p. 4.

59 Ibid., p. 10; Olcott, as note 44 above, pp. 83–123.

60 See the perceptive discussion of Russian economic policy and its role in strengthening the dependence of former Soviet republics, including those of Central Asia, on Moscow by Bertil Nygren in his chapter in this volume.

61 Martha Brill Olcott, 'State Building and Security Threats in Central Asia', in Andrew C. Kuchins (ed.), *Russia after the Fall* (Washington, DC: Carnegie Endowment for International Peace, 2002), p. 231.

62 Legvold, as note 25 above, p. 201.

9
Russia, Iran and the Nuclear Question: The Putin Record

Robert O. Freedman

> The construction of the Bushehr nuclear power station is nearing completion, and we are ready to continue collaboration with Iran in the sphere of nuclear power engineering, taking into consideration our international nonproliferation obligations, and to look for mutually acceptable political solutions in this area.
>
> Vladimir Putin, in a message to the new
> Iranian President, Mahmud Ahmadinezhad[1]

Introduction

Of all the countries of the Middle East Russia's closest relationship is with the Islamic Republic of Iran. While Russia's sale of the Bushehr nuclear power station is central to Iranian–Russian relations, several other facets of the relationship are of almost equal importance. These include trade, which by 2005 reached the level of $2 billion per year;[2] Russian arms sales to Iran, which include jet fighters and submarines; and diplomatic cooperation in the Caucasus and Central Asia. Both countries also have sought to prevent US hegemony in the world. There are, however, several areas of conflict in the relationship, the most important of which is the legal status of the Caspian Sea. However, by February 2005, when Moscow and Iran signed an agreement for the supply of Russian uranium to the Bushehr reactor, the two countries can be said to have reached the level of a tactical, if not yet a strategic, alliance.

After discussing Putin's domestic and foreign policies and briefly reviewing Russian–Iranian relations in the Yeltsin era, this essay will analyse Putin's policy toward Iran, especially in regard to the nuclear issue, and place it within the broader context of Russia's commitment to re-establishing itself as a major actor in world affairs.

Putin's domestic and foreign policies

One of the most striking aspects of the Putin presidency has been his ability to bring the quasi-independent players in Russian domestic and foreign policy of the Yeltsin era under much tighter centralized control. Thus, Putin has all but eliminated the political influence of oligarchs Boris Berezovsky, Vladimir Gusinsky and Mikhail Khodorkovsky and taken over their media outlets. He has replaced Yevgeny Adamov, head of the Ministry of Atomic Energy, who had a habit of trying to make nuclear deals with Iran not approved by the Kremlin.[3]

Other important political figures whom Putin has replaced include the director of the powerful gas monopoly, Gazprom, heavily involved in Turkey and Central Asia. The Defence Ministry; had its leader, Defence Minister Igor Sergeev, replaced by the Secretary of the National Security Council, Sergei Ivanov. Two other holdovers from the Yeltsin era were also removed – Prime Minister Mikhail Khazyanov and Foreign Minister Igor Ivanov. Putin also changed interior ministers, set up plenipotentiaries to oversee Russia's 89 regions, and consolidated Russia's arms sales agencies, in an effort to gain greater control over a major source of foreign exchange. Putin also emphasized improving Russia's economy, not only through the sale of arms, oil and natural gas, but also by selling high tech goods such as nuclear reactors and by expanding Russia's business ties abroad. Indeed, business interests have played an increasingly significant role in Putin's foreign policy.

Making Putin's task easier was the support he received from the Duma, especially from his Edinstvo (Unity) party – now the enlarged United Russia Party – in contrast to the hostile relations Yeltsin had with the Duma from 1993 until his resignation as President in December 1999. Indeed, the Duma elections of December 2003 greatly increased Putin's support, weakening both the communist and liberal parties, which were his main opponents, and he scored an overwhelming victory in the 2004 presidential elections.

Overall, Putin's central foreign policy aim has been to strengthen the Russian economy in the hope that, in the not too distant future, Russia might regain its status as a great power. In the interim he has sought to create an 'arc of stability' on Russia's frontiers, so that economic development can proceed as rapidly as possible. This was one of the reasons Putin embraced an improved relationship with Turkey and ended Russian opposition to the Baku–Ceyhan pipeline. In theory at least, Putin's goal would appear to require a policy of increased cooperation with the economically advanced West, led by the United States.

At the same time, mindful of voices in the Duma, as well as those in the security apparatus and the Russian foreign ministry unhappy at Moscow's appearing to play 'second fiddle' to the United States after 9/11, Putin has on occasion asserted an independent position for Russia, as Moscow's behaviour during the recent war in Iraq and the more assertive Russian policy in 2005 indicated. Increasingly Russian foreign policy appears to be seeking to create the 'multipolar world' advocated by former Russian Foreign Minister and Prime Minister Yevgeny Primakov, who is now a Putin adviser. The tension between these two alternative thrusts of Russian foreign policy, cooperating with the United States but also competing with it, clearly impacts the Russian–Iranian relationship.

This tension became increasingly evident following a series of reversals encountered by Putin in 2004. Following the replacement of Edouard Shevardnadze as President of Georgia in December 2003 by the much more pro-Western Mikhail Saakashivili, Putin suffered an embarrassing failure in Ukraine in November and December 2004 when, following the mass demonstrations of the 'Orange Revolution', the pro-Western Viktor Yushchenko defeated the pro-Russian candidate Victor Yanukovich in a presidential re-election that Putin had publicly opposed. Making matters worse for Putin was the debacle at Beslan in September 2004 when a Chechen rebel attack on a school led to the loss of more than 300 Russian lives following a bungled rescue mission. While Putin sought to capitalize on the incident by tightening control over Russia's governors (he would now appoint them) and political parties, as well as by blaming outside powers for wanting to dismantle Russia, the Beslan incident underlined Putin's major failure – his inability to bring the Chechen rebellion under control. Domestically, Putin also had problems in 2005. His efforts to transform 'payments in kind' to cash payments stirred up opposition from Russian pensioners, while his heavy-handed prosecution of oligarch Mikhail Khodorkovsky led to renewed capital flight from Russia and a chilling of the atmosphere for foreign investment.

As we shall see, these events put Putin on the defensive and challenged the image he wanted of a strong leader of a strong state and were to play a major role in Putin's decision to go ahead with the supply of nuclear fuel to the Bushehr reactor in February 2005, despite serious American objections.

Russian and Iran: the Yeltsin legacy

The rapid development of Russian–Iranian relations under Yeltsin had its origins in the latter part of the Gorbachev era. After alternately supporting first Iran and then Iraq during the Iran–Iraq war, by the end of the war Gorbachev had clearly tilted toward Iran.[4] The relationship between the two countries was solidified in June 1989 with Hashemi Rafsanjani's visit to Moscow, where a number of major agreements, including one on military cooperation, were signed. The military agreement permitted Iran to purchase highly sophisticated military aircraft from Moscow including MIG-29s and SU-24s to replace losses incurred during the eight-year war with Iraq. Iran's military dependence on Moscow grew as a result of the 1990–91 Gulf war. Not only did the United States become the dominant military power in the Gulf, with defence agreements with a number of GCC states, but also Saudi Arabia, Iran's most important Islamic challenger, acquired massive amounts of US weaponry. Given Iran's need for sophisticated arms, the pragmatic Iranian leader, Hashemi Rafsanjani, was careful not to alienate either the Soviet Union or Russia. Thus, when Azerbaijan declared its independence from the Soviet Union in November 1991, Iran, unlike Turkey, did not recognize its independence until after the USSR collapsed. Similarly, despite occasional rhetoric from Iranian officials, Rafsanjani ensured that Iran kept a relatively low profile in Azerbaijan and the newly independent states of Central Asia, emphasizing cultural and economic ties rather than Islam as the centrepiece of their relations. The Russian leadership basically saw Iran as acting very responsibly in Central Asia and Transcaucasia, and this was one of the factors which encouraged it to continue supplying Iran with modern weaponry – including submarines – despite strong protests from the United States.

Indeed, the Russian supply of weapons to Iran became an issue of increasing concern to the United States, and in 1995, US Vice-President Al Gore and Russian Prime Minister Viktor Chernomydin signed an agreement under which Moscow would cease supplying Iran with weapons, once existing contracts were fulfilled in the year 1999.[5] At the same time Yeltsin promised American President Bill Clinton that Russia, which had agreed to sell Iran an atomic reactor, would not build a nuclear centrifuge plant for Iran.

During Kozyrev's tenure as Russia's Foreign Minister (1991–95), Russian–Iranian relations developed rapidly. In addition to the economic gains from sales of arms and nuclear reactors for Russia, Yeltsin could use the close Russian–Iranian relationship to demonstrate to the nationalists in his Duma that he was independent of the United States, much as he could in the case of Russian–Iraqi relations. Oil and natural gas development was a third important Russian interest in Iran. Again, despite US objections, in 1997, GASPROM, along with the French company Total, signed a major agreement with Iran to develop the South Pars gas field. Finally, a greatly weakened Russia had found Iran a useful ally in dealing with several very sensitive Middle Eastern, Caucasian, Transcaucasian, and Central and Southwest Asian political hotspots. During the Yeltsin era, these included Chechnya, where Iran kept a very low profile in the first Chechen war, despite the use of Islamic themes by the Chechen rebels in their conflict with Russia; Tajikistan, where Iran helped Russia achieve a political settlement, albeit a shaky settlement; Afghanistan, where both Russia and Iran stood together against Taliban efforts to seize control over the entire country; and Azerbaijan, which neither Iran, with a size-able Azeri population of its own, nor Russia under Yeltsin wished to see emerge as a significant economic and military power. In addition, as NATO expanded eastward, many Russian nationalists called for a closer Russian–Iranian relationship as a counterbalance, especially as Turkey was seen by some Russians as closely cooperating with its NATO allies, in expanding its influence in both Transcaucasia and Central Asia.[6] Indeed an article in the newspaper *Segodnia* in late May 1995 noted:

Cooperation with Iran is more than just a question of money and orders for the Russian atomic industry. Today a hostile Tehran could cause a great deal of unpleasantness for Russia in the North Caucasus and in Tajikistan if it were really to set its mind to supporting the Muslim insurgents with weapons, money and volunteers. On the other hand, a friendly Iran could become an important strategic ally in the future.

NATO's expansion eastward is making Russia look around hurriedly for at least some kind of strategic allies. In this situation the anti-Western and anti-American regime in Iran would be a natural and very important partner.[7]

These interests and policies were already in place when Yevgeny Primakov became Foreign Minister in January 1996, and he sought to further deepen the relationship. Nonetheless, he also had to cope with increasing frictions in Russian–Iranian relations. First, in December 1996, then Russian Defence Minister Igor Rodionov – while Primakov was in Tehran – described Iran as a possible military threat to Russia, given Russia's weakened position.[8] Second, because of Iran's economic problems, it did not have enough hard currency to pay for the weapons and industrial equipment it wanted to import from Russia. Indeed, despite predictions of several billions of dollars in trade, Russian–Iranian trade was only $415 million in 1996, less than Russia's trade with Israel.[9] Third, Russian supplies of missile technology to Iran caused increasing conflict with the United States (and Israel). Although Russia in late 1997 very publicly expelled an Iranian diplomat for trying to smuggle missile technology, and in January 1998 promised to stop selling 'dual use' equipment to Tehran, by 1999 the issue had become a serious irritant in Russian–American relations, with particularly sharp criticism of Moscow coming from the US Congress.[10]Fourth, since 1995, Iran has increasingly thrust itself forward as an alternative export route for Central Asian oil and natural gas, in direct conflict with the efforts of the hardliners in the Russian government to control these oil and gas exports, as a means of limiting the freedom of action of the Central Asian states. While Iran, which remained dependent on Russian exports of military equipment, sought to defuse this problem by trying to organize tripartite projects with Russia and the Central Asian states, Iranian availability as an alternate export route was a concern for Moscow, one that threatened to become even more severe if there were a rapprochement between the United States and Iran.[11]Finally, the two countries disputed the division of the Caspian Sea. Iran, with little oil of its own in its Caspian coastal shelf, had opposed the Russian–Kazakh agreement of July 1998, which partially divided the Caspian Sea, and continued to call for an equal sharing of the sea's resources, with Iran getting a 20 per cent share, rather than the 12–13 per cent its length of coastline would have qualified it for.[12]

The election of Mohamed Khatami as Iran's President in May 1997 gave rise to the possibility of a rapprochement with the United States. Khatami, following his election, began to promote a policy of domestic reform and liberalization, along with a policy of rapprochement with the Arab world, Europe and the United States. Unfortunately for Khatami and the possibility of an improvement in US–Iranian relations, a conservative counterattack in the summer of 1998 forced an end to his efforts toward a rapprochement. Meanwhile, during the summer of 1998 a successful Iranian missile test strengthened the position of those in the United States who called for the sanctioning of Russian companies that provided Iran with missile help. With the collapse of the Russian economy in August 1998, Russia's government was hard put to resist the US pressure and indeed promised it would do its utmost to prevent the transmission of missile technology to Iran. A further complication to the US–Russian relationship came with what proved to be a temporary elevation of Primakov to the position of Russian Prime Minister in September 1998, following the economic crisis. Primakov, and the communist forces in the Duma who supported him, wanted a tougher line toward the United States, and their advocacy became more shrill following the US bombing of Iraq in December 1998 and its bombing of Serbia in spring 1999.

At the same time, Yevgeny Adamov, then head of Russia's Atomic Energy Ministry, continued to press for the sale of additional nuclear reactors to

Iran, something the United States strongly opposed. In November 1998, Adamov visited Tehran and, to spur the lagging Bushehr nuclear reactor construction project, signed an agreement which transformed Bushehr into a turnkey project in which Russian technicians would build the project whose target date for completion was set for May 2003.[13] However, Russian–Iranian relations were complicated by the Kosovo crisis, where Iran championed the Albanian Kosovars and Russia the Serbs, and even more by Russia's decision to invade Chechnya in August 1999, leading to the killing of numerous Muslim Chechens, something which Iran, as current head of the Islamic Conference, had to protest, albeit mildly.

Putin and Iran

Policy before 9/11

Chechnya was only one of the problems in Russian–Iranian relations facing Putin when he became Russia's President in January 2000. The second problem was the overwhelming victory of the moderates in Iran's Majlis (parliamentary) elections in February 2000. This had to be of concern to Moscow because for many of the reformers who were elected an improvement in US–Iranian relations (and the expected improvement of the Iranian economy that would result once the United States removed economic sanctions) was an important policy goal.[14] Yet, the moderate Parliament found itself checkmated by the conservative forces in the government and by the Iranian supreme religious authority, Ayatollah Khameini, who opposed their reform efforts. Iranian President Khatami was not able to overcome them.[15] Indeed, in a speech at the UN in September 2000, Khatami berated the United States for its condemnation of Iran for the arrest and conviction of a group of ten Iranian Jews as spies – a development which had further strained US–Iranian relations. The Iranian President, who had met Russian President Putin the previous day, also stated that he hoped to forge a closer relationship with Russia:

> We share a lot of interests with Russia. We both live in one of the most-sensitive areas of the world. I believe the two countries can engage in aviable and strong relationship. Russia needs a powerful and stable Iran A stronger relationship would allow both countries to marginalize external powers that are seeking destructive ends and which do not belong in the region.[16]

The Khatami statement seemed to put aside, at least in the short term, the possibilities of a US–Iranian rapprochement, and together with Iran's low profile in the rapidly escalating Chechen war may have led Putin to uni-laterally abrogate the Gore–Chernomyrdin agreement of 30 June 1995, under which Russia was to have ended all military sales to Tehran by 31 December 1999. This decision risked US sanctions, ranging from a ban on the use of Russian rockets for satellite launches to the discourage-ment of US investments in Russia, and to US pressure on the IMF not to reschedule Russian debts. While improving Russian–Iranian relations and clearly contributing to Russian arms exports, the decision to abro-gate the Gore–Chenomyrdin agreement was a blow to US–Russian rela-tions.[17] However, Putin's decision set the stage for Khatami's visit to Moscow in March 2001.

The Caspian Sea dispute, along with military cooperation, were high on the agenda of Khatami's visit to Moscow. The Iranian ambassador to Moscow, Mehdi Safari, in an apparent attempt to solicit support from Rosoboronoexport, dangled the prospect of $7 billion in arms sales to Iran, prior to the Khatami visit.[18] This followed an estimate of up to $300 million in annual sales by Rosoboronoexport director Viktor Komardin.[19]

Meanwhile, US–Russian relations had sharply deteriorated, as the new Bush Administration had called for the abrogation of the ABM Treaty and for the expansion of NATO into the Baltic States. Making matters worse, soon after taking office, the Administration had angered Moscow by bombing Iraqi anti-aircraft installations and by expelling a number of alleged Russian spies. Given this background of deteriorating US–Russian relations, one might have expected more to come out of the Putin–Khatami summit than actually happened. To be sure, Putin formally announced the resumption of arms sales, Khatami was awarded an honorary degree in philosophy from Moscow State University and was invited to tour Moscow's contribution to the international space station. Former Russian Foreign and Prime Minister Yevgeny Primakov waxed eloquently over the Khatami visit, calling it the biggest event in the history of relations between Tehran and Moscow.[20] Yet the treaty that emerged from the meeting (titled 'The Treaty on Foundations of Relations and Principles of Cooperation') merely stated that 'if one of the sides will be exposed to an aggression of some state, the other side must not give any help to the aggressor'.[21] This was far from a mutual defence treaty and something that would allow Moscow to stand aside should the United States, one day, attack Iran. No specific mention was made of any military agreements during the summit, and Russian deputy defence minister Alexander Lushkov, possibly in a gesture to the United States, stated, 'The planned treaty will not make Russia and Iran strategic partners, but will further strengthen partnerlike, neighborly relations'.[22]

As far as the Bushehr nuclear reactor issue was concerned, despite US protests, Putin (who as noted above was anxious to sell Russian nuclear reactors abroad) and Khatami stated that Russia would finish work on the complex, and the director of the Izhorskie Machine Works stated that the first reactor unit would be completed in early 2004, and 'as soon as the equipment for the first reactor leaves the factory, a contract for the second nuclear reactor will be signed'.[23]

Following Khatemi's visit to Moscow the Caspian Sea issue again generated problems for Russian–Iranian relations. On 23 July 2001, Iranian gunboats, with fighter escorts, harassed a British Petroleum research ship, forcing BP to suspend its activities in the region, which was located within the sea boundary of Azerbaijan according to a Russian–Azeri agreement, but according to Tehran lay in the 20 per cent share of the Caspian that it unilaterally claimed.[24] The fact that Turkey subsequently sent combat aircraft to Baku (the arrangement to send the aircraft, however, predated the Caspian Sea incident) complicated matters for Moscow, as the last thing Moscow wanted was a conflict to arise between Turkey and Iran, both of which Putin was cultivating.

The impact of 9/11

Putin's decision to draw closer to the United States after 9/11 and, particularly, his acquiescence in the deployment of US troops in Central Asia was dimly viewed by Tehran. Iranian radio noted on 18 December following the US military victory in Afghanistan, 'some political observers say that the aim of the US diplomatic activities in the region is to carry out certain parts of US foreign policy, so as to expand its sphere of influence in Central Asia and the Caucasus, and this is to lessen Russia's traditional influence in the region'.[25]

A second problem in post-9/11 Russian–Iranian relations dealt with the Caspian Sea. When, again because of Iranian obstinacy, the April 2002 Caspian summit failed, Putin moved to assert Russian authority in the Caspian. This took three forms: first, there was a May 2002 agreement with Kazakhstan jointly to develop the oil fields lying in disputed waters between them; second, a major Russian naval exercise, witnessed by Russian Defence Minister Sergei Ivanov, took place in the Caspian in early August 2002, on the 280th anniversary of Peter the Great's naval campaign in the Caspian, with 60 ships and 10,000 troops. Both Kazakhstan and Azerbaijan participated, and Putin called the purpose of the exercise 'part of the war against terrorism'.[26] Finally, in September 2002, Putin and Azeri leader Gaidar Aliev signed an agreement dividing the seabed between them, but holding the water in common.[27]

Iran, however, sought to demonstrate that it would not be cowed by the Russian military move, and in September 2003, while the Iranian foreign ministry spokesman, Hamid-Reza Asefi was stressing that the militarization of the Caspian Sea would never ensure the security of littoral states, Iran launched its 'Paykan' missile boat into the Caspian 'to protect the interests of the Iranian nation'.[28]

Nuclear issues take centre stage in the relationship 2002–05

Interestingly enough, while Russian–Iranian tension rose over the Caspian, Russian nuclear reactor sales and arms sales continued. In July 2002, just a few weeks before the major military exercises on the Caspian, Moscow announced that not only would it finish Bushehr (despite US opposition), but also stated it had begun discussions on the building of five additional reactors for Iran.[29] It remained unclear at the time, however, whether or not the spent fuel would be sent back to Russia so that it could not be made into nuclear weapons.

As Moscow stepped up its nuclear sales to Tehran, the United States sought to dissuade Russia through both a carrot-and-stick approach, threatening on the one hand to withhold $20 billion in aid for the dismantling of the old Soviet military arsenal, while on the other hand promising $10 billion in additional aid for Moscow.[30] Meanwhile support for the Chechens, who had seized a theatre in Moscow in October 2002, by Iranian newspapers, including those close to Khameini, raised questions in the minds of at least some Russians as to whether Moscow was backing the wrong side in the US–Iranian dispute over the Iranian nuclear programme.[31]

In looking at Moscow's unwillingness to cooperate with Washington on the nuclear issue there appear to be four central reasons. First, the sale of the reactor earns hard currency for Russia, and Putin cannot be sure that at a time of escalating deficits in the United States even if President Bush promised large sums of money to Russia, that the US Congress would allocate them. Second, once the first reactor was operating, Iran has repeatedly hinted to Moscow that it will purchase a number of additional reactors. Third, the Bushehr reactor and the factories in Russia which supply it employ a large number of Russian engineers and technicians and thus help keep Russia's nuclear industry alive – something Putin hopes will help not only earn Russia much needed hard currency but also help in the high tech development of the Russian economy. Finally, by standing firm on Bushehr, Putin could demonstrate to domestic audiences Russia's independent policy *vis-à-vis* the United States, as both the Duma and presidential elections neared.

Yet, such a policy held dangers for Moscow. First, as noted above, it served to alienate the United States, despite constant Russian protestations that the Bushehr reactor would only be used for peaceful purposes. Second, especially as revelations emerged about the extent of the Iranian nuclear programme, Moscow ran the danger that either the United States or Israel, might attack the Bushehr reactor. The problem became especially serious for Russia in December 2002, when a series of satellite photographs revealed that, in addition to Bushehr, Iran was building two new nuclear facilities, one a centrifuge plant near the city of Natanz and the other a heavy water plant near the city of Arak.[32] Initially, Russia downplayed the development, with the Director of Minatom, Alexander Rumantsev, stating that the photos taken of the plants were not sufficient to determine their nature, and, in any case, the Russians had nothing to do with the two plants. Throughout early 2003, he changed his position about Iranian nuclear developments several times[33] and by March asserted that Russia could not tell whether Iran was secretly developing nuclear weapons: 'While Russia is helping Iran build its nuclear plant (at Bushehr) it is not being informed by Iran on all the other projects currently underway.'[34] Following its initial successes in the Iraq war, the United States stepped up its pressure on Russia to halt the Iranian nuclear weapons programme. In response, Russian Foreign Minister Igor Ivanov noted in an Interfax interview at the end of May 2003 that Russia wanted all Iranian nuclear programmes to be under the supervision of the IAEA.[35] Then, following the Bush–Putin talks in St Petersburg in early June 2003, when Bush was at the height of his international influence following the fall of Baghdad, Putin asserted that the positions of Russia and the United States on Iran were closer than people thought. However, he added that 'the pretext of an Iranian nuclear weapons programme (could be used) as an instrument of unfair competition against Russian companies'.[36]

By early June 2003, it appeared that the United States was making two demands on Russia, *vis-à-vis* the Bushehr reactor. First, although the United States wanted Russia to end all support for Bushehr, at the minimum, it argued that Moscow should not supply any nuclear fuel to the Bushehr reactor unless Iran agreed to send all used fuel back to Moscow. Second, Moscow should also withhold the nuclear fuel until Iran signed an additional protocol with the IAEA permitting that agency unannounced visits to all Iranian nuclear facilities. On the latter issue, both the G-8 (of which Russia is a member) and the EU also pressured Iran. Indeed, the G-8 statement issued in early June noted: 'We urge Iran to sign and implement the IAEA Additional Protocol without delay or conditions.

We offer our strongest support to comprehensive IAEA examination of this country's nuclear program.'[37]

The question, of course, was not only how far Iran would go to comply, but how far Russia would go to pressure Iran. In this there appeared to be some initial confusion in Moscow. While British Prime Minister Tony Blair asserted that Moscow had agreed not to deliver nuclear fuel until Iran signed the IAEA protocol, a Russian Foreign Ministry spokesman stated that Moscow would only freeze construction on the Bushehr plant if Iran refused to agree to return all spent nuclear fuel to Russia, and that Iran was not required to sign the protocol, because 'the protocol is an agreement that is signed on a voluntary basis'.[38]

Meanwhile, perhaps to deflect some of the US pressure, Minatom Minister Rumanstev announced that the Bushehr reactor would be completed in 2005, not 2004, as originally planned. While he blamed the delay on the need to replace the reactor's original German parts, it could well be that this was an important gesture to the United States.[39]

Then, on 12 September 2003, the IAEA, of which Russia is a member, gave Tehran a deadline of 31 October to provide full information about its nuclear programme to show that it was not secretly building nuclear weapons, and furthermore urged Iran to freeze its uranium enrichment programme. While the tough wording of the message prompted the walk-out of the Iranian delegation from the Vienna IAEA meeting, the question now became how Russia would react to the situation. Interestingly enough, at the time Russia's Deputy Foreign Minister Sergei Kislyak tried to soft pedal the IAEA report by saying Iran should not see the 31 October deadline as 'an ultimatum'.[40] However, in September a dispute between Russia and Iran had broken out over who would pay for the return of the spent fuel from the reactor. Complicating matters further for Putin on the eve of his visit to the United States in late September, was the US sanctioning of a Russian arms firm (Tula Instrument Design Bureau) for selling laser-guided artillery shells to Iran. Fortunately for Putin, Bush's position at the time of the summit was weaker than it had been when the two leaders last met in June. Guerrilla warfare had erupted in Iraq and the United States was beginning to have trouble dealing with it. Indeed, Washington had turned to the UN in an effort to get additional troops, along with monetary aid to rebuild Iraq. Along with a sputtering American economy, Iraq had become a major issue in US politics, as Bush's standing in US polls had begun to drop. Consequently, while Bush raised the issue of Iran with Putin, the most he could extract from the Russian leader was the somewhat vague statement that 'It is our conviction that we shall give a clear but respectful signal to Iran about the necessity to continue and expand its cooperation with the IAEA'.[41] In addition, Bush proved unable to get Putin to agree to cease construction on the Bushehr reactor.

The EU took the initiative from Moscow when it sent a delegation to Tehran in late October 2003. The delegation succeeded in extracting from Iran, in return for a promise of high-tech cooperation, an agreement to stop enriching uranium temporarily and to sign the additional protocol, as well as to inform the IAEA of its past nuclear activities. Moscow hailed the Iranian action, and the head of the Iranian Security Council, Hassan Rowhani, came to Moscow on 11 November to announce formally that Tehran was temporarily suspending the enrichment of uranium and was sending that day a letter to the IAEA agreeing to the additional protocol.[42] Moscow exploited the visit saying that Iran was now in full compliance with the IAEA, and Putin said that now Russia and Iran would continue their nuclear cooperation.[43] Indeed, Foreign Ministry spokesman Alexander Yakovenko, eyeing the possibility of the sale of additional reactors to Tehran, something discussed during the Iranian delegation's visit, said Russia would now 'do its utmost to expedite the completion of Bushehr'.[44]

In part because of Russian (and EU) pressure, the Board of Governors of the IAEA in November 2003 decided not to refer Iran's nuclear programme to the UN Security Council. Nonetheless it did warn Iran against developing nuclear weapons and threatened to consider 'all options available' if Iran continued to conceal information about its nuclear facilities.[45] The United States took a tougher stance with John Bolton, then Undersecretary of State for Arms Control and International Security, warning that the United States was ready to use all options against rogue states believed to be developing weapons of mass destruction. Bolton also voiced scepticism that Iran would abide by its commitments to the IAEA.[46]

Bolton's scepticism soon proved to be well placed, because less than two months later revelations about Pakistan's nuclear proliferation policies, including to Iran, led IAEA Chief Muhammed ElBaradei to warn about the collapse of the non-proliferation system. The United States then called for closing a loophole in the nuclear non-proliferation treaty to prevent countries, such as Iran, from acquiring materials for their national atomic energy programs that could be used to build nuclear weapons.[47] In addition, IAEA inspectors found that Iran had hidden (and not told the IAEA about), among other things, an advanced P-2 centrifuge system that could be used for enriching uranium, along with a programme for producing polonium 210, which could be used as a neutron initiator for nuclear weapons.[48]

Meanwhile, as these revelations emerged, Moscow seemed unclear on how to react. Minatom's Deputy Minister Govorukhin played down

ElBaradei's warning of the possible collapse of the international nuclear non-proliferation system, and hailed Iran's cooperation with the IAEA.[49] By contrast, his superior Alexander Rumantsev supported ElBaradei, calling the situation 'extremely unpleasant' and went so far as to say that Russia, along with other countries, was going to give 'active consideration as to whether work on the establishment of national fuel cycles should be terminated in non-nuclear countries'[50] – something that would strike a serious blow against Iran's nuclear aspirations.

Consequently the central factor in Russian-Iranian relations in 2004 concerned when Russia would complete the Bushehr nuclear reactor. While there was progress on coordinating electricity grids via Azerbaijan, trade increased to the level of $2 billion per year, and Tehran and Moscow negotiated on further arms and civilian plane sales as well as on the Russian launch of an Iranian satellite,[51] Bushehr dominated the discourse, as Iran increasingly clashed with the International Atomic Energy Agency (IAEA). Even the division of the Caspian Sea, the other 'hot button' issue in the Russian–Iranian relationship seemed to be put on hold during this period with Russian Foreign Minister Sergei Lavrov noting in October 2004 that the Caspian Sea littoral states had only agreed on parts of eight of the 33 articles of the proposed Caspian Sea Legal Regime.[52]

Moscow's dilemma was basically twofold. Throughout 2004 either the IAEA continued to find that Iran was hiding information about its nuclear activities, or Iran was reneging on agreements it had already made with the IAEA and/or the EU-3 (Germany, France and England). This, in turn, brought heavy US pressure on Russia to hold off supplying nuclear fuel to the Bushehr reactor project it was constructing in Iran, lest Iranian efforts to develop a nuclear bomb be enhanced. Increasingly, as 2004 wore on, the Russian leaders appeared to be at least somewhat persuaded by the US argument and their criticism of Tehran mounted.In April Iran informed the IAEA that it intended to begin testing at its uranium conversion facility at Isfahan, after which it began to convert small amounts of natural uranium into uranium hexaflouride, the feed material used in centrifuges – an action that was a clear violation of the agreement signed with the EU-3 in October 2003.[53] Despite being criticized for this at the IAEA June 2004 Board of Governors meeting, Iran then notified the IAEA that it intended to resume manufacture of centrifuge components as well as to test and assemble centrifuges. This led the IAEA in September to threaten to refer Iran to the UN Security Council, if Tehran did not restore full suspension of its enrichment programmes, as well as grant IAEA inspectors access to Iranian nuclear facilities, and explain to the IAEA the extent and nature of Iran's uranium enrichment processing, specifically the role of P-2 centrifuges. A virtual repetition of the events in the fall of 2003 occurred, leading to an apparent agreement with Tehran to promise to temporarily stop enriching uranium in return for a promise of trade cooperation. After some additional delays by the end of November, Iran signed an agreement with the EU-3 to suspend all enrichment related and reprocessing activities 'on a voluntary basis', which included (1) the manufacture and import of gas centrifuges and their components; (2) the assembly, installation, testing or operation of gas centrifuges; and (3) undertaking any plutonium separation, or the construction or operation of any plutonium separation installation as well as all tests or production at any conversion installation. According to the agreement, Iran's suspension 'will be sustained while negotiations (with the EU-3) proceed on a mutually acceptable agreement on long-term arrangements'. In return the EU set up working groups with Iran on (1) political and security issues; (2) technology and cooperation; and (3) nuclear issues, with all working groups to report by 15 March 2005. The goal of the EU-3 was to have Iran permanently suspend its enrichment activities and end its nuclear fuel cycle programme, and the EU was prepared to offer Iran guarantees of fuel supply and management for Iran's nuclear power programme and also to help Iran acquire a light-water research reactor if Iran cancelled its plans to build a heavy-water research reactor.[54] Almost immediately, however, Iran seemed to back off from the agreement with Hassan Rowhani, Iran's chief negotiator, saying at a news conference, 'The length of the suspension will only be for the length of the negotiations with the Europeans and ... must be rational and not too long. We're talking about months, not years'.[55]

As these events unfolded, Russia faced a dilemma. On the one hand, as in 2003, the EU-3 deflected pressure from Russia and helped prevent not only a referral of Iran's nuclear programme to the UN Security Council, but also possible US and/or Israeli military action against Iran's nuclear installations. Indeed, Moscow could only welcome UK Foreign Minister Jack Straw's comments that force should not be used against Iran under any circumstances. On the other hand Moscow faced the possibility that, despite Iran's constant backsliding, the EU-3 Iran agreement of 30 November 2004 might actually take hold and, if so, the EU states could become competitors in Iran's nuclear market.[56]

What was clear was that, as Iran throughout 2004 and 2005 was seeking to wriggle out from its commitments to the IAEA and EU-3, Moscow appeared to take an increasingly tough tone with Tehran on nuclear issues. In June 2004, Putin threatened that 'Russia will halt its work at Bushehr if Iran refuses to behave in an open manner and fails to comply with the IAEA's demands'. Similarly, when meeting with French leader Jacques Chirac and German leader Gerhard Schroeder in September, Putin stated Russia's opposition to an 'expansion of the club of nuclear powers, notably through the addition of Iran'.[57] Then, in commenting on the tough September IAEA resolution, Rumantsev stated 'It is balanced and serves the interests of all parties'.[58]

While Russia proved supportive of the EU-3 negotiations with Iran, it reportedly opposed Iranian efforts to get the 20 centrifuges excluded from the agreement, something that was negatively commented on by the Iranian news agency Mehr.[59] Putin himself, as the final negotiations with the EU-3 wound down, made a not-so-veiled warning to Iran, stating 'We are engaged in bilateral negotiations with Iran. We are helping it use nuclear power for peaceful purposes. If final agreements are achieved, we will continue this cooperation'.[60] Then, when the agreement was reached at the end of November, and the subsequent IAEA report took a relatively tough stand against Iran, Deputy Foreign Minister Sergei Kislyak told Interfax that not only did Russia praise the IAEA resolution as 'well balanced', but 'we also welcome Iran's decision to freeze all uranium enrichment programs. This is a voluntary, trust building measure. We hope this decision will be reliably fulfilled'.[61] The Russian Foreign Ministry, in a statement issued after the IAEA resolution, reinforced Kislak's words, noting 'a full and sustained fulfilment of this voluntary undertaking, with due monitoring on the part of the IAEA is essential for the settlement of remaining issues regarding Iran's nuclear program'.[62]

Moscow's sharp rhetoric *vis-à-vis* Tehran began to fade in 2005. As mentioned above, in the latter part of 2004 Putin had suffered a number of embarrassing failures both internally and externally with the debacle in Beslan demonstrating just how far Putin was from 'normalizing' the situation in Chechnya, and the pro-Western 'Orange Revolution' in Ukraine, apparently indicating the defection of Russia's most important CIS neighbour. Consequently Putin seems to have decided that he had to demonstrate both his own, and Russia's, continuing importance in world affairs; and reinforcing his alliance with Iran was one way to do this.[63] The process included inviting Iran to join the Shanghai Cooperation Organization as an observer, and also inviting Iran to join the planned Caspian Sea security organization (Iran, under heavy pressure both from the United States and the European Union eagerly accepted both invitations). The two countries also stepped up their planning for a North–South transportation corridor through Azerbaijan. In addition, Moscow launched a satellite for Iran and discussed the possibility of the sale of submarine-launched missiles with a range of 200 km to be fitted on the submarines

Russia had sold to Iran.[64] Should the sale go through, it would greatly complicate the activities of the US fleet in the Persian Gulf–Indian Ocean region and be a major blow to US–Russian relations.

While these developments demonstrated a reinforced Russian–Iranian tie, the nuclear issue continued to occupy first place in the relationship. In early 2005, however, Iran was becoming increasingly critical of the delay in Russia's finalizing completion of the reactor. Indeed, a commentary by Mehdi Mohammadi in *Kehyan* in early January 2005 went so far as to assert that 'the breaches of promise, subterfuge and mischief-making of the Russians in the field of peaceful nuclear cooperation with the Islamic Republic of Iran is now a repeated saga'.[65] Whether or not the Iranian criticism was an important factor in Putin's decision-making is not yet known. However, Putin did realize that, in order to cement the relationship with Iran, which he saw as a foreign policy priority, he had to finalize the nuclear fuel agreement. Consequently, in late February 2005, Russia signed the final agreement for the supply of nuclear fuel to the Bushehr reactor.[66] Under the agreement all spent fuel was to be returned to Russia, thus, in theory at least, preventing its diversion into atomic weapons. The agreement came after a Bush-Putin summit in which the United States and Russia pledged to work together against nuclear proliferation,[67] and, as might be expected, the United States took a dim view of the Russian–Iranian agreement.

Perhaps emboldened by the agreement with Russia, Iran's then chief nuclear negotiator, Hassan Rowhani warned that Iran would never permanently cease enriching uranium, and if the United States sought sanctions at the UN Security Council, 'The security and stability of the region would become a problem'. Rowhani also stated that Iran was not happy with the pace of negotiations with the EU-3, and threatened to end the negotiations if there were no progress.[68]

Meanwhile, as the United States became increasingly bogged down in Iraq, it appeared to back off somewhat from its confrontation with Iran over the nuclear issue. Thus, in mid-March 2005, the United States agreed to join the EU in offering economic incentives to Iran if it gave up its nuclear programme.[69] At the same time, however, an Iranian Presidential campaign was now under way. While both the United States and the EU-3 hoped that the victor would be former Iranian President Hashemi Rafsanjani, with whom they felt they could make a deal, to their surprise an Islamic hard-liner, Mahmud Ahmadinizhad, the Mayor of Tehran, was elected President. Consequently, when the EU-3 presented its proposal to Ahmadinizhad's government on 5 August 2005, it was contemptuously rejected as a 'joke'.[70] The proposal called for a long-term

EU–Iranian relationship which combined security and economic incentives, including giving Iran access to international technologies for light-water reactors, in return for Iran agreeing not to withdraw from the nuclear non-proliferation treaty and keeping all Iranian nuclear facilities under IAEA safeguards.[71] The Iranian rejection may have been encouraged by a leaked US intelligence report in the *Washington Post* on 2 August 2005 which asserted that Iran was ten years away from acquiring a nuclear weapon.[72] The Iranians may well have seen the leak as an effort by the Bush Administration to deflect public pressure to take action against Iran by demonstrating that Iran would not have the bomb for a decade. In any case, an emboldened Iran, led by its hard-line President with the apparent support of Iran's supreme religious leader, the Ayatollah Khamenei, rejected the EU proposal and announced that it was resuming work at the uranium conversion plant at Isfahan, where it would transform uranium into nuclear fuel.[73] An angered EU-3 then cancelled further talks with Iran, and the issue was referred to the IAEA.[74]

As these events were transpiring, Russia sought to defuse the crisis, with the Russian Foreign Ministry issuing a statement on 9 August which asserted that 'it would be a wise decision on the part of Iran to stop enriching uranium and renew cooperation with the IAEA'.[75] Iran did not heed the Russian request, however, and international pressure on Iran grew at the end of August with French President Jacques Chirac warning that Iran would face censure by the UN Security Council if it did not reinstate a freeze on sensitive nuclear activities.[76] Russia, however, was now in a protective mode *vis-à-vis* Iran and chose not to go beyond its verbal call for Iran to stop enriching uranium. Thus, on 5 September 2005, the Russian Foreign Ministry stated that it was opposed to reporting Iran to the UN Security Council.[77]

However, Russia was made uneasy by the speech Ahmadinizhad gave at the UN in mid-September. Instead of diplomatically trying to assuage the opponents of Iran's nuclear programme, he delivered a fiery attack on the United States and Israel, going so far as to claim that the United States was poisoning its own troops in Iraq, while at the same time asserting that Iran would never give up its plans to enrich uranium.[78] This speech placed Iran on the defensive, as the members of the IAEA met in late September to decide what to do about its nuclear programme. At the beginning of the meeting the Russian Foreign Ministry issuing a statement that it considered proposals that Iran's nuclear programmes be referred to the UNSC to be 'counterproductive and nonconducive to the search for a solution to the problem by political and diplomatic methods'.[79] Nonetheless, following a heated debate Russia (along with

11 other countries) chose to abstain on an IAEA resolution which passed 22–1 that found that Iran's 'failures and breaches ... constitute non-compliance with Iran's agreement to let the international body verify that its nuclear program is purely peaceful'. The resolution went on to state that the 'absence of confidence that Iran's nuclear programme is exclusively for peaceful purposes has given rise to questions that are within the competence of the Security Council'. The resolution further called on Iran to resuspend conversion of uranium at its Isfahan plant and asked Tehran to return to negotiations with the EU-3.[80]

Russian behaviour at the IAEA meeting illustrated Moscow's ongoing dilemma in dealing with Iran. While Moscow did not want Iran to acquire nuclear weapons, it also did not want sanctions brought against one of its closest allies, which was also a very good customer, buying not only the Bushehr nuclear reactor (and possibly more in the future) but military equipment as well. Consequently, since the IAEA resolution did not explicitly call for sanctions, Moscow could perhaps claim a victory, while at the same time it did not alienate the EU-3, with which it was seeking increased economic and political cooperation or the United States. Nonetheless, by this time the United States was again seeking action against Iran, and US Secretary of State Condoleezza Rice travelled to Russia in mid-October 2005 to try to gain Russian support for sanctions. However, Russian Foreign Minister Sergei Lavrov stated that Russia wanted to pursue negotiations in the IAEA rather than go to the UNSC, noting 'We think that the current situation permits us to develop this issue and do everything possible within the means of this organization [the IAEA] without referring this issue to other organizations, so far'.[81] Putin echoed Lavrov's position in a telephone call to Ahmadinizhad in which he reportedly stated:

The need was stressed for decisions on all relevant issues to be made using political methods within the legal framework of the IAEA. In connection to this, the Russian President advocated the further development of Iran's cooperation with the IAEA, including with the aim of renewing the negotiations process.[82]

With these statements Russia had come down strongly on the side of Iran in its conflict with the EU-3 and the United States; because, without the threat of sanctions, there would be little incentive for Iran to change its policy. Nonetheless, Iran was to prove a difficult ally for Russia. With Russian Foreign Minister Lavrov on a visit to Israel as part of his trip to the Middle East after the Israeli Gaza disengagement, in a speech to Iranian students on 26 October at a programme called 'A world without

Zionism', Ahmadinizhad stated not only that Israel 'must be wiped off the map', but also that any country which recognizes Israel (presumably including Russia) 'will burn in the fire of the Islamic nation's fury'.[83] An uneasy Lavrov stated:

> What I saw on CNN is unacceptable. We will convey our standpoint to the Iranian side. We're inviting the Iranian ambassador to the Ministry of Foreign Affairs and will ask him to explain the motives behind this kind of statement.

He also noted that these kinds of statements 'do not facilitate the efforts of those who want to normalize the situation surrounding Iran'.[84] Two days later, however, while in Jordan, Lavrov changed his tone, stating 'our position on Iran remains unchanged. We favour cooperation through the IAEA in dealing with problems related to the Iranian nuclear program.'[85]

During the period between the two IAEA conferences, the Iranian record of compliance with IAEA directives was mixed. Iran, besides offering to resume negotiations with the EU-3, made a gesture to the IAEA by giving it access to a building at Parchin that the IAEA inspectors had wanted to enter. In addition the IAEA was allowed to interview Iranian specialists, and Iran also handed over additional documents to the IAEA.[86] However, one of the documents revealed that rogue Pakistani nuclear scientist, Abdul Khan, had provided Iran technical data to enable it to cast 'enriched, natural and depleted uranium metal into hemispheric forms' that would help Iran fit a nuclear warhead onto its missiles. In commenting on this development former nuclear inspector David Albright said the design is 'part of what you need ... to build a nuclear weapon. Although it's not a "smoking gun" proving Iran was developing nuclear weapons, the find cast doubts on previous Iranian assertions that it had no documents on making such arms'.[87]

Further complicating Iran's position as the IAEA meeting neared was Tehran's decision to reprocess another batch of uranium at its Isfahan nuclear facility. This brought a negative reaction from the French Foreign Ministry, whose spokesman stated: 'We consider that this is a decision which does not go in the right direction. It does not contribute to creating a climate of confidence between Iran and the international community'.[88] The Iranian Parliament then escalated the tension by voting 183 to 14 to stop IAEA inspection of its nuclear facilities, if Iran were referred to the UN Security Council by the IAEA.[89]

As this situation developed Moscow continued to oppose referring Iran to the UN Security Council, although holding out the possibility it could happen. Three days before the start of the IAEA meeting Russian Foreign Minister Sergei Lavrov stated, 'I do not rule out the possibility that the Iranian question might be sent to the Security Council if a real threat of the proliferation of weapons of mass destruction above all nuclear weapons arises. At the moment we do not see such a threat'.[90] Moscow also sought to defuse the crisis by working out a proposal with the EU-3 which would enable Iran domestically to convert uranium into uranium hexaflouride gas that is the precursor to making enriched uranium. The enrichment itself, however, would be done in Russia.[91] While the compromise defused the situation so that the 24 November IAEA meeting did not refer Iran to the UN Security Council, the question remained open how long Iran would enjoy its respite. First, at the time of the IAEA meeting Iran not only did not accept the EU-3–Russia compromise agreement, but many Iranian officials continued to demand the right to develop a full fuel cycle.[92] Second, members of the EU warned Iran that its time was not unlimited to accept the compromise as Peter Jenkins, Britain's IAEA delegate stated, 'Iran should not conclude that this window of opportunity will remain open in all circumstances. It won't be open for a great deal longer'.[93] Finally, in his report to the IAEA, Director General Mohamed ElBaradei, who had just been awarded a Nobel prize, urged Iran:

> to respond positively and without delay to the Agency's remaining questions related to uranium enrichment, and to the additional transparency measures we have requested. As I have stated before, these transparency measures are indispensable for the Agency to be able to clarify remaining outstanding issues – in particular, the scope and chronology of Iran's centrifuge enrichment programs. Clarification of these issues is overdue after three years of intensive verification efforts.[97]

The November 2005 IAEA meeting provides a useful point of departure for examining the nuclear issue in Russian-Iranian relations.

Conclusions

One central conclusion can be drawn from this study of Russian policy *vis-à-vis* Iran and its nuclear programme. It is that Moscow has been badly torn between its desire to maintain good relations with Iran, a diplomatic ally in many sensitive areas of Eurasia and a major purchaser of Russian arms (a $1 billion arms deal was signed just after the November 2005 IAEA meeting) and nuclear equipment, on the one hand, and, on the other hand, increasing pressure from the international community, especially the EU and the United States, to prevent Iran from acquiring nuclear weapons. Moscow has been on the horns of a dilemma on the Iranian nuclear issue because, on the one hand it does not want to alienate Iran, but on the other neither does it want to alienate the EU or the United States, nor does it wish Iran to acquire nuclear weapons, as Russian President Putin has said on numerous occasions. For this reason Russia has sought to chart a middle course between Iran and the West, seeking to minimize the damage to its relations with Iran, while at the same time seeking to respond to pressure from the United States and EU.

The pressure came in two forms. First, although the United States in particular was unhappy with Russia's decision to construct a nuclear reactor for Iran at Bushehr, at the minimum it called for the repatriation of the reactor's spent fuel to Russia, so that it could not be diverted into nuclear weapons. Russia complied with this request – despite Iranian opposition – and an agreement to this effect was signed in February 2005. It should also be noted that completion of the reactor was repeatedly delayed, although to what degree this was due to 'technical difficulties' or to Russian pressure on Iran to sign the fuel repatriation agreement is not yet known. Even though the agreement has been signed – in the face of US protests – it will be important to monitor closely how both Russia and Iran adhere to it, given the fact that the reactor is now due to become operational in mid-2006, and Putin has drawn closer to Iran to compensate for his losses in Ukraine and Beslan.

A second area of pressure from the EU and the United States has related to Iranian efforts to hide parts of its nuclear programme, something that became evident in December 2002. In the face of calls from the United States to impose UN sanctions on Iran, Russia joined with the EU to get Iranian acceptance of the additional protocol to the nuclear non-proliferation treaty which allows the IAEA to make unannounced inspection visits to Iranian nuclear installations.

Nonetheless, as negotiations between the EU-3 and Iran faltered in 2005 over a comprehensive agreement to give Iran economic and security benefits in return for abandoning its plans for a full nuclear cycle, and there were new revelations about Iran hiding parts of its nuclear programme, there were renewed calls for UN sanctions against Iran. Complicating matters for Moscow, and exacerbating its problem of choice were two new developments that had coalesced by autumn 2005. The first was a marked increase in the level of cooperation between the EU-3 and the United States over Iran, along with the electoral defeat of German Prime Minister Gerhard Schröder who had opposed US policy on Iran. Thus Moscow, for the first time, had to deal with a US–EU alignment on Iran.

The second factor was the election of a hard-line Islamic leader, Mahmud Ahmadinizhad as President of Iran who not only contemptuously rejected the EU-3 plan presented in August 2005, but also, by threatening to wipe Israel 'off the face of the map', raised serious questions about what Iranian leaders proclaimed were the "peaceful intentions" of their nuclear programme. The end result was an IAEA Board of Governors statement in September 2005 that threatened Iran with the possibility of sanctions, a statement on which Russia abstained. While Russia was able to defer a possible sanctions effort against Iran at the November 2005 IAEA meeting by negotiating a compromise offer to Iran with the EU-3 – supported by the United States – which allowed Tehran limited nuclear processing, in return for abandoning its plans for a full nuclear cycle, Iran has not yet accepted the offer, and should it not do so, perhaps counting on a weakened US unwillingness to press hard for sanctions at a time of record high oil prices, or hoping for a Russian (or Chinese) veto of a UN Security Council sanctions resolution, Russia will be hard put to decide what to do. While it has sought to put that day of decision off as long as possible, the time may be coming sooner rather than later when Moscow will have to choose between Iran and the West. Whether Putin will be able to finesse such a choice is a very open question.

Notes

1 'Russian Presidential service says [Russia is] ready for nuclear cooperation with Iran' Interfax 25 Oct. 2005 (Oct. 26 *FBIS: Russia*, 2005).
2 Ibid.
3 Anatoly Medetsky, 'Kiriyenko tapped to run Rosatom', *Moscow News*, 16 Nov. 2005.
4 For a study of Soviet policy toward the Iran–Iraq war, see Robert O. Freedman, *Moscow and the Middle East: Soviet Policy Since the Invasion of Afghanistan* (Cambridge: Cambridge University Press, 1991).
5 The Russian pledge and its later repudiation by Putin are discussed in James M. Goldgeier and Michael McFaul, *Power and Purpose: U.S. Policy Toward Russia After the Cold War* (Washington, DC: Brookings, 2003).
6 For a detailed discussion of these issues, see Robert O. Freedman, *Russian Policy Toward the Middle East Since the Collapse of the Soviet Union: The Yeltsin Legacy and the Challenge for Putin* (Seattle: Henry M. Jackson School of International Studies, University of Washington, 2001).
7 Pavel Felgenauer, 'Russia and Iran', *Segodnia*, 26 May 1995 (*Current Digest of the Post Soviet Press* [hereafter *CDSP*]. 47/21 (1995), p. 3).
8 Robert O. Freedman, 'Russia and Iran: A Tactical Alliance', *SAIS Review*, 17/2 (Summer–Fall 1997), p. 99.

9   Robert O. Freedman, 'Russian-Iranian Relations Under Yeltsin', *Soviet and Post-Soviet Review*, 25/3 (1999), p. 284.

10 See *New York Times*, 18 Nov. 1997; and *Kommersant Daily*, 22 Jan. 1998 (*CDSP*, 50/4 (1998), p. 22).

11 For a study of US–Iranian relations at this time, see Robert O. Freedman, 'American Policy Toward the Middle East in Clinton's Second Term', in Stephen J. Blank (ed.), *Mediterranean Security in the Coming Millenium* (Carlisle, P: Strategic Studies Institute of the US Army War College, 1999), pp. 371–416.

12 See Yuri Mezliakov, 'Legal Status of the Caspian Sea', *International Affairs* (Moscow), 45/1 (January 1999), p. 37.

13 Viktor Vishniakov, 'Russian-Iranian Relations and Regional Stability', *International Affairs* (Moscow), 45/1 (January 1999) p. 152.

14 This was clearly a concern of some of Russia's Iranian specialists. See N. M. Mamedova, 'Novii Etap Politichesko Zhizni Irana' [New Stage in the Political Life of Iran], in Vladimir Isaev (ed.), *Blizhnii Vostok i Sovremennost* (Moscow: Institute for the Study of Israel and the Near East, 2000), p. 132.

15 For an excellent study of Iranian politics at this time, see Shaul Bakhash, 'Iran: Slouching Toward the Twenty-first Century', in Robert O. Freedman (ed.) *The Middle East Enters the Twenty-first Century* (Miami: University Press of Florida, 2002), pp. 46–49.

16 Cited in *Washington Times*, 8 Sept. 2000. For his part, Putin had singled out Iran for special mention in his new foreign policy doctrine.

17 See Goldgeier and McFaul, as note 5 above, p. 302.

18 Cited in AFP, 22 Feb. 2001, 'Russia could earn 7 billion dollars from arms sales to Iran', *Russia Today On-line News Service*, 23 Feb. 2001.

19 Reuters, 11 Feb. 2001, 'Russia may sign Iran arms deal in 2001', *Russia Today On-line News Service*, 11 Feb. 2001.

20 See *Ettela'at* (Tehran), 'Iran-Russia discuss bilateral relations, regional cooperation', 13 March 2001.

21 Itar-Tass, 12 March 2001, cited in *FBIS Russia*, 12 March 2001.

22 Cited in Simon Saradzhyan, 'Visiting Khatami to deal for arms', *Moscow Times*, 12 March 2001.

23 Cited in Patrick Tyler, 'Russians question their coziness with Iran', *New York Times*, 16 March 2001.

24 Arif Useinov, 'Iranian gunboat diplomacy: Tehran is scaring investors away from the Caspian', *Vremia Novostei*, 25 July 2001 (*CDSP*, 53/30, pp. 19–20).

25 Radio Iran, 'U.S. military presence in Central Asia to lessen Russian influence', 10 Dec. 2001 (*FBIS-MESA*, 18 Dec. 2001.)

26 Alexander Reutov, 'Russia conclusively defines its borders on the Caspian', *Kommersant*, 24 Sept. 2002 (*CDSP*, 54/39, p. 17).

27 Ibid, p. 18.

28 Ambo News, 29 Sept. 2003, 'Paykan missile boat floats in Caspian'.

29 Cited in article by Sergei Leskov, *Izvestia*, 1 Aug. 2002 (*CDSP*, 54/31, pp. 17–18).

30 Ibid. p. 18.

31 Maxim Yugin, 'Ayatollahs support terrorists', *Izvestia*, 31 Oct. 2002 (*CDSP*, 54/44, p. 23).

32 For a useful survey of the Iranian nuclear installations, see Joseph Cirincione *et al.*, *Deadly Arsenals: Nuclear, Biological and Chemical Threats* (2nd edn, Washington, DC: Carnegie Endowment, 2005), ch. 15. See also William Broad

and David Sanger, 'Relying on Computer, U.S. Seeks to Prove Iran's Nuclear Aims', *New York Times*, 13 Nov. 2005.

33 See Guy Dinmore, 'Russia ready to supply N-fuel to Iran', *Financial Times*, 24 Dec. 2002; Guy Dinmore, 'U.S. raises fears over Iran's nuclear policy', *Financial Times*, 24 Feb. 2003.

34 Cited in Ali Akbar Dareini, 'Iran's first nuclear power plant 70 percent constructed', AP report, *Washington Times*, 12 March 2003.

35 Interfax, 28 May 2003, 'Moscow-Tehran cooperation gives no grounds for criticism – Russian Foreign Minister', (*FBIS-RUSSIA* Diplomatic Panorama, 28 May 2003).

36 Simon Saradzhyan, 'Russia needs Iran proof or incentives', *Moscow Times*, 3 June 2003.

37 Cited in *New York Times*, 3 June 2003, 'Primary points from the statements of the Group of 8'. See also Judy Dempsey, 'EU presses Iran on nuclear arms', *Financial Times*, 27 May 2003.

38 Cited in Vladimir Isachenko, 'Russia will ship nuclear fuel to Iran', *Washington Post*, 5 June 2003.

39 Cited in Ibid.

40 Cited in 'World Scene', *Washington Times*, 14 Sept. 2003.

41 Cited in Dana Milbank, 'Putin agrees in spirit but little else', *Washington Post*, 28 Sept. 2003.

42 Seth Mydans, 'Russia ready to help Iran with A-plant', *New York Times*, 11 Nov. 2003.

43 Ibid.

44 Cited in Tehran IRNA, 13 Nov. 2003, 'Russian spokesman calls meetings with Rowhani constructive', (*FBIS-MESA*, 13 Nov. 2003).

45 Cited in Judy Dempsey and Guy Dinmore, 'Nuclear monitor compromises on Iran', *Financial Times*, 27 Nov. 2003.

46 Cited in Guy Dinmore, 'All options are open, U.S. warns five "rogue" countries', *Financial Times*, 3 Dec. 2003.

47 'Stronger non-proliferation treaty sought by U.S.', *Financial Times*, 26 Jan. 2004.

48 See Scott Peterson, 'Evidence of possible work on nukes tests Iran's credibility', *Christian Science Monitor*, 26 Feb. 2004; and Carla Anne Robbins, 'U.N. report ties nuclear program to Iran's military', *Wall Street Journal*, 25 Feb. 2004.

49 Cited in Itar-Tass Report, 27 Jan. 2004, 'Russian Minister plays down IAEA's nuclear security fears', (*FBIS-RUSSIA*, 27 Jan. 2004).

50 Cited in Itar-Tass report, 5 Feb. 2004. 'Atomic energy minister fears non-proliferation safeguards may fail', (*FBIS-RUSSIA*, 5 Feb. 2004).

51 See Andrey Kioloskov, 'Who is lighting up Iran. Energy systems expand in synch', *Rossiskaya Gazetza*, 17 Dec. 2004 (*FBIS-RUSSIA* 17 Dec. 2004); and Tehran *IRNA*, 'Iran to purchase Russian Topolev passenger planes', 26 Nov. 2004 (*FBIS-MESA* 26 Nov. 2004).

52 *Ibid.*

53 Cited in Paul Hughes, 'Iran says nuclear freeze won't last long', *Reuters*, 30 Nov. 2004.

54 Straw's reported comments were: 'The prospect of it (war against Iran) is inconceivable ... I don't see any circumstances in which military action would be justified against Iran, full stop', Cited in 'Sigh of Relief', *Jordan Times*, 7 Nov. 2004.

55   Cited in *Iran Focus*, 30 Jan. 2007. <http://www.iranfocus.com/modules/news/>
56   Cited in Dmitry Suslov, 'Iranian Draw', *Russky Kuryer*, 13 June 2004 (*CDSP*, 56/24, p. 15).
57   Cited in Alexei Andreyev, 'Sochi Three', *Russky Kuryer*. 1 Sept. 2004 (*CDSP*, 56/35, p. 19).
58   Cited in Andrei Zlobin, 'Iran could face sanctions', *Vremya Novostei*, 20 Sept. 2004 (*CDSP*, 56/38, p. 22).
59   Mehr News Agency (Tehran), 'Russia's "secret" moves against Iran at IAEA revealed', 29 Nov. 2004 (*FBIS-MESA*, 29 Nov. 2004).
60   Interfax, 'Putin says [he] applauds Iran's decision to suspend uranium enrichment programs', 25 Nov. 2004 (*FBIS-RUSSIA*, 25 Nov. 2004).
61   Interfax, 'Russian Foreign Ministry welcomes [well-balanced] IAEA resolution on Iran', 30 Nov. 2004 (*FBIS-RUSSIA*, 30 Nov. 2004).
62   Itar Tass. 'Russia hopes Iran to continue cooperation with IAEA', 30 Nov. 2004 (*FBIS-RUSSIA*, 30 Nov. 2004).
63   During the early part of 2005, Putin decided to sell surface-to-air missiles to Syria, and he also visited Egypt, Israel and the Palestinian Authority in April.
64   *Kommersant*, 'Russia will equip Iranian subs with missiles', 5 July 2005. Cited in *Habalar Report*, 6 July 2005. See also *Agenstvo Voyennykh Novostey*, 'Russian shipyard plans to upgrade Iranian submarines with 200 km club-5 missile' (*FBIS-RUSSIA*, 6, July 2005).
65   Mehdi Mohammadi, 'Gone with the wind', *Keyhan*, Jan. 2005 (*FBIS-MESA*, 9 January 2005).
66   Scott Peterson, 'Russia fuels Iran's atomic bid', *Christian Science Monitor*, 28 Feb. 2005.
67   Peter Baker, 'U.S.-Russian pact aimed at nuclear terrorism', *Washington Post*, 24 Feb. 2005.
68   Cited in Nazila Fathi, 'Iran says it won't give up program to enrich uranium', *New York Times*, 6 March 2005.
69   David Sanger, 'U.S. and European allies agree on steps in Iranian dispute', *New York Times*, 11 March 2005.
70   Vision of the Islamic Republic of Iran (Tehran), 'Iran Foreign Ministry spokesman dismisses EU proposal as a "joke"; notes three "flaws"', 7 Aug. 2005 (*FBIS-MESA*, 8 Aug. 2005).
71   For the text of the EU proposals, see Mehr News Agency, 'Full text of EU nuclear proposals', 5 Aug. 2005 (*FBIS-MESA*, 6 Aug. 2005).
72   Cited in Dafna Linzer, 'Iran is judged 10 years from bomb', *Washington Post*, 2 Aug. 2005.
73   Cited in Dafna Linzer, 'Iran resumes uranium work, ignores warning', *Washington Post*, 9 Aug. 2005.
74   Kathrin Benhold, 'Europeans call off talks as Iran balks on nuclear issue', *New York Times*, 24 Aug. 2005.
75   RIA, 'Russian Foreign Ministry urges Iran to stop uranium conversion without delay', *Moscow Times*, 10 Aug. 2005.
76   Elaine Sciolino, 'Chirac warns Iran of penalty if it continues nuclear work', *New York Times*, 30 Aug. 2005.
77   'Russia opposes reporting Iran to UNSC', *New York Times*, 5 Sept. 2005.
78   Cited in Dafna Linzer, 'Iran's President does what U.S. diplomacy could not', *Washington Post*, 19 Sept. 2005.

79 Itar-Tass, 'Russia opposes referral of Iran to UN Security Council', 22 Sept. 2005 *(FBIS-RUSSIA*. 23 Sept. 2005).

80 For the full text of the IAEA resolution, see IAEA website, 'Implementation of the NPT safeguards agreement in the Islamic Republic of Iran'. Resolution adopted on 24 Sept. 2005.

81 Robin Wright, 'Rice is rebuffed by Russia on Iran', *Washington Post*, 16 Oct. 2005.

82 Interfax, 'Russia: Putin advocates Iran developing cooperation with the IAEA, renewing talks', 25 Oct. 2005 *(FBIS-RUSSIA*, 26 Oct. 2005).

83 Cited in Nazila Fathi, 'Iran's new President says Israel must be wiped off the map', *New York Times*, 27 Oct. 2005.

84 Cited in Ivan Groshkov, 'Iranian President's anti-Israeli remarks viewed; deemed dirty trick on Lavrov', *Nezavisimaya Gazeta*, 30 Oct. 2005 *(FBIS-RUSSIA*, 1 Nov. 2005).

85 Cited in Interfax, 'Moscow's position on Iran not influenced by Tehran's statement', 27 Oct. 2005 *(FBIS-RUSSIA*, October 28, 2005).

86 Statement to the Board of Directors by IAEA Director General Dr Mohamed ElBaradei, 24 Nov. 2005 (IAEA website); and IRNA, 'Full text of Iranian representative's address to the IAEA Board', 25 Nov. 2005 *(FBIS-MESA*, 27 Nov. 2005).

87 Cited in AP Report, 'Iran got black market warhead design – IAEA', *Jordan Times*, 20 Nov. 2000. See also Daphna Linzer, 'U.S. backs Russian plan to resolve Iran crisis', *Washington Post*, 19 Nov. 2005.

88 Cited in *Parisa Hafezi*, 'Iran signals defiance ahead of IAEA meeting', Reuters, 15 Nov. 2005. See also Richard Bernstein, 'Iran has resumed reprocessing uranium, diplomat said', *New York Times*, 17 Nov. 2005.

89 AP, 'Parliament approves bill to block UN nuclear agency inspections', *Jordan Times*, 20 Nov. 2005.

90 Itar-Tass, 'Russia sees "no reason" to refer Iran to UN Security Council', 21 Nov. 2005 *(FBIS-RUSSIA*, 22 Nov. 2005).

91 Rohan Sullivan, 'Bush backs Putin's Iran uranium plan', AP Report, *Moscow Times*, November 21, 2005. See also Roula Khalaf, 'EU-3 willing to explore new Iran nuclear talks', *Financial Times*, November 23, 2005.

92 Fars News Agency, 'Iran: MP says country must reject production of nuclear fuel in Russia', November 25, 2005 *(FBIS-MESA* November 26, 2005.)

93 Cited in George Jahn, 'EU accuses Iran, warns of sanctions', AP Report, *Washington Times*, November 25, 2005.

94 Cited in statement to the Board of Governors by IAEA Director General Dr Mohamed ElBaradei, 24 Nov. 2005 (IAEA website).

Conclusion: Russia as a Re-Emerging Great Power

Roger E. Kanet

The question posed at the beginning of this volume concerning the status of Russia as a great power remains unanswered fully. Has Russia regained the status of great power or, at least, is Russia on the verge of regaining great power status? The point most immediately relevant to a response to this question is the fact that Russia retains a very significant nuclear weapons capacity and, as a major nuclear power, virtually automatically has a voice in global and regional affairs. A second factor of importance, although one that has been developed comphrehensively in the preceding pages, is the fact that the Russian economy has been flourishing since the turn of the century. Yet, that growth has depended almost entirely upon the dramatic increase in world petroleum and natural gas prices. Russian industry is still floundering and generally non-competitive in the global market, and the domestic economy is based more on exchange than on production. It is questionable when the foundations of a comprehensive economy will be in place in Russia that will enable the country to compete in the global economy and that can serve as the base for a major role in world affairs that extends beyond the immediate post-Soviet region.

Finally, when one looks beyond the immediate future in attempting to assess the likely role of Russia in world affairs, another issue arises which only one author in this volume has mentioned – and which few analysts of Russian domestic or foreign policy have examined seriously to this point. This concerns the ongoing demographic catastrophe facing Russia. But, a very similar situation faces most European countries, whose indigenous populations will decline significantly in coming decades because of extremely low birth rates. But this issue, of which President Putin of Russia is well aware, is one that extends beyond the context of our analysis, even though it promises to undermine the overall base of Russian capabilities in competing in world affairs, as it will also undermine the foreign policy capabilities of most of the member countries of the European Union.

What emerges from the analyses presented in this vlume, beginning with those of Oldberg, Lomagin and Rukavishnikov, is a clear picture of a Russian leadership committed to re-establishing Russia's role as a great power. Great power status, however, cannot be based solely on military capabilities and, as Susanne Nies so very clearly reminds us, must include "soft power" capabilities, as well. Within the circle of states created out of the former Soviet Union, Russia has increasingly employed its central location and its re-emerging economic capabilities, especially its command of energy resources and their distribution, and collaboration with others in containing regional conflict – as Nies, Herd and Nygren point out – to influence political developments in the regions of greatest concern to Russia. In Central Asia and in relations with Asia more broadly, Moscow has used its economic clout, but also its military collaboration with regimes concerned about domestic opponents, to re-establish its influence despite challenges by the United States and China, as Berryman and Kanet note. In its relations with other former Soviet republics Russia has demonstrated its ability and its willingness to use is control over energy, its economic clout, as well as its direct involvement in domestic politics – sometimes quite brutally – in order to accomplish its foreign policy objectives.

As Russia looks beyond former Soviet space, it has wavered between collaboration with the United States and the West more generally in pursuing its struggle against domestic and international terrorist groups and challenging US and West European initiatives in other areas. Russian commentators, for example, view the Shanghai Cooperation Organization as a growing challenge to US global domination. Russia's policy toward the Iranian nuclear issue, as Freedman demonstrates, is strongly influenced by a desire to re-establish ties with states that share its concerns about potential US hegemony – as well as by long-term economic considerations. In a word, Russian policy toward Iran is part of a larger effort to re-establish a close relationship with important countries in the Global South.

Russia is not yet fully a great power, despite the commitment of its leadership to re-establishing Russian greatness. Yet, given its military capabilities, especially its nuclear arsenal, and assuming that its economy continues to expand as has over the last five or six years and that the demographic problems do not become too severe, Russia will likely gain significant influence in global affairs. It has already made great gains in re-establishing its role as an important global actor.

Postscript

In the months since the original completion of this manuscript Russian policy has generally not deviated from the picture presented in the foregoing analysis. Relations with the United Stated remain strained, with the ongoing war in Iraq, Iranian nuclear developments and the announced US decision to place anti-ballistic missiles in several Central European countries high on the agenda of issues dividing the two countries.

Russia's expanded use of the energy weapon, this time to punish Belarus has had a cooling effect on relations with some West European states and has reinforced the views of Russia's post-communist neighbours to the west of the importance of NATO membership for their long-term security.

Yet, as Rajan Menon and Alexander Motyl note in an important recent analysis,[1] the recent resurgence of Russia in world affairs is based largely on developments that are, potentially, quite ephemeral. Most important of these is the fact that what economic revival has occurred is based almost exclusively on the current high price of petroleum and natural gas. On almost all other indicators of economic prowess Russia ranks very poorly – 2.4% of global exports, 1.2% of worldwide imports – competitive with such countries as Thailand and Malaysia. A rapidly declining and aging population, a broken healthcare system, the inability to produce and retain talent, and declining 'soft power', all raise serious questions about the sustainability of Russia's recent revival in world affairs.

Even in those young countries along its borders where Russia has exercised the most influence in recent years – Ukraine, Belarus, Moldova, for example – there has been growing resistance to Russia. 'The Russian recovery is undeniable,' they conclude, 'but far less substantial than prevailing wisdom avers.' The desire of Moscow's leaders to reestablish Russia as a great power is clear, as we have seen. But it is possible that the world will have to live with a 'Russian petro-state that is weak, loud and potentially unstable.'[2]

Notes

1   Rajan Menon and Alexander J. Motyl, 'The Myth of Russian Resurgence', *American Interest: Policy, Politics, Culture, Digital*. (March–April 2007), available online at http://the-american-interest.com/ai2article.dfm?Id=258$mld=8
2   Ibid.

Index